First World War
and Army of Occupation
War Diary
France, Belgium and Germany

33 DIVISION
Divisional Troops
11 Field Company Royal Engineers
9 January 1915 - 30 May 1919

WO95/2414/1

The Naval & Military Press Ltd
www.nmarchive.com
Published in association with The National Archives

Published by

The Naval & Military Press Ltd

Unit 10 Ridgewood Industrial Park,

Uckfield, East Sussex,

TN22 5QE England

Tel: +44 (0) 1825 749494

www.naval-military-press.com

www.nmarchive.com

This diary has been reprinted in facsimile from the original. Any imperfections are inevitably reproduced and the quality may fall short of modern type and cartographic standards.

Contents

Document type	Place/Title	Date From	Date To
Heading	WO95/2414 Dec'15-May ' 19 II Field Coy R.E.		
Heading	33rd Division Divl Engineers 11th Field Company R.E. Dec 1915-May 1919. From 2 Div.		
Heading	33rd Division 11in Fd. Co. R.E Dec Vol XVII Dec 1915-May 1919.		
War Diary		01/12/1915	25/12/1915
War Diary		09/01/1915	31/01/1915
Heading	11 Co Fd Co R.E. Jan Vol XVII.		
War Diary		01/01/1916	28/01/1916
Miscellaneous	Appendix I.		
War Diary	Felmarg.	01/02/1916	29/02/1916
Heading	11 Fd Coy R.E. Vol XX.		
War Diary		01/03/1916	31/03/1916
Miscellaneous			
War Diary		01/04/1916	30/04/1916
War Diary	Cuinchy.	01/05/1916	30/06/1916
Heading	War Diary Of 11th Field Company R.E. From 1-7-16 To 31-7-16 Vol 24.		
War Diary	Cuinchy Front.	01/07/1916	11/07/1916
War Diary	Daours.	12/07/1916	12/07/1916
War Diary	Buire Sur L'Ancre.	13/07/1916	14/07/1916
War Diary	Meaulte.	14/07/1916	15/07/1916
War Diary	Mametz Wood.	15/07/1916	20/07/1916
War Diary	High Wood.		
War Diary	Mametz Wood.	21/07/1916	21/07/1916
War Diary	Buire Sur L'Ancre.	22/07/1916	31/07/1916
War Diary	Buire Sur L'Ancre.	27/07/1916	31/07/1916
Heading	Trenches July 16.		
Map	Western Portion Of Sheet 57c. S.W.		
Heading	Trenches July 16.		
Heading	11 Fd Coy R.E Vol XXI.		
Heading	33rd Divisional Engineers 11th Field Company R.E August 1916.		
Heading	War Diary Of 11th Field Company R.E. From 1/8/16 To 31/8/16 Vol 25.		
War Diary	Buire Sur L'Ancre.	01/08/1916	06/08/1916
War Diary	Valley E Of Mametz Wood.	07/08/1916	11/08/1916
War Diary	Bazentin.	12/08/1916	12/08/1916
War Diary	Le Grand.	12/08/1916	31/08/1916
Heading	War Diary Of 11th Field Company R.E For Month Of September 1916 Vol 2.		
War Diary	Pierregot.	01/09/1916	01/09/1916
War Diary	Boisbergues.	02/09/1916	03/09/1916
War Diary	Wavans.	04/09/1916	04/09/1916
War Diary	Blangeval.	05/09/1916	07/09/1916
War Diary	Petit Bouret Sur Canche Oppy.	08/09/1916	09/09/1916
War Diary	La Bazeque Farm.	10/09/1916	11/09/1916
War Diary	Bienvillers And Fonquevillers.	12/09/1916	13/09/1916
War Diary	Fonquevillers.	13/09/1916	13/09/1916
War Diary	Hannescamp.	13/09/1916	13/09/1916

War Diary	Fonque Villers.	14/09/1916	14/09/1916
War Diary	Hannescamp.	14/09/1916	14/09/1916
War Diary	Fonquevillers And Hannescamp.	15/09/1916	28/09/1916
War Diary	Gaudiempre.	29/09/1916	30/09/1916
Heading	War Diary Of 11th Field Coy R.E. From 1st Oct 1916 To 31st Oct 1916. Vol 22.		
War Diary	Milly.	01/10/1916	02/10/1916
War Diary	Doullens.	03/10/1916	06/10/1916
War Diary	Bayencourt.	07/10/1916	07/10/1916
War Diary	Hebuterne.	08/10/1916	17/10/1916
War Diary	Milly.	18/10/1916	19/10/1916
War Diary	Ville Sous Corbie.	20/10/1916	21/10/1916
War Diary	Briquetterie.	22/10/1916	23/10/1916
War Diary	Cuillemont.	24/10/1916	24/10/1916
War Diary	Lesboeufs.	24/10/1916	31/10/1916
Map	To be used in conjunction with Daily work Report. Appendix 2.		
Map	Appendix 1.		
Heading	War Diary Of 11th Field Company Royal Engineers From 1st Nov 1916 To 30th Nov 1916 Vol 23.		
War Diary	Lesboeufs.	01/11/1916	05/11/1916
War Diary	Guillemont.	06/11/1916	06/11/1916
War Diary	Meaulte.	07/11/1916	11/11/1916
War Diary	Carnoy.	12/11/1916	28/11/1916
War Diary	Vaux.	29/11/1916	30/11/1916
Heading	War Diary Of 11th Field Company R.E From 1.12.16 To 31.12.16 Vol 24.		
War Diary	Vaux.	01/12/1916	07/12/1916
War Diary	Morlancourt.	08/12/1916	08/12/1916
War Diary	Camp III.	09/12/1916	10/12/1916
War Diary	Maurepas.	11/12/1916	27/12/1916
War Diary	Buigny L'Abby.	28/12/1916	31/12/1916
Heading	33rd Div 212th F.C.R.E. Vol I 121/7928.		
Heading	War Diary Of 11th (Field) Co., R.E., From January 1st 1917 To January 31st 1917 (Volume).		
War Diary	Buigny L'Abbe' (Abbeville 1:100,000).	01/01/1917	17/01/1917
War Diary	Camp III L.2.b.2.9 (Albert Sheet Combined 1:40000) G.8.c.6.6. (Albert Sheet).	18/01/1917	20/01/1917
War Diary	P.G. Ourcel H.5.6.7.3 (Albert Sheet).	20/01/1917	31/01/1917
Miscellaneous	Report On Right Bde Area 33rd Divl Front.	23/01/1917	23/01/1917
Map	Sketch Co Inter Mediate Lane On Right Brigade Section.		
Map	Sketch Of The Ommiecourt Loop Defences.		
Map		23/01/1917	23/01/1917
Miscellaneous			
Heading	War Diary Of 11th Field Company R.E From 1/2/17 To 28/2/17 Vol 26.		
War Diary	P.C. Ourcel H.5.C.7.3 (Albert Comb Sheet 1/40,000).	01/02/1917	28/02/1917
War Diary	P.C. Ourcel H.5.C.7.2. Albert Comb Sheet 1/40,000.	23/02/1917	28/02/1917
Heading	War Diary Of 11th (Field) Co R.E. From March 1st 1917 To March 31st 1917 (Volume) Vol 27.		
War Diary	P.C. Oursel H.11.a.5.9 Ref. Map Albert Comb 1/40,000.	01/03/1917	06/03/1917
War Diary	Suzanne.	07/03/1917	07/03/1917
War Diary	Camp 13 K.22.C.4.7 Ref Map Albert (Comb) 1/40,000.	08/03/1917	08/03/1917
War Diary	Camp 13.	09/03/1917	23/03/1917

War Diary	Lamotte Brebiere.	24/03/1917	31/03/1917
Heading	War Diary Of 11th (Field) Company. R.E. From April 1st 1917 To April 30th 1917 (Volume).		
War Diary	Lamotte Brebieres.	01/04/1917	02/04/1917
War Diary	Villers Bocage.	03/04/1917	03/04/1917
War Diary	Beauval.	04/04/1917	04/04/1917
War Diary	Grouches.	05/04/1917	06/04/1917
War Diary	St Amand.	07/04/1917	07/04/1917
War Diary	Balleulmont.	08/04/1917	12/04/1917
War Diary	Boiry Becquerelle.	13/04/1917	27/04/1917
War Diary	Balleulmont.	28/04/1917	30/04/1917
Map	Appendix 1.		
Operation(al) Order(s)	33 Div. Order No. 177. Appendix II.	21/04/1917	21/04/1917
Operation(al) Order(s)	98th Infantry Brigade Order No. 132.	22/04/1917	22/04/1917
Operation(al) Order(s)	19th Infantry Brigade-Order No.228.	22/04/1917	22/04/1917
Heading	War Diary Of 11th (Field) Co R.E From May 1st 1917 To May 31st 1917 (Volume). Vol 29.		
War Diary	Bailleul Mont.	01/05/1917	01/05/1917
War Diary	Monchy-Au Bois.	02/05/1917	11/05/1917
War Diary	Hamelincourt.	12/05/1917	30/05/1917
War Diary	Bailleulmont.	31/05/1917	31/05/1917
Operation(al) Order(s)	33 Div. Order No. 185. Appendix A.	16/05/1917	16/05/1917
Operation(al) Order(s)	33 Div. Order No. 189. Appendix A 2.	18/05/1917	18/05/1917
Miscellaneous	A Form. Messages And Signals. Appendix A.		
Miscellaneous	33 Div. G.83.	19/05/1917	19/05/1917
Miscellaneous	B.M. 10. Appendix A.	19/05/1917	19/05/1917
Miscellaneous	19th Infantry Brigade Instructions No. 2.	19/05/1917	19/05/1917
Miscellaneous	Amendments to 19th Inf. Bde Ins. No. 1.	19/05/1917	19/05/1917
Miscellaneous	19th Infantry Brigade-Ins. No. 1.	19/05/1917	19/05/1917
Miscellaneous	Amendments To Brigade Order No. 238.	19/05/1917	19/05/1917
Operation(al) Order(s)	19th Infantry Brigade-Order No. 238.	16/05/1917	16/05/1917
Miscellaneous	19th Infantry Brigade Instructions No. 4. Appendix B.	20/05/1917	20/05/1917
Miscellaneous	33 Div. Operations-20 May 1917. Appendix C.	22/05/1917	22/05/1917
Map	Aeroplane Reconnaissance 3.30 pm. May 23 1917.		
Operation(al) Order(s)	19th Infantry Brigade-Order No. 246. Appendix D.	26/05/1917	26/05/1917
Heading	War Diary Of 11th (Field) Co. R.E. From June 1st 1917 To June 30th 1917 (Volume-). Vol 30.		
War Diary	Bailleulmont.	01/06/1917	20/06/1917
War Diary	Boiry-Becquerelle.	21/06/1917	30/06/1917
Heading	War Diary Of 11th Field Co. R.E From 1-7-17 To 31-7-17 (Volume) Vol 31.		
War Diary	Monchy.	01/07/1917	01/07/1917
War Diary	Acheux.	02/07/1917	02/07/1917
War Diary	Naours.	03/07/1917	03/07/1917
War Diary	Lachaussee.	04/07/1917	04/07/1917
War Diary	Conde-Folie.	05/07/1917	31/07/1917
Miscellaneous	Training Programme Of 11th (Field) Co. R.E From July 16th 1917 To July 21st 1917.	16/07/1917	16/07/1917
Miscellaneous	Training Programme Of 11th (Field) Co. R.E From July 9th To July 14th 1917. Appendix I.	09/07/1917	09/07/1917
Miscellaneous			
Map	Hindenburg Line And Sensee Valley. Scale 1/12000.		
Miscellaneous	11th (Field) Co. R.E Marching In State.	30/07/1917	30/07/1917
Miscellaneous		20/04/1917	20/04/1917
Heading	War Diary Of 11th (Field) Company R.E (Volume) From 1st Aug 1917 To 31st August 1917.		

War Diary	Conde-Folie.	01/08/1917	01/08/1917
War Diary	Bray-Dunes.	02/08/1917	19/08/1917
War Diary	Nieuport.	20/08/1917	28/08/1917
War Diary	Coxyde.	29/08/1917	29/08/1917
War Diary	Pt. Synthe.	30/08/1917	31/08/1917
Heading	War Diary Of 11th (Field) Company R.E. (Vol.) September 1917.		
War Diary		01/09/1917	30/09/1917
Operation(al) Order(s)	33 Div. Order No. 250. Appendix "A".	24/09/1917	24/09/1917
Operation(al) Order(s)	Appendix "B" To 33 Div. Order No. 230.		
Diagram etc	Visual Scheme.		
Diagram etc	Wireless And Power Buzzer Scheme.		
Operation(al) Order(s)	Appendix "C" To 33 Div. Order No. 230. Machine Gun Barrage.	24/09/1917	24/09/1917
Operation(al) Order(s)	Appendix "E" To 33 Div. Order No. 230. Synchronization Of Watches.	24/09/1917	24/09/1917
Operation(al) Order(s)	All recipients of Appendix "C", 33 Div. Order No. 230.	24/09/1917	24/09/1917
Operation(al) Order(s)	Appendix "D" to 98th Inf. Bde. Order No. 170.		
Operation(al) Order(s)	Appendix "E" To 98th Inf. Bde. Order No. 170. Instructions Regarding Prisoners.		
Operation(al) Order(s)	Appendix "B" to 98th Inf. Bde. Order No. 170.		
Miscellaneous			
Operation(al) Order(s)	98th Inf. Bde. Order No. 170.	25/09/1917	25/09/1917
Operation(al) Order(s)	Appendix "D" To 33 Div. Order No. 230. Of September 24, 1917. Work Of R.E. And Pioneers.	24/09/1917	24/09/1917
Miscellaneous			
Map	Message Map.		
Miscellaneous	Message Form.		
Operation(al) Order(s)	98th Inf. Bde. Order No. 171.	25/09/1917	25/09/1917
Operation(al) Order(s)	33 Div. Order No. 231.	25/09/1917	25/09/1917
Miscellaneous	Special Order Of The Day by Major-General P. Wood, C.B., C.M.G. Commanding 33rd Division.	29/09/1917	29/09/1917
War Diary	Troisvilles Ref Map 57 B.	01/09/1917	03/09/1917
War Diary	Waggonville.	04/09/1917	04/09/1917
War Diary	Sartbara Ref Map 51 1/40,000.	05/09/1917	06/09/1917
War Diary	Berlaimont Sheet 51.	07/09/1917	14/09/1917
War Diary	Locquignol Ref Map 51.	15/09/1917	16/09/1917
War Diary	Clary Sheet 57 B.	17/09/1917	30/09/1917
Heading	War Diary Of 11th Fd Coy R.E. From 1st October To 31st October 1917. Vol 34.		
War Diary	Dickebusch.	01/10/1917	07/10/1917
War Diary	Westoutre.	07/10/1917	07/10/1917
War Diary	Sheet 28 T.10.a.5.9. On Wulverghem.	08/10/1917	08/10/1917
War Diary	Neuvle Eglise Road.	08/10/1917	10/10/1917
War Diary	Sheet 28 T.10.a.5.9 On Neuve Eglise.	11/10/1917	11/10/1917
War Diary	Wolverghem Road.	12/10/1917	19/10/1917
War Diary	Sheet 28 T.10.a.5.9 Or Neuve Eglise.	20/10/1917	21/10/1917
War Diary	Wulverghem Road.	22/10/1917	29/10/1917
War Diary	Sheet 28 T.10.a.5.9 On Neuve Eglise.	30/10/1917	30/10/1917
War Diary	Wulverghem Road.	31/10/1917	31/10/1917
War Diary	La Sotiere.	23/10/1918	24/10/1918
War Diary	Forest.	25/10/1918	25/10/1918
War Diary	Croix.	26/10/1918	26/10/1918
War Diary	Troisvilles.	27/10/1918	31/10/1918
Diagram etc	Sheet 28.J. (Belgium).		
Map			

Heading	War Diary Of 11th Field Company R.E (Volume) From November 1st 1917 To 30th November 1917.		
War Diary	On Neuve Eglise.	01/11/1917	01/11/1917
War Diary	Wulverghem Road.	01/11/1917	06/11/1917
War Diary	T.10.a.5.9 (Sheet 28).	01/11/1917	06/11/1917
War Diary	On Wulverghem.	07/11/1917	07/11/1917
War Diary	Neuve Eglise Rd.	08/11/1917	08/11/1917
War Diary	T.10.a.5.9 (Sheet 28).	09/11/1917	13/11/1917
War Diary	Hazebrouck Sheet S.A. 100 Yds N Of 1st T In Merris.	14/11/1917	17/11/1917
War Diary	Camp In Ypres I.2.c.5.5. (Sheet 28).	18/11/1917	22/11/1917
War Diary	Camp In Ypres I.2.c.5.5. Horse Line H.11 Central (Sheet 28).	23/11/1917	30/11/1917
Heading	War Diary Of 11th (Field) Co. R.E Volume From 1st December 1917 To 31st December 1917.		
War Diary	I.2.c.5.5. (Ref Map Sheet 28) On Ypres.	01/12/1917	01/12/1917
War Diary	St. Jean Rd.	02/12/1917	12/12/1917
War Diary	I.2.c.5.5 On St. Jean.	13/12/1917	14/12/1917
War Diary	Ypres Road.	14/12/1917	17/12/1917
War Diary	Ypres-St-Jean Rd. I.2.c.5.5. (Sheet 28).	18/12/1917	21/12/1917
War Diary	Menin Gate I.8.b.3.4. (Sheet 28).	21/12/1917	31/12/1917
Heading	War Diary Of 11th Field Coy R.E. (Volume) From 1st January 1918 To 31st January 1918.		
War Diary	Menin Gate I.8.b.3.4 (Sheet 28).	01/01/1918	14/01/1918
War Diary	Menin Gate I.8.b.3.4.	27/01/1918	27/01/1918
War Diary	Salper Wick Hazebrouck 5 A Edition Z Belgium.	28/01/1918	28/01/1918
War Diary	Sheet 27A S.E. R.21.d.1.2.	29/01/1918	31/01/1918
Heading	War Diary Of 11th Fd Coy R.E. (Volume) From 1st February 1918 To 28th February 1918. Vol 38.		
War Diary	Salperwick Sheet 27 S.E R.21.d.1.2.	01/02/1918	19/02/1918
War Diary	Ypres Sheet 28 I.8.b.3.4.	20/02/1918	28/02/1918
Heading	War Diary Of 11th Field Company R.E. (Volume) From 1st March 1918 To 31st March 1918. Vol 39.		
War Diary	Ypres.	01/03/1918	13/03/1918
War Diary	Ypres I.8.b.3.4.	14/03/1918	31/03/1918
Heading	33rd Divisional Engineers 11th Field Company R.E. April 1918.		
Heading	War Diary Of 11th Fd Coy R.E. Volume From 1st April 1918 To 30th April 1918. Vol 40.		
War Diary	Menin Gate Ypres I.8.b.3.4 (Sheet 28).	01/04/1918	03/04/1918
War Diary	Ridge Camp Brandhoek	04/04/1918	06/04/1918
War Diary	Grande Rullecourt Billet 71.	07/04/1918	10/04/1918
War Diary	Farm At X.q.d.27. (Ref Sheet 27).	11/04/1918	14/04/1918
War Diary	X.2.c.22 (Sheet 27).	15/04/1918	16/04/1918
War Diary	R.34.a.50.85 (Sheet 27).	17/04/1918	20/04/1918
War Diary	Aeroplane P.25 Central (Sheet 27).	21/04/1918	22/04/1918
War Diary	Q.8.c. (Sheet 27).	23/04/1918	30/04/1918
Heading	War Diary Of 11th (Field) Coy R.E. Volume From 1st May 1918 To 31st May 1918 Vol 41.		
War Diary	Steenvoorde Q.8.c. (Sheet 27).	01/05/1918	03/05/1918
War Diary	Sheet 27 L.9.d.0.1.	04/05/1918	31/05/1918
Heading	War Diary Of 11th Fd Coy R.E. Volume From 1st June 1918 To 30th June 1918 Vol 32.		
War Diary	Sheet 27 L.9.d.0.1 S.W Of Poperinghe.	01/06/1918	06/06/1918
War Diary	Sheet 28 G.10.b.20.	07/06/1918	30/06/1918
Heading	War Diary Of 11th (Field) Company R.E. (Volume) From 1st July 1918 To 31st July 1918. Vol 43.		

War Diary	Sheet 28 G.10.b.0.0.	01/07/1918	31/07/1918
Heading	War Diary Of 11th Fd Coy R.E. Volume From 1st August 1918 To 31st August 1918 Vol 44.		
War Diary	Sheet 28 G.10.b.0.0.	01/08/1918	16/08/1918
War Diary	Gaunt-Farm A.28.a.27. Sheet 28.	17/08/1918	18/08/1918
War Diary	Westrove (Hazebrouck Sheet N.W. 6 Houlle).	19/08/1918	19/08/1918
War Diary	Cahen (Calais Sheet 13).	20/08/1918	25/08/1918
War Diary	Affringues (8 Miles S.W Wizernes Hazebrack Sheet).	26/08/1918	27/08/1918
War Diary	Ivergnay (Billet No 51 Lens II Sheet).	28/08/1918	31/08/1918
Heading	War Diary Of 11th (Sheet) Coy R.E. Volume From 1st October 1918 To 30th September 1918. Vol 45.		
War Diary	Ivergny Billet 51 Lens 11 Sheet.	01/09/1918	14/09/1918
War Diary	Menin Gate I.8.b.3.4 Sheet 28.	15/01/1918	26/01/1918
War Diary	Ivergny Billet 51 (Lens 11 Sheet).	14/01/1918	15/01/1918
War Diary	Etricourt. Sheet 57 C S.E.	15/01/1918	26/01/1918
War Diary	Sheet 57. c. W.25.a.77.	27/01/1918	29/01/1918
War Diary	Sheet 57 B. S.W.	30/01/1918	30/01/1918
Heading	War Diary Of 11th (Field) Coy R.E. Volume From 1st October 1918 To 31st October 1918 Vol 46.		
War Diary	Limerick Post Sheet 57c. S.W. X.22.c.0.2.	01/10/1918	07/10/1918
War Diary	X.18.a.25.90 Sheet 57 C S.W Just S Of Honnecourt	08/10/1918	08/10/1918
War Diary	Hurtevant Farm 0.21.d.38 Sheet 57 B.	09/10/1918	09/10/1918
War Diary	Troisvilles.	10/10/1918	12/10/1918
War Diary	Elincourt.	13/10/1918	22/10/1918
Miscellaneous	11th Field Coy. R.E.	07/10/1918	07/10/1918
Miscellaneous	11th Field Coy. R.E.	27/10/1918	27/10/1918
Miscellaneous	Commune De Clary. Clary, Le 14 October 1918.	14/10/1918	14/10/1918
Miscellaneous	To All Recipients Of 33rd Div. Routine Orders.		
Heading	War Diary Of 11th (Field) Coy R.E. (Volume) From 1st November 1918 To 30th November 1918 Vol 47.		
Heading	War Diary Of 11th (Field) Coy R.E. Volume From 1st December 1918 To 31st December 1918 Vol 48.		
War Diary	Clary.	01/12/1918	01/12/1918
War Diary	Fouilloy Corbie.	02/12/1918	04/12/1918
War Diary	Vraignes (Dieppe Sheet).	05/12/1918	31/12/1918
Heading	War Diary Of 11th (Field) Coy R.E. Volume From 1st January 1919 To 31st January 1919 Vol 49.		
War Diary	Rouen.	01/01/1919	09/01/1919
War Diary	Le Havre.	10/01/1919	31/01/1919
Heading	War Diary Of 11th (Field) Company R.E. Volume From 1st February 1919 To 28th February 1919 Vol 50.		
War Diary	Harfleur Near.	01/02/1919	01/02/1919
War Diary	Le Havre.	02/02/1919	28/02/1919
War Diary		07/02/1919	27/02/1919
War Diary		26/02/1919	26/02/1919
Heading	War Diary Of 11th (Field) Company R.E. Volume From 1st March 1919 To 31st March 1919 Vol 51.		
War Diary	Harfleur Near Le Havre.	01/03/1919	15/03/1919
War Diary		13/03/1919	22/03/1919
War Diary		21/03/1919	31/03/1919
Heading	War Diary Of The 11th (Field) Company Royal Engineers Volume From 1st April 1919 To 30th April 1919. Vol 52.		
War Diary	Camp 8 (a) Harfleur Nr Le Havre.	02/04/1919	23/04/1919
Heading	War Diary Of 11th (Field) Company R.E. Volume From May 1st 1919 To May 31st 1919. Vol 53.		

War Diary Camp 8 (A) Harfleur Nr. Le Havre. 02/05/1919 30/05/1919

WO 95/2414

(1)

Dec '15 — May '19

11 Field Coy R.E.

33RD DIVISION
DIVL ENGINEERS

11TH FIELD COMPANY R.E.

DEC 1915 - MAY 1919

FROM 2 DIV

862

~~2nd Div~~

11th 7th Co. R.E.

Dec.

Vol XVII

33rd Division

transferred to XXXIII Dec 2nd

Dec 1915
|
May 1919

Army Form C. 2118.

Instructions regarding War Diaries and Intelligence Summaries are contained in F. S. Regs., Part II. and the Staff Manual respectively. Title pages will be prepared in manuscript.

WAR DIARY

~~or~~

~~INTELLIGENCE~~ SUMMARY.

(Erase heading not required.)

11th Field Company R.E.

December 1915.

Place	Date	Hour	Summary of Events and Information	Remarks and references to Appendices
Dec	1		No 1 Sect & the majority of No 2 Sect, with 200 24th R.F by day continued work on 2nd line.	
			No 3 Sect with 100 24th RF by day continued work on HUNTER ST.	
			No 4 Sect continued work on billets in ANNEQUIN	
			Part of No 2 Sect repaired two covered sentry posts in ORCHARD REDOUBT & deep dugout in TUNNEL ST	
			Two sections of 226th Fd Coy were attached to my Nos 1 & 3 Sections for instruction & work	
			Capt Sim took OC 226th Fd Coy round the line & showed him work in hand & contemplated which he is taken over	
			The 2nd line machine-gun wire is now all marked out with a front row of pickets so that 226 will be able to carry on without difficulty	
	2nd		Today the 11th Fd Coy ceases to belong to 2nd Division & is transferred to the 33rd Div (at present in the GIVENCHY & FESTUBERT front).	
			Company moved to billet in GORRE F.3.d.	
			Capt Sim & officers of Nos 3 & 4 Sect reconnoitred BARNTON ROAD, a communication breastwork not finished which has to be continued	

2353 Wt. W2544/1454 700,000 5/15 D. D. & L. A.D.S.S./Forms/C. 2118.

Instructions regarding War Diaries and Intelligence Summaries are contained in F. S. Regs., Part II. and the Staff Manual respectively. Title pages will be prepared in manuscript.

WAR DIARY
or
INTELLIGENCE SUMMARY.
(Erase heading not required.)

Army Form C. 2118.

Place	Date	Hour	Summary of Events and Information	Remarks and references to Appendices
			For the present 3 & 4 Sect with infantry parties are to continue Barnton Rd & the new support breastwork line N & S of it. Nos 1 & 2 Sects to be employed on billets.	
	3rd		No 3 Sect with 100 21st RF by night worked in BARNTON TRENCH — mostly carrying up hurdles. 25 were put in position & wired	
			No 4 Sect with 100 21st RF by night continued filling in breastwork. The hurdles are already in position but require adjustment & staying in places. Most of the work is shovel work here but ground is so water-logged that work is necessarily very slow.	
			Nos 1 & 2 Sect cleaning up & improving billets	
			Lt Clifton rode over to LE CAUROI & advised O.C. North Irish Horse about shelters for his horse lines.	
	4th		No 1 Sect completed drying room at FERME DU ROI & started foot bath room	
			No 2 Sect laid & raised boards that had floated away in BARNTON RD.	
			No 3 Sect same as 3rd with 200 inf in 2 reliefs	
			No 4 Sect " " " " " " " "	

2353 Wt. W2544/1454 700,000 5/15 D. D. & L. A.D.S.S./Forms/C. 2118.

Instructions regarding War Diaries and Intelligence Summaries are contained in F. S. Regs., Part II. and the Staff Manual respectively. Title pages will be prepared in manuscript.

WAR DIARY
or
INTELLIGENCE SUMMARY.
(Erase heading not required.)

Army Form C. 2118.

Place	Date	Hour	Summary of Events and Information	Remarks and references to Appendices
	5th		Same as 4th	
	6th		No 1 Sect continued footbath room & started a 20-seat covered latrine in ECHOLE DES FILLES BETHUNE. Also started 3 useful huts in transport lines of 1st SR GORRE.	
			No 2 Sect raising boards in BARNTON TRENCH by day	
			Nos 3 & 4 Sect rested (no infantry parties available).	
	7th		No 1 Sect completed footbath room & continued latrine	
			No 2 Sect continued the 3 huts	
			Nos 3 & 4 Sect worked at night raising parapet of PIONEER TRENCH with sandbags. No infantry parties	
	8th		No 1 Sect finished latrine at ECHOLE DES FILLES & continued the 3 huts	
			No 2 Sect raised boards in PIONEER ROAD	
			No 3 Sect with 100 inf improved the tramway E of LE PLANTIN by laying sandbags between the sleepers	
			No 4 Sect with 50 inf put 11 bridges over dykes from QUINQUE RUE Road to post No 2 on front line.	

2353 Wt. W2544/1454 700,000 5/15 D. D. & L. A.D.S.S./Forms/C. 2118.

Instructions regarding War Diaries and Intelligence Summaries are contained in F. S. Regs., Part II. and the Staff Manual respectively. Title Pages will be prepared in manuscript.

WAR DIARY
or
INTELLIGENCE SUMMARY
(Erase heading not required.)

Army Form C. 2118

Place	Date	Hour	Summary of Events and Information	Remarks and references to Appendices
	15		Same as 14th No 3 Sect started a emplacement for MG R 10 & carried on with dugout for same	
	16		Same as 15th. No 4 Sect finished the Infantry deep dugout in HUNTER ST. Also the wire of MG R1 along TOWER RESERVE TRENCH. No 3 Sect finished the dugout of MG R10	
	17		Company rested. No work done.	
	18		No 1 Section continued the 4 emplacements and dugouts in brickstacks 10 & 12. No 2 Sect continued emplacement & dugout in Ry Embkt for MG R6 (end of Banbury Cross. Also wiring reserve line at night. No 3 Sect continued emplacement R10 in TOWER RESERVE TRENCH. Also finished deep dugout in MARYLEBONE Rd & started another further south in same trench. No 4 Sect finished strengthening emplacement MG S6 in IKEY TERRACE & continued the wiring of reserve line S of road. Lt ANDERSON went on leave	

1875 Wt. W593/826 1,000,000 4/15 J.B.C. & A. A.D.S.S./Forms/C. 2118.

Instructions regarding War Diaries and Intelligence Summaries are contained in F. S. Regs., Part II. and the Staff Manual respectively. Title Pages will be prepared in manuscript.

WAR DIARY
or
INTELLIGENCE SUMMARY

(Erase heading not required.)

Army Form C. 2118

Place	Date	Hour	Summary of Events and Information	Remarks and references to Appendices
	19		Same as 18th. MG R6 finished. (BANBURY CROSS)	
	20		Same as 19th except No 4 Sect.	
			No 4 Sect started 2 deep dugouts in RESERVE LINE, one just S of OLD KENT ROAD & the other just S of LOVERS LANE (ESPERANTO TERRACE)	
	21		Same as 20th No 3 Section finished MG R10. No 2 Sect finished the wiring of the Reserve Line	
			6 Men No 3 Sect started an emplacement for an indirect fire MG in CUINCHY. It was a special mounting & had to be erected on an absolutely level platform & bolted down so that the Zero line was on 100° true bearing.	
	22		No 1 Section finished MG 4 & 4a in brickstack 12 & the dugouts for them	
			Also continued MG 3a & 3b in brickstack 10.	
			No 2 Sect rested	
			No 3 Sect finished indirect fire MG emplacement in CUINCHY	
			Also started revetting interior of deep dugout in GLASGOW ROAD	
			also continued deep dugout in MARYLEBONE Rd	
			No 4 Sect continued 2 deep dugouts, CUINCHY SUPPORT & ESPERANTO TERRACE	

1875 Wt. W593/826 1,000,000 4/15 J.B.C. & A. A.D.S.S./Forms/C. 2118.

Instructions regarding War Diaries and Intelligence Summaries are contained in F. S. Regs., Part II. and the Staff Manual respectively. Title Pages will be prepared in manuscript.

WAR DIARY
or
INTELLIGENCE SUMMARY

(Erase heading not required.)

Army Form C. 2118

Place	Date	Hour	Summary of Events and Information	Remarks and references to Appendices
	23		Same as 22nd No 3 Sect finished revetting deep dugout GLASGOW ROAD No 2 Sect started deep dugout under embankment Railway Hollow for garrison of THE BULGE. Also, with help from garrison started the repair of the defences of CUINCHY SUPPORT POINT No 3 Sect started infantry deep dugout in TOWER RESERVE TRENCH	
	24		Same as 23rd In addition Lt BALCOMBE took charge of a party of 50 Infantry & dug a "sap" from our front line to a new crater just S of LABASSEE Rd (about 35x). 8 of No 3 Sect worked at the entrance to the sap out of the trench in 2 reliefs.	
	25		No 1 Sect continued emplacements & dugouts MG S3A & MG S3b in Brickstack 10 also started repairing dugout behind No 7 brickstack of Trench Mortar battery No 2 Sect continued dugout in RAILWAY HOLLOW & repair of CUINCHY SUP PT No 3 Sect continued dugouts in TOWER RESERVE TR & MARYLEBONE Rd and also finished entrance to ~~the~~ sap. Party of 30 infantry ~~with~~ under Lt BALCOMBE improved sap	

1875 Wt. W593/826 1,000,000 4/15 J.B.C. & A. A.D.S.S./Forms/C. 2118.

Instructions regarding War Diaries and Intelligence Summaries are contained in F. S. Regs., Part II. and the Staff Manual respectively. Title pages will be prepared in manuscript.

WAR DIARY
or
INTELLIGENCE SUMMARY.
(*Erase heading not required.*)

Army Form C. 2118.

Place	Date	Hour	Summary of Events and Information	Remarks and references to Appendices
	9th		No 1 Sect continued 3 huts. Two are now finished & the third about half done	
			No 2 Sect Continued boarding sides of PIONEER TR.	
			No 3 Sect loading pontoon wagons in BETHUNE.	
			No 4 Sect with 50 Inf made 6 bridges over dykes between posts 1 & 2 in front line.	
	10th		Company moved to CANTRAINNE by march route Lt BALCOMBE leave.	
	11th		" " " BURECQ to rest billets by march route.	
	#		Fetched 2 pontoon wagon - loads of stores from MANQUEVILLE	
	12th		Company rested & cleaned up equipment, arms etc.	
			Fetched remainder of stores from MANQUEVILLE (6 wagon loads) ↖ Lt ANDERSON returned from leave,	
	13th		Inspection of Company by OC	
			Carpenters employed on making 4 - seat latrine at billet	
			Remainder checked & cleaned tools in cart.	
	14th		One hours section drill in morning	
			No 2 Sect started dressing room at bath house BOURECQ	

2353 Wt. W2544/1454 700,000 5/15 D. D. & L. A.D.S.S./Forms/C. 2118.

Army Form C. 2118.

Instructions regarding War Diaries and Intelligence Summaries are contained in F. S. Regs., Part II. and the Staff Manual respectively. Title pages will be prepared in manuscript.

WAR DIARY
or
INTELLIGENCE SUMMARY.

(Erase heading not required.)

Place	Date	Hour	Summary of Events and Information	Remarks and references to Appendices
			Remainder of Company making latrines for billets	Interpreter De BARDY
			No 4 Sect also made 2 sentry boxes for 33rd Div HQ at BUSNES	left me for 226th Coy RE
	15		No 3 & 4 Sections & Headquarters of Company bathed in the morning	
			Nos 1, 2, 4 Section drill for 1 hour in morning	
			No 1 Sect continued latrines	
			No 2 Sect " dressing room at bath house BOURECQ	
	16		One hours drill in the morning	
			No 2 Sect continued dressing room at bath house BOURECQ	
			Remainder continued latrines	
			In the afternoon football match, Sappers v drivers	
	17		Nos 1 & 2 Section left me for a months attachment to 222nd & 212th Fd Coy respectively, a section of each of these companies joined me in their place.	
			1 NCO & 10 men each of Nos 3 & 4 Section gave exhibition of wiring at L'ECLEME	
			Remainder of No 3 Sect continued dressing room at bath-house BOURECQ	
			" " No 4 " erected type machine gun emplacement at BOURECQ	
	18		Route march. Football match in the afternoon.	

2353 Wt. W2544/1454 700,000 5/15 D. D. & L. A.D.S.S./Forms/C. 2118.

Instructions regarding War Diaries and Intelligence Summaries are contained in F. S. Regs., Part II. and the Staff Manual respectively. Title pages will be prepared in manuscript.

WAR DIARY
or
INTELLIGENCE SUMMARY.
(Erase heading not required.)

Army Form C. 2118.

Place	Date	Hour	Summary of Events and Information	Remarks and references to Appendices
	19		Sunday rest.	
			The Company paraded on road at 11 am on the road in BOURECQ & saluted Gen French on his return to England as he passed.	
	20		No 3 Sect continued dressing room for bath-house BOURECQ	
			No 4 Sect improved MG Emplacement also started foundations (brick piers) for recreation room 78' x 28' at NORRENT FONTES	
			Sect 212th Coy (attached) commenced strengthening magazine dugouts at RE Park ~~BOUR~~ BERGUETTE STATION	
			Sect 222nd Coy (attached) made good a bridge into a field for 33rd D.A.C. at BERGUETTE	
	21		Two attached sections continued work on magazine dugouts at BERGUETTE	
			No 3 Sect continued bath house dressing room & put shelves in clean linen store	
			Also finished off 6 4-seat latrines	
			No 4 Sect continued work on recreation hut at NORRENT FONTES	
	22		Lt BALCOMBE returned from leave	
			Work same as 21st	

2353 Wt. W2544/1454 700,000 5/15 D. D. & L. A.D.S.S./Forms/C. 2118.

Instructions regarding War Diaries and Intelligence Summaries are contained in F. S. Regs., Part II. and the Staff Manual respectively. Title pages will be prepared in manuscript.

WAR DIARY
or
INTELLIGENCE SUMMARY.
(Erase heading not required.)

Army Form C. 2118.

Place	Date	Hour	Summary of Events and Information	Remarks and references to Appendices
	23		Same as 21st	
			Work on magazine dugouts finished	
			Also finished & delivered two more 4 seat latrines & made a large map-table for Hq RA 33rd Div.	
	24		No 4 Sect & section 212th Coy continued Recreation Hut at NORRENT FONTES	
			Sect 222nd Coy delivered two latrines & rejoined their own Company for Christmas	
			No 3 Sect installed geyser apparatus at bath-house BOURECQ. This necessitated a good deal of structural alteration to huts & also the laying of a cold water supply main to cistern of geyser	
			My No 1 & 2 sections rejoined me for Christmas in the evening.	
	25		Christmas day. No work	
	26		No 3 Sect improved arrangements at Bath house ~~~~ BOURECQ. This is now finished	
			No 4 Sect & sect 212th Coy continued work on REcreation hut. All the foundations & sides are finished & work has been handed over to in-coming unit.	
			My nos 1 & 2 sections left me again & section of 222nd Co returned to me	
	27		Company marched to old billets in ANNEQUIN. N for work in CUINCHY with 98th Bde	

2353 Wt. W2544/1454 700,000 5/15 D. D. & L. A.D.S.S./Forms/C. 2118.

Instructions regarding War Diaries and Intelligence Summaries are contained in F. S. Regs., Part II. and the Staff Manual respectively. Title pages will be prepared in manuscript.

WAR DIARY
or
INTELLIGENCE SUMMARY.
(Erase heading not required.)

Army Form C. 2118.

Place	Date	Hour	Summary of Events and Information	Remarks and references to Appendices
	28		Officers reconnoitred line	
			1 NCO with working party of RA worked on Adv Bde Hq dugout	
			Remainder of company cleaning billets etc.	
	29		No 4 Sect Artillery observation post at COWL HOUSE. Clearing away old strutting & sandbag work to make a brick tower	
			Made ~~covered~~ covered 1-seat latrine for Bde Hq.	
			No 3 Sect at night reclaiming THE BULGE	
			Sect 212th Co at night worked on mending revetment of OLD KENT ROAD	
			Sect 222nd Co at night clearing & revetting HUNTER ST (with 50 infantry)	
	~~30~~		2 men with artillery party carried on with Adv Bde Hq dugout.	
	30		Same as 29th except Sect of 222nd Co	
			Sect of 222nd Co was divided into 3 equal parts & worked with the three regiments in the line removing cylinders from front line & making up parapets.	
			2 men enlarging flues of soup-kitchen in HARLEY ST.	
			1 NCO & 1 Man was attached permanently to each battalion in the line for small jobs.	

2353 Wt. W2544/1454 700,000 5/15 D. D. & L. A.D.S.S./Forms/C. 2118.

Instructions regarding War Diaries and Intelligence Summaries are contained in F. S. Regs., Part II. and the Staff Manual respectively. Title pages will be prepared in manuscript.

WAR DIARY
or
INTELLIGENCE SUMMARY.
(Erase heading not required.)

Army Form C. 2118.

Place	Date	Hour	Summary of Events and Information	Remarks and references to Appendices
	30		1 Company 18th Middlesex pioneers worked on cleaning GLASGOW ROAD. This company has been put under my orders for work while the 33rd Div is up in the line.	
	31		Same as 30th. No 4 Sect also ~~[illegible]~~ worked at finishing off the brick tower obs post at MOUNTAIN HOUSE. Sapper HENRETTY killed by fragment of shell.	
			[illegible] Capt RE O.C. 11th Fd Coy RE	

2353 Wt. W2544/1454 700,000 5/15 D. D. & L. A.D.S.S./Forms/C. 2118.

2
~~33~~ Dn

Hie Jo Co. Ple.

Jan

Vol XVIII

Instructions regarding War Diaries and Intelligence Summaries are contained in F. S. Regs., Part II. and the Staff Manual respectively. Title Pages will be prepared in manuscript.

WAR DIARY ~~or~~ ~~INTELLIGENCE SUMMARY~~

(Erase heading not required.)

11th Field Company RE / January 1916.

Army Form C. 2118

Place	Date	Hour	Summary of Events and Information	Remarks and references to Appendices
January	1st	—	No 4 Sect started brick tower observation post in COWL HOUSE & continued Tower in MOUNTAIN HOUSE. Also ~~continued~~ continued enlarging flues in soup-kitchen in HARLEY ST. No 3 Sect continued revetting the BULGE at night. Also started to repair leak in tank in BATH HOUSE at ANNEQUIN. Also continued sheeting interior of Adv Bde Hq dugout in No 6 Siding. Sect of 222nd Coy (attached) continued clearing & revetting HUNTER ST with 50 Inf. Sect of 212th Coy (attached) continued removing cylinders from front line & making good the parapet Pioneer Coy worked on clearing BERKSHIRE LANE & HERTFORD ST.	
	2nd		No work was possible by day on account of heavy bombardment. At night parts of No 3 & 4 Sects helped 16th KRR in A, repair their trenches. Part of No 4 Sect blinded a window in Estaminet near COWL HOUSE by letting down floor of room above Plumbers No 3 Sect ~~wo~~ continued repair of tank at bath-house in ANNEQUIN	

1875 Wt. W593/826 1,000,000 4/15 J.B.C. & A. A.D.S.S./Forms/C. 2118.

Instructions regarding War Diaries and Intelligence Summaries are contained in F. S. Regs., Part II. and the Staff Manual respectively. Title Pages will be prepared in manuscript.

WAR DIARY
or
INTELLIGENCE SUMMARY
(Erase heading not required.)

Army Form C. 2118

Place	Date	Hour	Summary of Events and Information	Remarks and references to Appendices
	3		No 4 Sect — 1 NCO & 3 men continued COWL HOUSE tower 1 NCO & 1 man at night repaired strutting of KINGSCLERE obs station Remainder at night put out 120^x of French Wire in front of front line trench immediately S of LA BASSEE Rd	
			No 3 Sect — 1 NCO + 1 man with parts of RA continued lining Bde Hq dugout. Remainder put out 70^x of French wire in front of front line trench immediately N of LA BASSEE Rd.	
			Sect of 212th Coy (attached) dug trench from front lip of crater in front of BRICKSTACKS KEEP to join up with front line (top of REGENT ST)	
			Sect of 222nd Coy (attached) dug trench along rear lip of crater to join up with REGENT ST & form new front face of KEEP	
			Pioneers as 1st	
	4		No 3 Sect continued repair of tank & dugout. Also helped 16th KRR at night repairing front line trench across LA BASSEE Rd.	
			No 4 Sect finished enlarging flues of Soup Kitchen in HARLEY ST. Also continued work at COWL HOUSE & again re-strutted KINGSCLERE	

1875 Wt. W593/826 1,000,000 4/15 J.B.C. & A. A.D.S.S./Forms/C. 2118.

Army Form C. 2118

Instructions regarding War Diaries and Intelligence Summaries are contained in F. S. Regs., Part II. and the Staff Manual respectively. Title Pages will be prepared in manuscript.

WAR DIARY
or
INTELLIGENCE SUMMARY
(Erase heading not required.)

Place	Date	Hour	Summary of Events and Information	Remarks and references to Appendices
			Sect 212th Co (attached) worked at night reopening trench along North side of No 3 brickstack to form Northern face of THE KEEPS	
			Sect 222nd Coy rested. Required for day work tomorrow.	
			Pioneers as on 1st	
	5		No 3 Sect finished the tank at bath HOUSE ANNEQUIN, also continued the Bde Hqr dugout. Remainder with 30 Infantry continued revetting THE BULGE	
			No 4 Sect continued COWL HOUSE & MOUNTAIN HOUSE towers	
			Sect 222nd Coy with 50 Inf continued revetting HUNTER ST	
			Sect 212th Coy continued North face of BRICKSTACKS KEEP	
			Pioneers finished BERKSHIRE LANE, continued HERTFORD ST, & started pumping water out of COLDSTREAM LANE.	
	6th		Nos 3 & 4 Sects as on 5th	
			Sect 222nd Coy as on 5th. Also mended 4 shell holes in LA BASSEE Rd CAMBRIN	
			Sect 212th Coy rested.	
	7		Pioneers as on 5th	

1875 Wt. W593/826 1,000,000 4/15 J.B.C. & A. A.D.S.S./Forms/C. 2118.

Instructions regarding War Diaries and Intelligence Summaries are contained in F. S. Regs., Part II. and the Staff Manual respectively. Title Pages will be prepared in manuscript.

WAR DIARY
or
INTELLIGENCE SUMMARY
(Erase heading not required.)

Army Form C. 2118

Place	Date	Hour	Summary of Events and Information	Remarks and references to Appendices
	7		Nos 3 & 4 Sects as on 5th	
			Pioneers finished clearing HERTFORD ST & continued COLDSTREAM LANE	
			The attached section of 212th & 222nd Coys rejoined their own companies & my Nos 1 & 2 Sects rejoined my Company.	
	8th		No 1 Sect started clearing tunnel at PARK LANE REDOUBT. Also mended entrance to deep dugout in STAFFORD REDOUBT	
			No 2 Sect with 50 Inf worked on HUNTER ST. also with 50 inf started reclaiming DAWSON ST	
			Nos 3 & 4 Sects as on 6th	
			Pioneers continued COLDSTREAM LANE clearing & started clearing parts of GRAFTON ST.	
	9th		No 1 Sect continued work on tunnel in PARK LANE REDOUBT & also helped garrison of BRICKSTACKS KEEP to "make it good" where it had been damaged by the mine explosion	
3P 12/15			Nos 2 Sect with 50 inf continued work on HUNTER ST. Also with 50 inf by night started new trench from DAWSON ST to LOCK to form a new approach to B2 Subsection to avoid PONT FIXE which is being badly shelled every day	

1875 Wt. W593/826 1,000,000 4/15 J.B.C. & A. A.D.S.S./Forms/C. 2118.

Instructions regarding War Diaries and Intelligence Summaries are contained in F. S. Regs., Part II. and the Staff Manual respectively. Title Pages will be prepared in manuscript.

WAR DIARY
or
INTELLIGENCE SUMMARY
(Erase heading not required.)

Army Form C. 2118

Place	Date	Hour	Summary of Events and Information	Remarks and references to Appendices
			Nos 3 & 4 Sects same as 5th	
			~~As~~ Pioneers same as 8th	
	10th		No 1 Sect as on 9th	
			No 2 Sect Finished HUNTER ST as far as RE work is concerned.	
			No 3 Sect as on 5th, also started machine gun emplacement in No 2 Brickstack. This entails tunnelling through the stack & will be a long job.	
			No 4 Sect as on 5th	
			Pioneers continued COLDSTREAM LANE, boarded part of GRAFTON ST & revetted part of BERKSHIRE LANE.	
	11th		No 1 Sect as on 9th, also made up entrance to Bomb Store in CUINCHY SUP. PT.	
			No 2 Sect prepared ~~8~~ trestles for new footbridge across canal just W of lock also with 100 inf by night continued new trench from DAWSON ST to LOCK (SKEYS TRENCH) also with 50 inf at night cleared top part of BERKSHIRE LANE of mud which had been put on fire steps.	
			No 3 Sect with 20 inf by night continued THE BULGE. Also continued mine into BRICKSTACK NO 2 & started one into the RUINED MILL for another M.G. Emplacement	
			No 4 Sect as on 5th	
			Pioneers as for 10th	

1875 Wt. W593/826 1,000,000 4/15 J.B.C. & A. A.D.S.S./Forms/C. 2118.

Army Form C. 2118

Instructions regarding War Diaries and Intelligence Summaries are contained in F. S. Regs., Part II. and the Staff Manual respectively. Title Pages will be prepared in manuscript.

WAR DIARY
or
INTELLIGENCE SUMMARY
(Erase heading not required.)

Place	Date	Hour	Summary of Events and Information	Remarks and references to Appendices
	12		No 1 Sect as for 10th	
			No 2 Sect made half bridge over canal at LOCK	
			Also with 50 inf at night continued clearing forward end of BERKSHIRE LANE	
			No 3 Sect as for 11th	
			No 4 Sect as for 5th	
			Pioneers continued work on COLDSTREAM LANE, BERKSHIRE LANE, & GRAFTON ST	
	13		No 1 Sect as for 10th	
			No 2 Sect completed bridge over canal at lock. Also with 50 inf by day continued revetting BERKSHIRE LANE & with 100 inf by night continued SKEYS TRENCH	
			No 3 completed work on BULGE & continued the two MG emplacements	
			No 4 Sect as for 5th	
			Pioneers continued COLDSTREAM LANE & started work on big drain (WILLOW GUT) in B,	
	14		No 1 Sect worked on ~~No~~ 4 Mg emplacements in 2nd line	
			No 2 Sect continued revetting BERKSHIRE LANE	
			No 3 Sect worked on MG emplacements in RUINED MILL & BRICKSTACK No 2	
			No 4 Sect as for 5th	
			Pioneers as for 13th	

1875 Wt. W593/826 1,000,000 4/15 J.B.C. & A. A.D.S.S./Forms/C. 2118.

Army Form C. 2118

Instructions regarding War Diaries and Intelligence Summaries are contained in F. S. Regs., Part II. and the Staff Manual respectively. Title Pages will be prepared in manuscript.

WAR DIARY
or
~~INTELLIGENCE SUMMARY~~
(Erase heading not required.)

Place	Date	Hour	Summary of Events and Information	Remarks and references to Appendices
	15		No 1 Sect as for 14th. No 2 Sect as for 14th No 3 Sect, Mg emplacements in BRICKSTACKS NO2 & RUINED MILL ~~No 4 Sect~~ also continued clearing TUNNEL in PARK LANE REDOUBT & started strengthening 3 deep dugouts in OXFORD ST No 4 Sect strengthened all the cellars & dugouts at No 1 HARLEY ST (dressing Station) Pioneers worked on clearing COLDSTREAM LANE & the two drains in B1 (WILLOW CUT & FRONT LINE CUT)	
	16		Capt Sim went on leave. No 1 Sect as before No 2 Sect as before No 3 Sect as before. No 4 Sect Completed artillery O.P. in MOUNTAIN HOUSE. and commenced work on making an emplacement under the Ry Bridge ~~xxxx~~ near the RAILWAY HOLLOW from which to use a captured ~~xxxxxxx~~ German searchlight and with making the approaches to the place practicable for the same. Pioneers completed the opening of COLDSTREAM LANE and commenced revetting the E end of OLD KENT ROAD where it is very shallow. They also continued the drainage of the front line N of the Canal.	

1875 Wt. W593/826 1,000,000 4/15 J.B.C. & A. A.D.S.S./Forms/C. 2118.

Army Form C. 2118

Instructions regarding War Diaries and Intelligence Summaries are contained in F. S. Regs., Part II. and the Staff Manual respectively. Title Pages will be prepared in manuscript.

WAR DIARY
or
~~INTELLIGENCE SUMMARY~~
(Erase heading not required.)

Place	Date	Hour	Summary of Events and Information	Remarks and references to Appendices
	17		No 1 Section & No 2 Section as before No 3 Section worked in dugouts as before and finished opening up of BROOK ST. No 4 Section as before. Pioneers as before except that platoon which had cleared out COLDSTREAM LANE commenced clearing out OXFORD ST between OLD KENT RD & COLDSTREAM LANE.	
	18		No 1 2 & 3 & 4 Sections as on the day previous. The work of Nos 2 & 4 Sections was greatly interrupted by hostile shell fire. Pioneers worked as on previous day.	
	19		Work as for previous day.	
	20.		Nos 1 2 & ~~4~~ sections as before No 3 section took on in addition to previous day the reclaiming of deep dugouts in MARYLEBONE RD Pioneers as before.	
	21		No 1 Section completed the M.G. emplacement in the E face of the BRICK STACKS KEEP otherwise as in previous day Nos 2 & 3 ~~sections~~ & 4 sections as in previous day Pioneers as above.	

1875 Wt. W593/826 1,000,000 4/15 J.B.C. & A. A.D.S.S./Forms/C. 2118.

Army Form C. 2118

Instructions regarding War Diaries and Intelligence Summaries are contained in F. S. Regs., Part II. and the Staff Manual respectively. Title Pages will be prepared in manuscript.

WAR DIARY
or
INTELLIGENCE SUMMARY

(Erase heading not required.)

Place	Date	Hour	Summary of Events and Information	Remarks and references to Appendices
	22		Nos 1 + 2 sections as before. No 3 section as before but in addition undertook with a party of 30 infantry the resolving of the BULGE which had been blown in the previous day by 5.9" shells and big aerial torpedos No 4 Section completed the approaches + emplacement for the searchlight and commenced work on reclaiming parapets and alterations to BRICKSTACKS KEEP. Searchlight section commenced taking the searchlight into position. After reaching the COWL HOUSE further work was stopped by bright moonlight. B, section had been inspected by the C.O. 18th Middlesex (pioneers) who decided to put more men on the drainage of it. The half coy working S of the Canal was shifted over to the N and another half company put in to replace it. The G.O.C. 19th Inf Bde decided that more help should be given to the Inf in A2 for work in the front line so work by the platoon in OXFORD ST was stopped and they commenced on deepening firestepping and thickening parapets in A2 between Sap No 10 + JERUSALEM HILL. The revetting of OLD KENT RD was carried on with.	

1875 Wt. W593/826 1,000,000 4/15 J.B.C. & A. A.D.S.S./Forms/C. 2118.

Instructions regarding War Diaries and Intelligence Summaries are contained in F. S. Regs., Part II. and the Staff Manual respectively. Title Pages will be prepared in manuscript.

WAR DIARY
or
INTELLIGENCE SUMMARY
(Erase heading not required.)

Army Form C. 2118

Place	Date	Hour	Summary of Events and Information	Remarks and references to Appendices
	23		No 1 Section as before	
			No 2 Section, no infantry being available helped the searchlight section to install the light in position.	
			No 3 & No 4 continued as before. No work done in BULGE no party from infantry being available.	
			Pioneers as before	
	24		Nos 1 3 & 4 as before No 2 continued work in BERKSHIRE LANE no infantry available	
			Pioneers as before.	
			Capt GEH. SIM returned from leave	
			2/Lt R.E. FRYER went on leave.	

1875 Wt. W593/826 1,000,000 4/15 J.B.C. & A. A.D.S.S./Forms/C. 2118.

Instructions regarding War Diaries and Intelligence Summaries are contained in F. S. Regs., Part II. and the Staff Manual respectively. Title Pages will be prepared in manuscript.

WAR DIARY
or
INTELLIGENCE SUMMARY
(Erase heading not required.)

Army Form C. 2118

Place	Date	Hour	Summary of Events and Information	Remarks and references to Appendices
	25		No 1 Sect continued MG Emplacements in 2nd line & BRICKSTACK No 2 & RUINED MILL (SHORT CUT) No 2 Sect with 50 Inf at night continued revetting BERKSHIRE LANE No 3 Sect with 20 Inf at night continued repair of THE BULGE. Also continued repair of TUNNEL (A1) & deep dugouts in MARYLEBONE RD & OXFORD ST No 4 Sect with 50 Inf at night continued improvements to BRICKSTACKS KEEP	
	26		No 1 Sect as before Part of No 2 Sect worked in BERKSHIRE LANE dug-outs by day. Also mended one of the two holes in Overhead Railway HEARTFORD ST (broken by shells) No 3 Sect continued dugout strutting in OXFORD ST & MARYLEBONE RD. Former are now finished All night work stopped on account of anticipated attack which never came off	
	27		Same as 25th. No infantry parties available	
	28		No 1 Sect ditto No 2 Sect at night continued repair of Overhead Ry HEARTFORD ST. Also renewed Canvas Screens across PONT FIXE	

Instructions regarding War Diaries and Intelligence Summaries are contained in F. S. Regs., Part II. and the Staff Manual respectively. Title pages will be prepared in manuscript.

WAR DIARY
or
INTELLIGENCE SUMMARY.
(Erase heading not required.)

Army Form C. 2118.

Place	Date	Hour	Summary of Events and Information	Remarks and references to Appendices

APPENDIX I

Account of the cutting of the German wire with Bangalore Torpedo in connection with raids on the nights of 6/7 & 7/8 June 1915.

Raid of the night 6/7.

Object of the operation was to cut a gap in the enemys wire to allow infantry raiding party to get through into German Trench.

Previous Reconnaissance I was not told till mid-day 6th that a Torpedo was required so no previous reconnaissance on the part of my officer was possible. The Infantry officer in charge of the raiding party had, however, been out with a party the previous night & cut away some of the wire with wire cutters. He estimated the remaining uncut wire as about 20 ft broad & very thick. I detailed Lieut ANDERSON for the job & he took with him Sergt FIELD & 4 sappers

Preparation of the Torpedo 3 lengths (30') of torpedo filled with Ammonal were obtained from BETHUNE, 1st Army Workshops with tin primer complete. It was decided to fire it electrically from the trench. Leads, detonator & exploder were all

Instructions regarding War Diaries and Intelligence Summaries are contained in F. S. Regs., Part II. and the Staff Manual respectively. Title pages will be prepared in manuscript.

WAR DIARY
or
INTELLIGENCE SUMMARY.
(Erase heading not required.)

Army Form C. 2118.

Place	Date	Hour	Summary of Events and Information	Remarks and references to Appendices

carefully tested in the afternoon & the "primer made up with ammonal & electric detonator & attached to the leads before starting. Joints were soldered & insulated. A No 8 detonator & 3' of safety fuze were also inserted in the primer in case the electrical method should fail.

The whole apparatus was carried up to our trenches (just N of the brickstacks) by the party that was going to use them & everything was ready at 9.30 pm on the site.

The placing of the torpedo The party of sappers left the trench at 10.20 pm in the following order:—

(1) Lieut ANDERSON (accompanied by 2Lt Mc Roberts, o/c raiding party, as guide) with front length of the torpedo.

(2) Sergt FIELD with centre length of torpedo.

(3) 1 Sapper with rear length of torpedo

(4) 1 Sapper with the ends of leads with primer complete attached

(5) 1 Sapper about 20x behind No 4 ~~with~~ easing out the leads

(6) 1 Sapper paying out the leads off drum in the trench.

As soon as the party had got to the german wire the infantry officer came

WAR DIARY
or
INTELLIGENCE SUMMARY.
(Erase heading not required.)

Place	Date	Hour	Summary of Events and Information	Remarks and references to Appendices
			back and got out the raiding party, who took cover behind a bank about 20x to 30x from the german wire. Meanwhile Lieut ANDERSON pushed the torpedo through the wire.	
			When all was fixed all the RE party returned to the trench.	
			The torpedo made a slight noise going through the wire, rather like a mouse squeaking, but the Germans took no notice of it. When placed the nose of the torpedo was touching the german parapet.	
			A signal had been arranged to let the raiding party know when the torpedo was going to be fired. Lt ANDERSON was to fire 3 revolver shots in quick succession, wait 10 seconds & then fire.	
			The artillery forward observing officer had a telephone alongside the exploder so there was no difficulty about warning the artillery.	
			The placing of the torpedo took a little over an hour.	
			The firing of the torpedo The torpedo was fired as arranged. The electrical firing worked excellently and the entanglement was destroyed, leaving a gap absolutely clear of wire 10' to 15' broad through which the raiding	

Instructions regarding War Diaries and Intelligence Summaries are contained in F. S. Regs., Part II. and the Staff Manual respectively. Title pages will be prepared in manuscript.

WAR DIARY
or
INTELLIGENCE SUMMARY.
(Erase heading not required.)

Army Form C. 2118.

Place	Date	Hour	Summary of Events and Information	Remarks and references to Appendices
			party went. Artillery opened within 20+ seconds of the explosion, which took place at 11.45 pm	
			After the raiding party had all returned the leads were quietly rolled in from the trench & my party returned to billets.	
			<u>Raid of the night 7/8.</u>	
			This operation had exactly the same object as the raid of the previous night & was carried out in a very similar manner. The main differences were as follows.	
			(1) I had about 5 days warning of the raid. Lieut BALCOMBE was detailed for the job & he made 2 reconnaissances with Cpl SAUNDERS (No 3 Sect), one on his own & one with the infantry officer who was to carry out the raid. The exact spot was therefore known beforehand (20x N of the LA BASSEE Road)	
			(2) The German wire was about 15x away from the german parapet here & not close up as in the former raid. It was about 20' deep & fairly thick.	
			(3) No attempt had been made to cut it previously.	
			(4) The Infantry officer did not accompany the sapper party as this was not necessary	

T2134. Wt. W708–776. 500000. 4/15. Sir J. C. & S.

Instructions regarding War Diaries and Intelligence Summaries are contained in F. S. Regs., Part II. and the Staff Manual respectively. Title pages will be prepared in manuscript.

WAR DIARY
or
INTELLIGENCE SUMMARY.
(Erase heading not required.)

Army Form C. 2118.

Place	Date	Hour	Summary of Events and Information	Remarks and references to Appendices
			(5) The party was spotted by the enemy while placing the torpedo & 2 bombs were thrown at them. No damage was done & the work went on.	
			(6) 2 men were left in the trench to pay out leads instead of one. This was learnt the previous night.	
			Otherwise the procedure was an exact replica of the previous night and the explosion was perfectly successful in cutting the wire.	
			Lessons learnt from the two raids.	
			(1) Take every precaution beforehand. Test everything. Leave nothing to chance.	
			(2) Do the whole thing with your own sappers. Dont let an infantry man touch any part of the torpedo, leads or exploder during the operation. You cannot guarantee success ~~if~~ unless the whole thing is done entirely by R.E.	
			(3) See that every man knows exactly what the scheme is & how it is to be carried out.	
			(4) Pick your men but dont ask for volunteers.	
			(5) A few bombs wont do you much harm & dont get rattled by them. Lie low till it quiets down & then get on with the job.	

T2134. Wt. W708–776. 500000. 4/15. Sir J. C. & S.

Army Form C. 2118

WAR DIARY
~~or~~
~~INTELLIGENCE SUMMARY~~
(Erase heading not required.)

Instructions regarding War Diaries and Intelligence Summaries are contained in F. S. Regs., Part II. and the Staff Manual respectively. Title Pages will be prepared in manuscript.

11th FIELD Coy RE
33rd DIVISION
FEBRUARY 1916.

2

Place	Date	Hour	Summary of Events and Information	Remarks and references to Appendices
				Vol XIX
February	1st		Work continued in the CUINCHY FRONT (A_1, A_2 & B, Sectors)	
			No 1 Sect continued MG emplacements in OLD MILL & BRICKSTACK No 2, also concealing those in RESERVE LINE by night.	
			No 2 Sect finished revetment of HERTFORD ST where it had been blown in.	
			Remainder of Company packing wagons etc for move to rest area. This move was cancelled about 9pm.	
			At night searchlight at bridge in A_2 was run. The night was misty & though the light was excellent it could not reach german trenches.	
	2nd		No 1 Sect Same as 1st	
			No 2 Sect with 50 Inf at night continued revetment of BERKSHIRE LANE	
			No 3 Sect " 30 " " " " " " BULGE	
			No 4 Sect " 15 " " " " improvements to BRICKSTACKS KEEP.	
	3rd		Same as 2nd. No 4 Sect had 30 infantry. 2/Lt Fryer returned from leave.	
	4th		No 1 Sect Same as 1st All the RESERVE LINE MGs are now completed & occupied	
			No 2 Sect with 50 Inf continued BERK LANE & dogs leg. Filled in old part of BERKS LANE cut off by dogs leg. Started clearing dogs leg of LOVERS LANE & building loopholed traverse	

1875 Wt. W593/826 1,000,000 4/15 J.B.C. & A. A.D.S.S./Forms/C. 2118.

Instructions regarding War Diaries and Intelligence Summaries are contained in F. S. Regs., Part II. and the Staff Manual respectively. Title Pages will be prepared in manuscript.

WAR DIARY
or
INTELLIGENCE SUMMARY
(Erase heading not required.)

Army Form C. 2118

Place	Date	Hour	Summary of Events and Information	Remarks and references to Appendices
			No 2 Sect also started work on COFFEE BAR in ANNEQUIN (fitting doors, counters, stoves etc) 4 men	
			No 3 Sect strengthened deep dugouts in MARYLEBONE Rd & ESPERANTO ST; also with 30 inf at night continued work on the BULGE.	
			No 4 Sect with 20 inf at night continued improvements to brickstacks KEEP & commenced wiring.	
	5th		Same as 4th also put up number boards for all boyaux between front line (26 to 51) The BULGE is now finished.	
	6th		No 1 Sect continued MG emplacement in OLD MILL & also improved the emplacement in front line E of BULGE (widened loophole) No 2 Sect dogs legs of BERKS, LOVERS, COLDSTREAM lanes with 50 Inf at night No 3 Sect continued strengthening deep dugouts in ESPERANTO ST (MARYLEBONE Rd dugouts are now finished). Also started 4 dugouts in SPOIL BANK No 4 Sect with 20 Inf continued keeps & wiring of same.	

1875 Wt. W593/826 1,000,000 4/15 J.B.C. & A. A.D.S.S./Forms/C. 2118.

Instructions regarding War Diaries and Intelligence Summaries are contained in F. S. Regs., Part II. and the Staff Manual respectively. Title Pages will be prepared in manuscript.

WAR DIARY
or
INTELLIGENCE SUMMARY
(Erase heading not required.)

Army Form C. 2118

Place	Date	Hour	Summary of Events and Information	Remarks and references to Appendices
	7th		Same as 6th — no Infantry.	
	8th		Same as 6th Capt Pressey went on leave. Wiring of ~~keep~~ BRICKSTACKS KEEP finished 4 Men No 2 Sect started erection of TARRANT HUT at Bde. Hq LE PREOL Closed all sluices (that were not broken) at CUINCHY LOCK.	
	9th		Same as 6th Framework for dugout for 2 officers put up at No1 HARLEY ST. Sandbagging to be done by RAMC At night searchlight was run between 9 & 9.30 pm. It was very clear & german trenches could be seen from the mine craters at DUCKS BILL on the left for a sweep of 60° to the right A German wiring party was picked up in the beam & fired on by a LEWIS GUN in B1 & dispersed. Germans opened MG fire on the light & got one hit which bent ~~the~~ one leaf of the shutter. This was put right next day. No artillery fire was opened.	

1875 Wt. W593/826 1,000,000 4/15 J.B.C. & A. A.D.S.S./Forms/C. 2118.

Instructions regarding War Diaries and Intelligence Summaries are contained in F. S. Regs., Part II. and the Staff Manual respectively. Title Pages will be prepared in manuscript.

WAR DIARY
or
INTELLIGENCE SUMMARY
(Erase heading not required.)

Army Form C. 2118

Place	Date	Hour	Summary of Events and Information	Remarks and references to Appendices
	10th		No1 Sect continued work on MG emplacements in OLD MILL & started dugout for MG S3	
			No2 Sect continued erection of TARRANT HUT at Bde Hq. & Coffee bar in ANNEQUIN also reserve line dogs legs with 50 infantry at night.	
			No3 Sect, working continuously in 3 reliefs started 2 deep dugouts for MG, 1 & 3	
			No4 Sect " " " " " " " " " " 5 & S7	
			Two reliefs of 40 infantry for Nos 3 & 4 Sections	
	11th		Same as 10th Coffee bar ANNEQUIN now completed.	
	~~11~~		Sect 222nd Fd Coy (Lent) started deep dugout for MG 6 & ordinary strong dugout for MG 8 (N of Canal) with 25 infantry for carrying	
	12th		Same as 11th	
	13th		Same as 11th	
	14th		Same as 11th	
	15th		Same as 11th Dugout for MG 3 finished.	
	16		Same as 15th. Dugouts for MG 1, 5, S7 finished. Infantry dugouts in SPOIL BANK continued Capt Pressey returned from leave.	

1875 Wt. W593/826 1,000,000 4/15 J.B.C. & A. A.D.S.S./Forms/C. 2118.

Instructions regarding War Diaries and Intelligence Summaries are contained in F. S. Regs., Part II. and the Staff Manual respectively. Title Pages will be prepared in manuscript.

WAR DIARY
or
INTELLIGENCE SUMMARY
(Erase heading not required.)

Army Form C. 2118

Place	Date	Hour	Summary of Events and Information	Remarks and references to Appendices
	17th		No 1 Sect continued emplacements in OLD MILL (S1 & S1a)	
			also completed dugout in Brickstack 2 for MG (S 3)	
			Started tunnel into Brickstack 12 for MG S 4 A	
			No 2 Sect continued dogs legs Reserve line with 80 Inf at night. Also new piece of GRAFTON ST.	
			Also put up partition etc in Tarrant Hut at Bde Hq LE PREOL	
			No 3 Sect continued the 5 dugouts in SPOIL BANK & timbered new dugout dug by Inf in ESPERANTO TER. Started 2nd entrance for dugout of MG S 5 (CABBAGE PATCH)	
			No 4 Sect started dugout with 2 entrances under No 12 Brickstack for Coy Hq.	
			Also started 2nd entrance & dugout for MG S 6 (off IKEY TERRACE)	
			Also started new mined emplacement for MG S 7 out of dugout just completed	
			Sect 222nd Coy completed dugout for MG 7 & continued dugout for MG 6	
			Sluices at CUINCHY LOCK partially opened to avoid flooding mine.	
			Lieut CLIFTON went on leave	
	~~18th~~ 18th		Same as 17th	
	19th		Same as 17th	
			Part No 2 Sect started revetment of portion of HARLEY ST (This took 3 days)	
			2 Men No 3 Sect reclaimed & re-timbered dugout in MARYLEBONE Rd (one week)	

1875 Wt. W593/826 1,000,000 4/15 J.B.C. & A. A.D.S.S./Forms/C. 2118.

Army Form C. 2118

Instructions regarding War Diaries and Intelligence Summaries are contained in F. S. Regs., Part II. and the Staff Manual respectively. Title Pages will be prepared in manuscript.

WAR DIARY
or
INTELLIGENCE SUMMARY
(Erase heading not required.)

Place	Date	Hour	Summary of Events and Information	Remarks and references to Appendices
	20		Same as 17th except No 3 Sect took on dugout for MG 6 as sect 222nd Coy was removed. Only 1 dugout on SPOIL BANK carried on with.	
	21		Same as 20th. Dugout for emplacement MG S3 completed by No 1 Sect 4 Men No 4 Sect started timbering entrance to Sap 14 (3 days work)	
	22		4 Men No 4 Sect continued sap 14 Remainder of company rested.	
	23		Same as ~~20th~~ 21st	
	24		Same as 21st No 2 Sect having finished the dogs-legs etc of reserve line started ~~emplace~~ mine to emplacement for MGR6 (end of BANBURY CROSS). 60' to go	
	25		Same as 24th. 1 dugout in SPOIL BANK finished. Lt CLIFTON returned from leave	
	26		Same as 24th Dugout in MARYLEBONE Rd finished.	
	27		Same as 26th Dugout in GLASGOW Rd (retimbering) started.	
	28th		Same as 27th Dugout for MG 6 finished.	

1875 Wt. W593/826 1,000,000 4/15 J.B.C. & A. A.D.S.S./Forms/C. 2118.

Instructions regarding War Diaries and Intelligence Summaries are contained in F. S. Regs., Part II. and the Staff Manual respectively. Title Pages will be prepared in manuscript.

WAR DIARY
or
INTELLIGENCE SUMMARY
(Erase heading not required.)

Army Form C. 2118

Place	Date	Hour	Summary of Events and Information	Remarks and references to Appendices
	29		No 1 Sect continued work on MGs S1 & S1A (old mill) These are nearing completion & will be finished about 4.3.16. A drawing of these will accompany next months diary.	
			Also continued S4A (in No12 Stack). Chamber completed, only requires loophole & table	
			Also started drive into stack for MG S3A.	
			No 2 Sect finished tables etc for Tarrant Hut at Bde Hq.	
			Also finished tunnel for MG R6. Emplacement & dugout remain to be done.	
			No 3 Sect finished second entrance & strengthening dugout for MG S5	
			Also continued dugouts in SPOIL BANK 3 remain to be finished, all in hand	
			Also finished re-timbering dugout in GLASGOW Rd	
			No 4 Sect continued 2nd entrance & dugout for MG B6. This should be finished about 7.3.16	
			Also continued emplacement for MG S7. Chamber finished, loophole to be put in, should be finished about 7.3.16.	
			Also continued dugout for COY Hq under Brickstack 12. Nearing completion	
			Note About 100 Infantry were employed each day as carriers etc for the various jobs, also removing & emptying sandbags.	

E. E. Allen Capt RE
O.C. 11th Fd Coy R.E.

1875 Wt. W593/826 1,000,000 4/15 J.B.C. & A. A.D.S.S./Forms/C. 2118.

2/33

11 Fd Coy R.E.

Vol XX

Instructions regarding War Diaries and Intelligence Summaries are contained in F. S. Regs., Part II. and the Staff Manual respectively. Title Pages will be prepared in manuscript.

WAR DIARY
or
INTELLIGENCE SUMMARY
(Erase heading not required.)

Army Form C.

11th Field Company RE
March 1916.

Place	Date	Hour	Summary of Events and Information	Remarks and references to Appendices
MARCH.	1		No 1 Sect continued Machine gun emplacements in OLD MILL, Brickstacks 10 & 12,	
			No 2 Sect continued the emplacement & dugout for MGR6, end of BANBURY CROSS	
			No 3 Sect continued 3 dugouts for Infantry in SPOIL BANK	
			No 4 Sect continued 2nd entrance to dugout for MG in IKEY TERRACE, also emplacement for MG ~~R~~ S7 in ABINGDON LANE, also dugout for Coy Hq under Brickstack 12	
	2		Same as 1st.	
			No 3 Sect also started strong dugout for MGR7 in SPOIL BANK.	
	3		Same as 2nd No 3 Sect started deep dugout for MG2 in WATERLOO PLACE in shifts	
	4		Same as 2nd. Coy Hq dugout under Brickstack 12 finished by No 4 Sect	
	5		Same as 4th Emplacements in OLD MILL now finished.	
	6		~~Same as 5th~~ No work done, Company rested. Inspection 4pm	
	7		No 1 Sect continued the 4 emplacements in brickstacks (working in reliefs)	
			No 2 Sect continued emplacement & dugout for MGR6, end of BANBURY CROSS (working in reliefs	

1875 Wt. W593/826 1,000,000 4/15 J.B.C. & A. A.D.S.S./Forms/C. 2118.

Instructions regarding War Diaries and Intelligence Summaries are contained in F. S. Regs., Part II. and the Staff Manual respectively. Title Pages will be prepared in manuscript.

WAR DIARY
or
INTELLIGENCE SUMMARY
(Erase heading not required.)

Army Form C. 2118

Place	Date	Hour	Summary of Events and Information	Remarks and references to Appendices
			No 3 Sect continued dugout for MG 2 in WATERLOO PLACE working in reliefs, also dugout for MG R7 in SPOIL BANK.	
			No 4 Sect continued ~~dugout~~ emplacement for MG S7 in ABBINGDON LANE. Also continued dugout for MG S6 in IKEY TERRACE. Also started deep dugout with 2 entrances for Infantry in HUNTER ST.	
	8		Same as 7th. No 3 Sect finished dugout for MG R7 in SPOIL BANK also 2 of the 3 infantry dugouts in SPOIL BANK	
	9th		Same as 8th. No 3 Sect finished dugout for MG 2 in WATERLOO PLACE & started two entrance deep dugout for inf in MARYLEBONE ROAD.	
			No 4 Sect completed the MG emplacement S7 in ABBINGDON LANE.	
	10th		No 1 Sect finished emplacement firing N out of Brickstack 12 & continued the other 3 (brickstacks 10 & 12), (working in reliefs)	
			No 2 Sect continued emplacement & dugout for MG R 6, end of BANBURY CROSS (working in reliefs)	

1875 Wt. W593/826 1,000,000 4/15 J.B.C. & A. A.D.S.S./Forms/C. 2118.

Army Form C. 2118

Instructions regarding War Diaries and Intelligence Summaries are contained in F. S. Regs., Part II. and the Staff Manual respectively. Title Pages will be prepared in manuscript.

WAR DIARY
or
INTELLIGENCE SUMMARY
(Erase heading not required.)

Place	Date	Hour	Summary of Events and Information	Remarks and references to Appendices
			No 3 Sect finished the 3rd infantry dugout in SPOIL BANK.	
			Also continued deep dugout with 2 entrances for Inf in MARYLEBONE Rd (in reliefs)	
			Also two started 2 MG emplacements in TOWER RESERVE TR, mined forward out of dugouts already made by 212th Coy RE (working in reliefs)	
			No 4 Sect continued dugout for MG S6 in IKEY TERRACE	
			Also continued deep dugout for Infantry in HUNTER ST (in reliefs)	
	11th		Same as 10th	
	12th		Same as 10th No 4 Sect at night also started improving the wire of MG R1 in front of TOWER RESERVE TRENCH (4 bays & festooned)	
			2 Men of No 2 Sect started small hut for Armourers Shop in ANNEQUIN N.	
	13th		Same as 12th No 2 Sect at night also started extending the wire of MG R10 northwards (4 bays & festooned) in front of TOWER RESERVE TRENCH.	
	14th		Same as 13th No 3 Sect finished emplacements R11 & R12	

1875 Wt. W593/826 1,000,000 4/15 J.B.C. & A. A.D.S.S./Forms/C. 2118.

Instructions regarding War Diaries and Intelligence Summaries are contained in F. S. Regs., Part II. and the Staff Manual respectively. Title Pages will be prepared in manuscript.

WAR DIARY
or
INTELLIGENCE SUMMARY
(Erase heading not required.)

Army Form C. 2118

Place	Date	Hour	Summary of Events and Information	Remarks and references to Appendices
			No 4 Sect continued the two deep dugouts in RESERVE LINE	
			Also started to renovate two entrances to dugouts in BRICKSTACKS KEEP	
	26		Same as 25th Lt BALCOMBE proceeded on leave.	
	27		Same as 26th	
			No 4 Sect finished the two entrances to dugouts in BRICKSTACKS KEEP	
			No 1 Sect finished the dugout behind brickstack 7 for T.M. Battery	
			No 3 Sect starting lowering the tunnel to MG R10 in TOWER RESERVE TR.	
	28		Same as 27th	
			No 4 Sect finished the deep dugout in reserve line near CUINCHY SUP PT	
			No 4 Sect started clearing & making good the two entrances to another dugout in BRICKSTACKS KEEP (knocked in by Minenwerfer) (Finished 30th)	
			No 2 Sect made a snipers post in a derelict MG emplacement in ABBINGDON LANE.	
			Lieut BALCOMBE went on leave.	
			" Lieut FRYER went to hospital.	
			I/NO No 4 Sect at night superintended the start of a dressing stn dugout in THE LANE	

1875 Wt. W593/826 1,000,000 4/15 J.B.C. & A. A.D.S.S./Forms/C. 2118.

Instructions regarding War Diaries and Intelligence Summaries are contained in F. S. Regs., Part II. and the Staff Manual respectively. Title Pages will be prepared in manuscript.

WAR DIARY
or
INTELLIGENCE SUMMARY
(Erase heading not required.)

Army Form C. 2118

Place	Date	Hour	Summary of Events and Information	Remarks and references to Appendices
	29		~~Same as 28th~~	
			No 1 Sect continued emplacements and dugouts MGS3a & MGS3b in Brickstack 10	
			No 2 Sect continued dugout in RAILWAY HOLLOW and repair of CUINCHY SUPPORT POINT	
			No 3 Sect finished alterations to tunnel to MG R10 & continued the two deep dugouts in TOWER RESERVE and MARYLEBONE ROAD	
			No 4 Sect continued deep dugout in ESPERANTO ST and started making second entrance & enlarging an existing dugout, same trench.	
			Dressing Station dugout in THE LANE continued.	
	30		Same as 29th.	
			No 3 Sect also started strengthening two old deep dugouts in BACK ST	
			No 3 Sect finished deep dugout in MARYLEBONE Rd	
			No 4 Sect " " " " ESPERANTO ST	
			No 4 Sect started enlarging & making 2nd entrance to another deep dugout in ESPERANTO ST	

1875 Wt. W593/826 1,000,000 4/15 J.B.C. & A. A.D.S.S./Forms/C. 2118.

Instructions regarding War Diaries and Intelligence Summaries are contained in F. S. Regs., Part II. and the Staff Manual respectively. Title Pages will be prepared in manuscript.

WAR DIARY
or
INTELLIGENCE SUMMARY
(Erase heading not required.)

Army Form C. 2118

Place	Date	Hour	Summary of Events and Information	Remarks and references to Appendices
	31		No 1 Sect finished emplacements & dugouts MGS3a & MGS3b in Brickstack No 10	
			No 2 Sect continued the dugout in Ry HOLLOW and repair of CUINCHY SUPPORT POINT	
			No 3 Sect continued deep dugout in TOWER RESERVE TRENCH & the repair of 2 dugouts in BACK STREET. Also started to repair deep dugout for MGR2 in STAFFORD REDOUBT	
			No 4 Sect continued the two deep dugouts in ESPERANTO ST & also superintended the dressing station dugout in THE LANE	
			NOTE All machine gun emplacements are now finished. Attached are drawings of some of the most interesting types made to supplement those attached to my February War Diary.	
			[signature] Capt RE O.C. 11th Fd Coy RE	

1875 Wt. W593/826 1,000,000 4/15 J.B.C. & A. A.D.S.S./Forms/C. 2118.

Army Form C. 2118

Instructions regarding War Diaries and Intelligence Summaries are contained in F. S. Regs., Part II. and the Staff Manual respectively. Title Pages will be prepared in manuscript.

WAR DIARY
or
INTELLIGENCE SUMMARY
(Erase heading not required.)

Place	Date	Hour	Summary of Events and Information	Remarks and references to Appendices
			No 3 Sect with 30 Inf at night continued THE BULGE	
			No 4 Sect with 20 Inf at night " BRICKSTACKS KEEP.	
			Note	
			Three sketches of the 4 machine-gun emplacements of the 2nd Line are appended.	
			[illegible] Capt RE O.C. 11th Fd Coy RE	

1875 Wt. W593/826 1,000,000 4/15 J.B.C. & A. A.D.S.S./Forms/C. 2118.

Instructions regarding War Diaries and Intelligence Summaries are contained in F. S. Regs., Part II. and the Staff Manual respectively. Title Pages will be prepared in manuscript.

WAR DIARY
or
~~INTELLIGENCE SUMMARY~~
(Erase heading not required.)

Army Form C. 2118

11th Field Company RE
~~Feb~~ April 1916

Place	Date	Hour	Summary of Events and Information	Remarks and references to Appendices
April	1		No 1 Sect, with 75 Infantry started to repair front face of BRADDEL POINT. (this work was afterwards countermanded so was not continued) No 2 Sect continued deep dugout in RAILWAY HOLLOW and repair of CUINCHY SUPPORT POINT. Also started trench to Bulge from dugout with 20 Infantry No 3 Sect finished infantry deep dugout in TOWER RESERVE TRENCH and continued repairing dugout MG R2 in STAFFORD REDOUBT No 4 Sect continued enlarging 2 deep dugouts in ESPERANTO ST and superintended the digging of dressing stn deep dugout in THE LANE	
	2		Rest day. No work done.	
	3		No 1 Sect, with 40 infantry at night, started two trench-mortar emplacements behind No 13 brickstack. Remainder same as 1st No 3 Sect finished one of the 4 dugouts in BACK ST and started reclaiming 2nd entrance to dugout in MARYLEBONE ROAD.	

1875 Wt. W593/826 1,000,000 4/15 J.B.C. & A. A.D.S.S./Forms/C. 2118.

Army Form C. 2118

Instructions regarding War Diaries and Intelligence Summaries are contained in F. S. Regs., Part II. and the Staff Manual respectively. Title Pages will be prepared in manuscript.

WAR DIARY
or
INTELLIGENCE SUMMARY
(Erase heading not required.)

Place	Date	Hour	Summary of Events and Information	Remarks and references to Appendices
	4		No 1 Sect, with inf at night, continued 2 trench Mortar Emplacements No 2 Sect Finished deep dugout in RAILWAY HOLLOW & continued repair of defences of CUINCHY SUPPORT POINT & digging trench to THE BULGE, & repair of BRICKSTACKS KEEP No 3 Sect Finished 2nd entrance to dugout in MARYLEBONE ROAD & repairs of dugout M & R 2 (STAFFORD REDOUBT) & started a Deep dugout in TOWER RESERVE No 4 Sect continued dressing station dugout in the LANE and enlargement of two deep dugouts in ESPERANTO TERRACE Lt BALCOMBE returned from leave.	
	5		Same as 4th No 3 sect started repair of 2 old deep dugouts in BACK STREET & an Infantry observation Post in PARK LANE COTTAGES	
	6th		Same as 5th	
	7th		Same as 5th. No 4 Sect finished one of the dugouts in ESPERANTO ST	
	8th		Same as 7th No 4 Sect started a tunnel connecting 2 deep dugouts under Brickstack 2 & finished the dressing station in THE LANE.	

1875 Wt. W593/826 1,000,000 4/15 J.B.C. & A. A.D.S.S./Forms/C. 2118.

Instructions regarding War Diaries and Intelligence Summaries are contained in F. S. Regs., Part II. and the Staff Manual respectively. Title Pages will be prepared in manuscript.

WAR DIARY
or
INTELLIGENCE SUMMARY
(Erase heading not required.)

Army Form C. 2118

Place	Date	Hour	Summary of Events and Information	Remarks and references to Appendices
	9		Same as 8th. No 4 Sect finished the second dugout in ESPERANTO ST	
			No 3 Sect finished the Inf Obs post in PARK LANE COTTAGES.	
			No 2 Sect started repair of gate of overhead railway across WILLOW Rd.	
	10		No 1 Sect continued the 2 trench-mortar emplacements & started 6 others. They employed about 100 inf daily for digging approaches etc.	
			No 2 Sect started erecting blanket-screens to dugouts throughout the line to keep out gas. Also continued repair of railway gate across WILLOW ROAD	
			No 3 Sect continued deep dugout in TOWER RESERVE, improvements to dugouts in BACK STREET & HIGH STREET	
			No 4 Sect continued tunnel between two deep dugouts under BRICKSTACK 2 & continued revetment of trench between new dugout in Ry HOLLOW & BULGE	
	11		Same as 10th. No 4 Sect finished the tunnel under BRICKSTACK 2	
	12		Same as 11th. No 4 Sect started digging new support line behind Back St with 100 infantry. Also finished revetting of Trench to THE BULGE.	
			No 3 Sect started tunnel across LA BASSEE Rd between front & support line	

1875 Wt. W593/826 1,000,000 4/15 J.B.C. & A. A.D.S.S./Forms/C. 2118.

Instructions regarding War Diaries and Intelligence Summaries are contained in F. S. Regs., Part II. and the Staff Manual respectively. Title Pages will be prepared in manuscript.

WAR DIARY
or
INTELLIGENCE SUMMARY
(Erase heading not required.)

Army Form C. 2118

Place	Date	Hour	Summary of Events and Information	Remarks and references to Appendices
	13		No 1 Sect continued 8 trench mortar emplacements No 2 Sect continued erecting blanket screens to deep dugouts & repairing gate of overhead railway across WILLOW ROAD No 3 Sect continued repair of dugouts in BACK ST & HIGH ST & tunnel across LA BASSEE Rd between front & Support line. No 4 Sect started repairs to & reclaiming of front line trenches S of Old Mill & superintended digging of new SUPPORT LINE behind BACK ST.	
	14		Same as 13th.	
	15		Same as 13th.	
	16		Same as 13th. Part No 2 Sect lent to No 1 Sect to make bomb-stores.	
	17		Same as 16th. No 1 Sect started 2 more TM Emplacements, 10 now in hand. No 2 Sect finished gas-proof screens to dugouts & gate of overhead railway No 3 Sect finished Tunnel under LA BASSEE ROAD & 2 of the BACK ST dugouts	
	18th		Rest day, no work done, Inspection of Coy by O C.	

1875 Wt. W593/826 1,000,000 4/15 J.B.C. & A. A.D.S.S./Forms/C. 2118.

Army Form C. 2118

Instructions regarding War Diaries and Intelligence Summaries are contained in F. S. Regs., Part II. and the Staff Manual respectively. Title Pages will be prepared in manuscript.

WAR DIARY
or
INTELLIGENCE SUMMARY
(Erase heading not required.)

Place	Date	Hour	Summary of Events and Information	Remarks and references to Appendices
	19		No 1 Sect & part of No 2 Sect continued work on 12 TM Emplacements No 3 Sect started deep dugout in LEITH WK (front line) & dugout under LA BASSEE Rd for Trench Mortar detachments No 2 Sect repairs to CUINCHY SUPPORT POINT with labour from the garrison No 4 Sect Traverses & improvements to front line S of Mill & superintending excavation of new support line behind BACK ST	
	20		Same as 19th except No 4 Sect No 4 Sect started 2 deep dugouts in HIGH ST & ST ANDREWS TR (Support line)	
	21		Same as 20th	
	22		Same as 20th	
	23		Same as 20th ~~No 1 Sect finished 2 of the T.M. Emplacements~~.	
	24		Same as 23rd	
	25		Same as 24th No 2 Sect stopped work on CUINCHY SUPPORT POINT and started deep dugout for M. G Officer under MACHINE GUN HOUSE	

1875 Wt. W593/826 1,000,000 4/15 J.B.C. & A. A.D.S.S./Forms/C. 2118.

Instructions regarding War Diaries and Intelligence Summaries are contained in F. S. Regs., Part II. and the Staff Manual respectively. Title Pages will be prepared in manuscript.

WAR DIARY
or
INTELLIGENCE SUMMARY
(Erase heading not required.)

Army Form C. 2118

Place	Date	Hour	Summary of Events and Information	Remarks and references to Appendices
	26		Same as 25th.	
	27		Same as 25th Capt Sim proceeded on leave.	
	28 } 29 } 30 }		No change in work.	

H. A. L. Pusley Capt RE.
for O.C. 11th Fd Co R.E.

1875 Wt. W593/826 1,000,000 4/15 J.B.C. & A. A.D.S.S./Forms/C. 2118.

33.

Army Form C. 2118

Instructions regarding War Diaries and Intelligence Summaries are contained in F. S. Regs., Part II. and the Staff Manual respectively. Title Pages will be prepared in manuscript.

WAR DIARY
or
~~INTELLIGENCE SUMMARY~~
(Erase heading not required.)

11th Field Coy R.E.
MAY. 1916.
Vol 22

Place	Date	Hour	Summary of Events and Information	Remarks and references to Appendices
CUINCHY	1/5/16		No 1 Section was occupied on making Trench Mortar emplacements for 2" trench Howitzer. 2 off COLDSTREAM LANE. behind brickstack 13. 2 behind brickstack 7. 2 off OLD KENT ROAD 2 off BOYAU 32 (OLD BOND ST) 2 by CAMBRIN LABASSÉE ROAD.	type sketch attached.
			No 2 Section was employed half the section assisting No 1 section ½ section making a dug out for H.Q. of M.G. officer under M.G. HOUSE. In addition this day 2 men repaired the overhead Ry in HERTFORD ST when blown in	
			No 3 Section was employed in making a dug out for Lewis Gunners in LEITH WALK (½ a section) and making a dugout under LABASSÉE ROAD for H.Q. T.M.	
			No 4 Section making deep dug outs for infantry one in HIGH ST & one in ST ANDREWS TR	

1875 Wt. W593/826 1,000,000 4/15 J.B.C. & A. A.D.S.S./Forms/C. 2118.

Instructions regarding War Diaries and Intelligence Summaries are contained in F. S. Regs., Part II. and the Staff Manual respectively. Title Pages will be prepared in manuscript.

Army Form C. 2118

WAR DIARY
or
INTELLIGENCE SUMMARY
(Erase heading not required.)

Place	Date	Hour	Summary of Events and Information	Remarks and references to Appendices
CUINCHY	2/5/16		No 1 Section as before No 2 Section as before. HERTFORD ST Railway repaired. in 2 places No 3 Section as before. also undertook retimbering of a dugout in BACK ST which had been shaken up by a minenwerfer. No 4 Section as before.	
	3/5/16		as for 2nd.	
	4/5/16		~~as for 2nd~~ Company had a rest day. a Battery in the neighbourhood of the billets was shelled with very heavy shells (calibre unknown) and one man seriously wounded.	
	5/5/16		as for 2nd. No 2 Section finished the T.M. Emplacement behind No 13 brickstack.	
	6		Capt Sim returned from leave No 1 Sect & ½ No 2 Sect continued Trench Mortar Emplacements throughout line. ½ No 2 Sect continued MG Ofr Dugout under MACHINE GUN HOUSE	

1875 Wt. W593/826 1,000,000 4/15 J.B.C. & A. A.D.S.S./Forms/C. 2118.

Instructions regarding War Diaries and Intelligence Summaries are contained in F. S. Regs., Part II. and the Staff Manual respectively. Title Pages will be prepared in manuscript.

WAR DIARY
or
INTELLIGENCE SUMMARY
(Erase heading not required.)

Army Form C. 2118

Place	Date	Hour	Summary of Events and Information	Remarks and references to Appendices
	6		No 3 Sect continued deep dugout under road at PARK LANE for TM Hq, also repairs to dugout in BACK ST & continued deep dugout for RFA in Boyau 21 No 4 Sect continued dugouts in ST ANDREWS TR ~~& finished one in~~ HIGH ST.	
	7		Same as 6th Dugout in HIGH ST finished. 4 out of the 12 TM Emplacements now finished.	
	8		Nos 1 & 2 Sects same as 6th No 2 Sect finished dugout at Machine Gun House No 3 Sect finished repairs to dugout in BACK ST No 4 Sect finished dugout in ST ANDREWS TRENCH. ½ No 4 Sect started preliminary work for "Special" ~~OP~~ observation post in front parapet near boyau 20	
	9		Nos 1 & ½ No 2 TM Emplacements ½ No 2 Sect with 20 Inf at night started wiring of support line OXFORD ST. & PARK LANE No 3 Sect continued deep dugouts at PARK LANE & Boyau 21 No 4 Sect continued work for Special OP	

1875 Wt. W593/826 1,000,000 4/15 J.B.C. & A. A.D.S.S./Forms/C. 2118.

Instructions regarding War Diaries and Intelligence Summaries are contained in F. S. Regs., Part II. and the Staff Manual respectively. Title pages will be prepared in manuscript.

WAR DIARY
or
INTELLIGENCE SUMMARY.
(Erase heading not required.)

Army Form C. 2118.

Place	Date	Hour	Summary of Events and Information	Remarks and references to Appendices
	10		No 1 & ½ No 2 continued work on T M Emplacements	
			½ No 2 Sect with 20 inf at night continued wiring support line OXFORD ST & PARK LANE	
			No 3 Sect continued deep dugouts at PARK LANE & Boyau 21	
			No 4 Sect started deep dugout for Coy Hq in TOWER RESERVE, also excavation for Norton Tube Well ~~at~~ in THE LANE, & finished the preliminary work for Special OP.	
	11		Same as 10th except wiring party No 2 Sect	
			½ No 2 Sect started cutting gaps in reserve line wire about every 75x	
	12		Same as 10th. Gaps in Reserve line wire finished & labelled.	
			2/Lt FRYER went on leave.	
	13		Same as 10th	
			No 4 Sect prepared & placed 5 bridges over trenches to make overland route for Special OP.	
	14		Same as 10th	
			Wiring of OXFORD ST & PARK LANE finished by No 2 Sect	

Army Form C. 2118.

WAR DIARY
or
INTELLIGENCE SUMMARY.
(Erase heading not required.)

Instructions regarding War Diaries and Intelligence Summaries are contained in F. S. Regs., Part II. and the Staff Manual respectively. Title pages will be prepared in manuscript.

Place	Date	Hour	Summary of Events and Information	Remarks and references to Appendices
	14		At night Special Coy, assisted by 5 men of No 4 Sect, put the special O P in parapet. This consisted of a steel box with loophole, & a wooden cover with plaster immitation of parapet. The steel box was in 2 parts, each a heavy & awkward load for 2 men. Carrying party took it from CAMBRIN SUP PT to front line over previously prepared route in 40 minutes. It took a little over an hour to place. The chamber under the box for observer to stand in had also been tunnelled out beforehand so that all that remained to be done was to remove a piece of the parapet & put in the O P in its place.	
	15		No 1 & ½ No 2 Sects continued work on T M Emplacements. ½ No 2 Sect prepared chevaux de frizes for blocking communication trenches leading into keeps No 3 Sect continued dugouts at PARK LANE & BOYAU 21 No 4 Sect continued Coy Hq dugout in TOWER RESERVE, finished off the interior of the Special O P, & continued work on the Norton Tube Well. This is now driven but little water obtained. Chamber blasted at bottom but still very little water	

T2134. Wt. W708–776. 50(000. 4/15. Sir J. C. & S.

Instructions regarding War Diaries and Intelligence Summaries are contained in F. S. Regs., Part II. and the Staff Manual respectively. Title pages will be prepared in manuscript.

WAR DIARY

or

INTELLIGENCE SUMMARY.

(Erase heading not required.)

Army Form C. 2118.

Place	Date	Hour	Summary of Events and Information	Remarks and references to Appendices
	16		Same as 15th	
			No 2 Sect finished the chevaux de frizes	
			No 3 Sect finished the deep dugout for TM Hq at PARK LANE	
			No 4 Sect started tunnel to new indirect-fire M G emplacement near BANBURY X through Ry Embkt	
			No 1 Sect finished 2 more TM emplacements. 6 are now finished & 6 in hand.	
	17		No1 & ½ No2 Sect continued TM emplacements	
			½ No 2 Sect started putting in loophole plates instead of box loop holes in dogs legs of the Reserve Line.	
			No 3 Sect continued dugout for RFA in boyau 21 & started a large platoon dugout (3 chambers & 4 entrances) in the reserve line GRAFTON ST.	
			No 4 Sect continued Coy Hq dugout in TOWER RESERVE, the Norton Tube Well, & the indirect fire M G Emplacement in BANBURY X.	

T2134. Wt. W708-776. 500000. 4/15. Sir J. C. & S.

Instructions regarding War Diaries and Intelligence Summaries are contained in F. S. Regs., Part II. and the Staff Manual respectively. Title pages will be prepared in manuscript.

WAR DIARY
or
INTELLIGENCE SUMMARY.
(Erase heading not required.)

Army Form C. 2118.

Place	Date	Hour	Summary of Events and Information	Remarks and references to Appendices
	18	-	N°1 SECTION & ½ N°2 SECTION continued T.M. EMPLACEMENTS; remainder of N°2 on loophole plates in RESERVE LINE, as yesterday.	
			N°3 SECTION as yesterday, & repairing tunnel under road between BOYAUX 30 & 31.	
			N°4 SECTION as yesterday.	
	19		N°1 SECTION & ½ N°2 SECTION as yesterday; remainder of N°2 with infantry on T-HEADS (DAWSON ST)	
			N°3 SECTION: Tunnel between BOYAUX 30 & 31 repaired; repairing damage to T.M. Hq. DUG-OUT under LA BASSÉE ROAD begun; R.F.A. DUG-OUT (BOYAU 21) continued.	
			N°4 SECTION: As yesterday	
			CAPT. H.A.S. PRESSEY goes on leave.	
	20		N°1 SECTION & ½ N° SECTION: As yesterday; remainder of N°2 begin deep BOMB-STORES (KINGSCLERE & COLDSTREAM LANE)	
			N°3 SECTION: As yesterday; R.F.A. DUG-OUT completed.	
			N°4 SECTION: As yesterday.	
			SEC-LIEUT. R.E. FRYER returns from leave.	

T2134. Wt. W708-776. 500000. 4/16. Sir J. C. & S.

Instructions regarding War Diaries and Intelligence Summaries are contained in F. S. Regs., Part II. and the Staff Manual respectively. Title pages will be prepared in manuscript.

WAR DIARY
or
INTELLIGENCE SUMMARY.
(Erase heading not required.)

Army Form C. 2118.

Place	Date	Hour	Summary of Events and Information	Remarks and references to Appendices
	21	-	Nº 1 SECTION & ½ Nº 2 SECTION: As yesterday; remainder of Nº 2, with infantry, continue T-HEADS and wire SUPPORT LINE between BRICKSTACKS 2 & 7.	
			Nº 3. SECTION: As yesterday.	
			Nº 4. SECTION: As yesterday. NORTON TUBE PUMP (at intersection of THE LANE & TOWER RESERVE TRENCH) completed.	
			CAPT. G.E.H. SIM leaves for ENGLAND to be invested by THE KING with MILITARY CROSS (on 24TH)	
	22	-	Nº 1. SECTION & ½ Nº 2. SECTION: As yesterday; remainder of Nº 2: as yesterday.	
			Nº 3. SECTION: As yesterday.	
			Nº 4. SECTION: As yesterday.	
			During evening, a/2/Cpl. NORTON C. 23601, & 28362 SAP. NEWTON. J, are wounded & admitted to hospital.	
	23	-	Nos 1. 3. & 4 SECTIONS & ½ Nº 2 SECTION on same work as yesterday up till 4 P.M. Owing to our prepared artillery bombardment on German front line system immediately SOUTH of LA BASSEE ROAD during evening & night, no work is done after 4 P.M. except by remainder of Nº 2 SECTION which carries on with T-HEADS (HERTFORD ST.) & with MACHINE GUN EMPLACEMENT (indirect fire) in BANBURY CROSS.	

T2134. Wt. W708-776. 500000. 4/15. Sir J. C. & S.

Instructions regarding War Diaries and Intelligence Summaries are contained in F. S. Regs., Part II. and the Staff Manual respectively. Title pages will be prepared in manuscript.

WAR DIARY
or
INTELLIGENCE SUMMARY.
(Erase heading not required.)

Army Form C. 2118.

Place	Date	Hour	Summary of Events and Information	Remarks and references to Appendices
-	24.	-	No. 1. SECTION: on T.M. EMPLACEMENTS as yesterday. (Tracing of T.M.E. attached hereto). No. 2. SECTION: Constructing BOMB STORES, & ~~fixing~~ placing a FIXED-RIFLE BATTY. at PUDDING LANE COTTAGES. No. 3. SECTION: As yesterday No. 4. SECTION: as yesterday	
-	25	-	Work as yesterday. In addition No. 2. SECTION, with infantry, continue wiring SUPPORT LINE in BRICKSTACKS.	
-	26	-	Work as yesterday.	
-	27	-	Work as yesterday. CAPT. SIM returned from "investiture" leave.	
	28		Rest day, no work done Capt PRESSEY returned from leave II/Lt CLIFTON went on leave	

T2134. Wt. W708–776. 500000. 4/15. Sir J. C. & S.

Instructions regarding War Diaries and Intelligence Summaries are contained in F. S. Regs., Part II. and the Staff Manual respectively. Title pages will be prepared in manuscript.

WAR DIARY
or
INTELLIGENCE SUMMARY.
(Erase heading not required.)

Army Form C. 2118.

Place	Date	Hour	Summary of Events and Information	Remarks and references to Appendices
	29		No 1 Sect & ½ No 2 Sect continued T.M. Emplacements ½ No 2 Sect bomb stores No 3 Sect deep dugout for Coy Hq in TOWER RESERVE TRENCH continued. Also alterations & adjustments to Norton Tube Well. No 4 Sect deep dugout for 1 platoon in Reserve line MACHINE GUN HOUSE	
	30		Same as 29th. No 2 Sect also looked after 240 Infantry digging Tee-heads in THE LANE.	
	31		Same as 30th.	
	NOTE		Attached are 4 plates showing the construction of the Trench Mortar Emplacements (for 2" T.Ms). 6 pairs are being constructed on the brigade front of which 4 pairs are completed & 2 in hand. [illegible] Capt RE O.C. 11th Field Coy RE	

T2134. Wt. W708–776. 500000. 4/15. Sir J. C. & S.

SECRET

Instructions regarding War Diaries and Intelligence Summaries are contained in F. S. Regs., Part II. and the Staff Manual respectively. Title pages will be prepared in manuscript.

WAR DIARY
or
INTELLIGENCE SUMMARY.
(Erase heading not required.)

Army Form C. 2118.

11th Field Company RE

JUNE 1916

Vol 23

2

Place	Date	Hour	Summary of Events and Information	Remarks and references to Appendices
CUINCHY	1/6/16		No 1 Sect ~~contd~~ & ½ No 2 Sect continued 4 Trench mortar emplacements. 8 are now finished ½ No 2 Sect continued deep bomb stores in Support & Reserve Lines No 3 Sect continued deep dugout for 1 platoon MACHINE GUN HOUSE No 4 Sect fixed gas-proof screens to 3 telephone dugouts, finished the large Coy Hq dugout at junction of TOWER RESERVE & THE LANE & continued Tee heads off communication trenches. Also continued indirect fire MG Emplacement in Ry Embkt.	
	2		No 1, 2, & 3 Sects same as 1st. No 4 Sect continued tee heads & indirect fire MG Empl and started a platoon deep dugout in STAFFORD REDOUBT	
	3		Same as 2nd	
	4		Same as 2nd	
	5		Same as 2nd	

Instructions regarding War Diaries and Intelligence Summaries are contained in F. S. Regs., Part II. and the Staff Manual respectively. Title pages will be prepared in manuscript.

WAR DIARY
or
INTELLIGENCE SUMMARY.
(Erase heading not required.)

Army Form C. 2118.

Place	Date	Hour	Summary of Events and Information	Remarks and references to Appendices
	6		Same as 2nd At night Lieut ANDERSON & 5 NCO's & Men No1 Sect accompanied a raiding party of the 13th Sussex with bangalore torpedo & cut enemys wire. An account of this operation will be found in APPENDIX I	APP I
	7		Same as 2nd At night Lieut BALCOMBE & 6 NCO's & men No 3 Sect accompanied a raiding party of the 14th Hants with bangalore torpedo & cut enemys wire. See APPENDIX I	APP I
	8		Same as 2nd. Tee heads all finished.	
	9		Same as 2nd	
	10		Same as 2nd Lieut BALCOME proceeded on leave.	
	11		Rest day. Inspection of Company by OC. No work done.	

Instructions regarding War Diaries and Intelligence Summaries are contained in F. S. Regs., Part II. and the Staff Manual respectively. Title pages will be prepared in manuscript.

WAR DIARY
or
INTELLIGENCE SUMMARY.
(Erase heading not required.)

Army Form C. 2118.

Place	Date	Hour	Summary of Events and Information	Remarks and references to Appendices
	12		Same as 2nd	
	13		Same as 2nd No 2 Sect also shored up a wall in CUINCHY SUPPORT POINT that was dangerous & mended a pump at KINGSCLERE No 4 Sect & part No 3 Sect (1 officer & 30 OR) attended memorial service to F. M Lord KITCHENER in BETHUNE. In consequence no work was done on the deep dugout in STAFFORD REDOUBT.	
	~~14~~			
	14		Same as 2nd 4 more TM Emplacements started in RESERVE LINE by No 1 Sect.	
	15		Same as 14th	
	16		Same as 14th	

T2134. Wt. W708–776. 500000. 4/15. Sir J. C. & S.

Instructions regarding War Diaries and Intelligence Summaries are contained in F. S. Regs., Part II. and the Staff Manual respectively. Title pages will be prepared in manuscript.

WAR DIARY
or
INTELLIGENCE SUMMARY.
(Erase heading not required.)

Army Form C. 2118.

Place	Date	Hour	Summary of Events and Information	Remarks and references to Appendices
	17		Same as 14th	
			No 1 Sect finished 2 more TM Emplacements in support line. 10 are now finished & the last 2 well in hand, being done by ½ No 2 Sect.	
	18		No 1 Sect continued 4 TM Emplacements in RESERVE LINE	
			No 2 Sect continued 2 TM Emplacements in SUPPORT LINE, finished deep bomb store (6 in support line, 4 in Reserve line, 1 at KINGSCLERE have been made) & started repair of HERTFORD ST Ry which has been broken in 3 places by shell.	
			No 3 Sect continued deep platoon dugout at MACHINE GUN HQ & started work on telephone deep dugout at WOBURN ABBEY, (Adv Bde Hq). This last work taken over from 222nd Fd Coy R.E.	
			No 4 Sect continued deep dugout at STAFFORD REDOUBT & work at dressing station No 1 HARLEY ST. This also taken over from 222nd Fd Coy RE & consists in finishing off large concrete roof, digging approach trenches from HERTFORD ST, & making up approaches from the cellar of the house.	
			Lt ANDERSON proceeded on leave.	

T2134. Wt. W708–776. 500000. 4/15. Sir J. C. & S.

Instructions regarding War Diaries and Intelligence Summaries are contained in F. S. Regs., Part II. and the Staff Manual respectively. Title pages will be prepared in manuscript.

WAR DIARY
or
INTELLIGENCE SUMMARY.
(Erase heading not required.)

Army Form C. 2118.

Place	Date	Hour	Summary of Events and Information	Remarks and references to Appendices
	19 ~~20~~		No 1 Sect continued 4 TM Emplacements Reserve line.	
			No 2 Continued 2 TM Emplacements Support line & started 2 Reserve line, finished repair of HERTFORD ST Railway, & continued work on Brick O P (THE VINEYARD) taken over from 222nd Coy R E	
			No 3 Sect continued platoon dugout M G HOUSE & signal dugout Adv Bde Hq & continued brick O P (TOWER OF BABEL) taken over from 222nd Fd Coy RE	
			No 4 Sect continued deep dugout STAFFORD REDOUBT & work at dressing station No 1 HARLEY ST.	
			Lieut BALCOMBE returned from leave.	
	20		Same as 19th	
	21		Rest day. No work done	
	22		~~Nos 1 & 2 Sect Same as 19th~~ Work stopped temporarily on deep dugout STAFFORD RED & the two O. P's	
			No 1 Sect continued 4 T. M. Emplacements reserve line	
			No 2 Sect continued 2 T. M. Es in Support & 2 in Reserve lines.	

T2134. Wt. W708–776. 500000. 4/15. Sir J. C. & S.

Instructions regarding War Diaries and Intelligence Summaries are contained in F. S. Regs., Part II. and the Staff Manual respectively. Title pages will be prepared in manuscript.

WAR DIARY
or
INTELLIGENCE SUMMARY.
(Erase heading not required.)

Army Form C. 2118.

Place	Date	Hour	Summary of Events and Information	Remarks and references to Appendices
			also, with 8 men No 4 Sect started filling up shell holes in LA BASSEE Rd from BRADDELL POINT forward & making the road good.	
			No 3 Sect continued dugouts at M.G. HOUSE & ADV. Bde Hq & built two bridges over trenches NE & NW of M.G. HOUSE to take guns.	
			No 4 Sect started construction of bridge over front trench LA BASSEE Rd for lorries (3 tons) & continued work on No 1 HARLEY ST.	
	23		No 4 Sect finished bridge front line LA BASSEE Rd	
			No 2 Sect finished making up roadway of LA BASSEE Rd.	
			No 3 Sect started strengthening existing bridges & tunnels across LA BASSEE rd to take lorries	
			Otherwise Same as 22nd.	
	24		No 1 Sect continued 4 Trench Mortar Emplacements reserve line.	
			No 2 Sect finished 2 T.M. Emplacements support line & continued 2 reserve line also started filling up shell-holes etc on CUINCHY road from Support point forward.	

T2134. Wt. W708–776. 500000. 4/15. Sir J. C. & S.

Instructions regarding War Diaries and Intelligence Summaries are contained in F. S. Regs., Part II. and the Staff Manual respectively. Title pages will be prepared in manuscript.

WAR DIARY
or
INTELLIGENCE SUMMARY.
(Erase heading not required.)

Army Form C. 2118.

Place	Date	Hour	Summary of Events and Information	Remarks and references to Appendices
			No 3 Sect finished deep dugout for 1 platoon MACHINE GUN HOUSE, also continued Signal dugout at Adv Bde Hq. Also continued strengthening LA BASSEE Rd trench - bridges & tunnels	
			No 4 Sect continued work at dressing Station No 1 HARLEY ST. Also made bridge across CLIVE ROAD & started 2 across OXFORD ST & SEYMOUR ST to take guns	
	25		Same work as 24th continued	
	26		Same as 24th All bridges on LA BASSEE Rd finished by No 3 Sect	
			Bridges over ~~CLIVE Rd &~~ OXFORD ST & SEYMOUR ST finished by No 4 Sect	
			Making up of the M.G. HOUSE road finished by No 2 Sect.	
	27		No 1 Sect continued 4 TM Emplacements Reserve line	
			No 2 Sect Continued 2 TM Emplacements Reserve line, also O P, THE VINEYARD	
			No 3 Sect continued Signal dugout Adv Bde Hq & O P TOWER OF BABEL	

Instructions regarding War Diaries and Intelligence Summaries are contained in F. S. Regs., Part II. and the Staff Manual respectively. Title pages will be prepared in manuscript.

WAR DIARY
or
INTELLIGENCE SUMMARY.
(Erase heading not required.)

Army Form C. 2118.

Place	Date	Hour	Summary of Events and Information	Remarks and references to Appendices
			No 4 Sect continued deep dugout STAFFORD REDOUBT and work on dressing Station No 1 HARLEY ST	
	28		Same as 27th.	
			In addition No 3 Sect made 2 gas-cylinder emplacements in front line, one for 4 cylinders at head of Sap TWO & one for 6 cylinders north end of PORTLAND Rd.	
			Lt ANDERSON returned from leave.	
	29		Same as 27th	
			Lt ANDERSON mentioned in despatches (for 2nd Time) & Sergt HOLMES (Mention)	
	30		Same as 27th	
			In addition No 3 Sect mended break in overhead railway HERTFORD ST & deepened trench under one of the new bridges NW of MG HOUSE.	
			[signature] Capt, R.E. Commdg. 11th Coy. R.E.	

T2134. Wt. W708–776. 50000. 4/15. Sir J. C. & S.

CONFIDENTIAL 33rd R.E. XXXIII 2

Vol 24

WAR DIARY

OF

11th FIELD COMPANY R.E.

FROM 1-7-16 To 31/7/16.

SECRET

Instructions regarding War Diaries and Intelligence Summaries are contained in F. S. Regs., Part II. and the Staff Manual respectively. Title pages will be prepared in manuscript.

WAR DIARY

or

~~INTELLIGENCE SUMMARY.~~

(Erase heading not required.)

Army Form C. 2118.

11th Field Company RE

JULY 1916

Place	Date	Hour	Summary of Events and Information	Remarks and references to Appendices
CUINCHY FRONT	1st July.		No 1 Sect + ½ No 2 Sect continued 6 T.M. Emplacements in Reserve Line. ½ No 2 Sect continued brick tower OP (THE VINEYARD) No 3 Sect continued Signal dugout for Adv Bde Hq near WOBURN ABBEY & brick tower OP (TOWER OF BABEL No 2) No 4 Sect continued entrances to dressing station Dugout at No 1 HARLEY ST & large platoon dugout at STAFFORD REDOUBT.	
	2nd		Same as 1st No 3 Sect finished ~~pl~~ signal dugout at WOBURN ABBEY.	
	3rd		Rest day. No work done. Inspection of Company, equipment etc by O.C.	
	4th		No 1 & ½ No 2 Sect continued 6 TM Emplacements Reserve Line. ½ No 2 Sect continued Brick OP (THE VINEYARD). Also superintended the digging of new trench N of M.G. HOUSE ~~by~~ night. No 3 Sect continued brick O.P. (TOWER OF BABEL No 2) and took over the	

Instructions regarding War Diaries and Intelligence Summaries are contained in F. S. Regs., Part II. and the Staff Manual respectively. Title pages will be prepared in manuscript.

WAR DIARY
or
INTELLIGENCE SUMMARY.
(Erase heading not required.)

Army Form C. 2118.

Place	Date	Hour	Summary of Events and Information	Remarks and references to Appendices
			reclaiming & revetment of COVENTRY STREET (front line) from Pioneers.	
			No 4 Sect continued platoon dugout at STAFFORD REDOUBT and started work on brick OP in DISTILLERY, PONT FIXE, taken over from 222nd Fd Coy RE.	
			Lieut ANDERSON left Company to take over duties of Adjt RE 33rd Div.	
	5th		Same as 4th	
	6th		Same as 4th	
			In the afternoon received orders that Coy would hand over work in line & move out on evening of 7th.	
	7th		One shift on the 6 in TM Emplacements & on the deep dugout in STAFFORD RED.	
			Remainder of Company packing, loading pontoons, cleaning up etc.	
			Work in line was taken over by officers of 227th & 234th Fd Coys (39th Div).	
			All maps & stores handed over.	
			Capt Sim & Lt BALCOMBE took these officers round the works etc and explained everything to them.	

T2134. Wt. W708–776. 500000. 4/15. Sir J. C. & S.

Instructions regarding War Diaries and Intelligence Summaries are contained in F. S. Regs., Part II. and the Staff Manual respectively. Title pages will be prepared in manuscript.

WAR DIARY
or
INTELLIGENCE SUMMARY.
(Erase heading not required.)

Army Form C. 2118.

Place	Date	Hour	Summary of Events and Information	Remarks and references to Appendices
			Company paraded at 8.15 pm and marched to billets at VENDIN (NW of BETHUNE), arriving 10.45 pm.	
			NOTE. The 11th Company has now been working in the CUINCHY area without a relief from Dec 27th 1915 to July 7th 1916 (6⅓ months). On the average it had a rest day about once a fortnight. By this arrangement no doubt a great amount of work was accomplished, but at the expense, to a certain extent, of the efficiency of the Company as regards marching, drill, etc. I consider that it is absolutely essential for the Field Company to be taken off the work for a week or 10 days about every 3 months for the purpose of training. It would not only add to the efficiency of the Company but prevent officers and men becoming "stale," which is absolutely unavoidable when a company is kept continuously on work in one place for over 6 months.	
	8th		Company rested till evening. Paraded 8 pm & marched to FOUQUEREUIL STN and started entraining at 9 pm. All entrained by 11 pm. Train left FOUQUEREUIL at midnight.	

T2134. Wt. W708–776. 500000. 4/15. Sir J. C. & S.

Instructions regarding War Diaries and Intelligence Summaries are contained in F. S. Regs., Part II. and the Staff Manual respectively. Title pages will be prepared in manuscript.

Army Form C. 2118.

WAR DIARY
or
INTELLIGENCE SUMMARY.
(Erase heading not required.)

Place	Date	Hour	Summary of Events and Information	Remarks and references to Appendices
	9th		Train arrived at LONGUEAU (SE of AMIENS) at 8am. Company detrained and marched to VAUX (NNW of AMIENS), arriving in billets 1.45 pm.	
	10th		Informal inspection of Company & horses by CE 2nd Corps (Brig-Gen. GOODBY) Lecture to officers & NCO's by OC on March Discipline. The company had shown itself very ignorant of this subject on the march on 9th. (This was of course due to lack of training in marches and was no fault of anybody as the company has had no opportunity for this sort of training) At 2.30 pm received orders to be ready to move at 4.30 pm. This order was cancelled at 5.30 pm.	
	11th		1 hours Section & Company drill. Received orders 6.15 pm to move to DAOURS via POULAINVILLE, ALLONVILLE and BUSSY-LES-DOURS and join 19th Bde. at once Marched off 7.30 pm and arrived 12 midnight, bivouacked between the SOMME & the Railway, S of VECQUEMONT.	

T2134. Wt. W708-776. 500000. 4/15. Sir J. C. & S.

Instructions regarding War Diaries and Intelligence Summaries are contained in F. S. Regs., Part II. and the Staff Manual respectively. Title pages will be prepared in manuscript.

WAR DIARY
or
INTELLIGENCE SUMMARY.
(Erase heading not required.)

Army Form C. 2118.

Place	Date	Hour	Summary of Events and Information	Remarks and references to Appendices
DAOURS	12		Handed in Packs to store in DAOURS	
			Paraded at 1·45pm & joined into 19th Bde behind 2nd RWF on the march at road junction N of DAOURS.	
			Marched with brigade to BUIRE-SUR-L'ANCRE via LA NEUVILLE, BONNAY and, HEILLY, arriving in billets at 6·30pm. Very hot and dusty march.	
BUIRE SUR L'ANCRE	13.		Company rested all day.	
	14		Company "stood to" at 3.25am being then dismissed under orders to move at ½ hours notice.	
MEAULTE			Marched off at 11am. Tool carts accompanied the Sappers and marched with Brigade to MEAULTE, arriving 2.10pm. All other transport with brigade transport B échelon.	
			Moved out of MEAULTE and bivouaced in field by BECORDEL-BECOURT, F13 a.19 arriving at 7.15pm.	
MAMETZ WOOD.	15		Moved off in early morning arriving to S Edge of MAMETZ WOOD. there had 8 O.R killed & 17 O.R. wounded by shell fire. Bivouaced being in reserve with 19th I.B. Pontoon waggons carrying materials	

2353 Wt. W2544/1454 700,000 5/15 D. D. & L. A.D.S.S./Forms/C. 2118.

Instructions regarding War Diaries and Intelligence Summaries are contained in F. S. Regs., Part II. and the Staff Manual respectively. Title Pages will be prepared in manuscript.

WAR DIARY
or
INTELLIGENCE SUMMARY
(Erase heading not required.)

Army Form C. 2118

Place	Date	Hour	Summary of Events and Information	Remarks and references to Appendices
MAMETZ WOOD	16		Company moved with 19th Bde to E side of MAMETZ WOOD at 3 am. Tool carts with the company. Ponton waggons & forage cart & Tool cart horses at FRICOURT. Remainder of transport with B Echelon 19th I.B.	
do	16		No 4 section made a Shelter for Signals 19th I.B. 2 hours work. No 3 – made 2 Platforms for observers in the MILL at S 9 c 3.10. 5 hours night work. No 1 & 4 Secs erected 250x of wire entanglement (100x double bay 150x single bay) round strong point in cemetery of BAZENTIN LE PETIT S 8 b.8.1. using 300 screw pickets & 100 coils barbed wire. time 4 hours. Casualties 1 O.R. wounded (Shell shock)	
do	17		No 3 Sec improving Bde H.Q. dug out & holes for company etc. Squared up the dump S of BAZENTIN LE PETIT. By night Nos 1 & 4 Secs finished wiring of cemetery entanglement 18' wide medium height wire. time taken 3 hours. Neighbourhood of bivouac heavily shelled by day. No stores could be got to dump. One O.R. wounded in bivouac.	

1875 Wt. W593/826 1,000,000 4/15 J.B.C. & A. A.D.S.S./Forms/C. 2118.

Instructions regarding War Diaries and Intelligence Summaries are contained in F. S. Regs., Part II. and the Staff Manual respectively. Title Pages will be prepared in manuscript.

WAR DIARY
or
INTELLIGENCE SUMMARY
(Erase heading not required.)

Army Form C. 2118

Place	Date	Hour	Summary of Events and Information	Remarks and references to Appendices
MAMETZ WOOD	18	9.30 am to 5 p.m.	By day No 1 Sec continued on support point at S 8 d 5.7. Traverses, fire steps + M.G emplacement. Work interrupted continuously by heavy bombardment	
	18th 19	7.30 pm to 3 am	By night No 3 Sec assisting R.W.F to make two strong points about 60x ahead of our front line S 8 a 9.9 + S 2 d 6.1. Small posts for 8 men wired well in front.	
		8 pm 2.30 am	No 4 Sec continued strong point at S 8 a.9.7. Squaring up and fire stepping front face.	
			No casualties.	
	19th		No work.	

1875 Wt. W593/826 1,000,000 4/15 J.B.C. & A. A.D.S.S./Forms/C. 2118.

Instructions regarding War Diaries and Intelligence Summaries are contained in F. S. Regs., Part II. and the Staff Manual respectively. Title pages will be prepared in manuscript.

WAR DIARY
or
INTELLIGENCE SUMMARY.
(Erase heading not required.)

Army Form C. 2118.

Place	Date	Hour	Summary of Events and Information	Remarks and references to Appendices
MAMETZ WOOD	20th		Action of the 11th Field Co. R.E. in the assault on High Wood 20.7.16.	One map MARTINPUICH area attached
			Ref. Map:- Trench map area of Martinpuich 1/20,000.	
			Dispositions:- The Company was attached to the 19th I.B. and was ordered to move up with them and consolidate certain strong points after the wood had been captured.	
			Strong points were to be made at S.4.b.2.0, S.4.a.7.7, S.4.a.2.7, S.3.b.8.2 and a keep to be made.	
			As there were 5 strong points to be made and the Company had practically only 3 Sections available, one having been badly cut up previously, 2 Sections of the 222nd Field Company were attached under orders of Capt. Sim.	
		12 mn.	The Company was ordered to parade at 12 mn with the exception of No. 2 Section and Capt. PRESSEY who were left behind in reserve. They moved off and picking up stores at the dump at S.14.b.1.5 moved up & formed in line behind the 20th R.F.	
			Of the 19th I.B. the dispositions were that the 1st CAMERONIANS and the	

2353 Wt. W2544/1454 700,000 5/15 D. D. & L. A.D.S.S./Forms/C. 2118.

Instructions regarding War Diaries and Intelligence Summaries are contained in F. S. Regs., Part II. and the Staff Manual respectively. Title pages will be prepared in manuscript.

WAR DIARY
or
INTELLIGENCE SUMMARY.
(Erase heading not required.)

Army Form C. 2118.

Place	Date	Hour	Summary of Events and Information	Remarks and references to Appendices
HIGH WOOD			5th S.R. were to assault the wood from the S.W. face; the 20th R.F. to line up and, entering the wood from its S face, to work up, clearing it. The 11th Field Company to move up in rear of the 20th R.F. and when the wood had been totally cleared of the enemy, to make the strong points as ordered.	
			Capt. PRESSEY reported to the H.Q. 19th I.B., which was adjacent to the bivouac of the 11th Co. R.E., and remained there until Capt. SIM was reported wounded at 10.30 A.M. when he went up.	
		3 am.	From reports gathered from those present, the assault went absolutely as expected, the 5th S.R. and the CAMERONIANS carrying their objectives. The clearing of the wood, however, was too hurried, evidently not being taken systematically, the clearing parties moving in compact bodies up the open spaces, leaving many snipers and not clearing the dug outs. There is no doubt that the enemy retired into his dug-outs, and when the parties had passed, came out, mounted his M.G's and shot down & sniped the parties which had passed through.	

2353 Wt. W2544/1454 700,000 5/15 D. D. & L. A.D.S.S./Forms/C. 2118.

Instructions regarding War Diaries and Intelligence Summaries are contained in F. S. Regs., Part II. and the Staff Manual respectively. Title pages will be prepared in manuscript.

WAR DIARY
or
INTELLIGENCE SUMMARY.
(Erase heading not required.)

Army Form C. 2118.

Place	Date	Hour	Summary of Events and Information	Remarks and references to Appendices
HIGH WOOD			The construction of the German dug-outs in this district renders throwing bombs down them a futile proceeding. It is my opinion that parties of R.E. should accompany the clearing party, moving in rear of them and blow in the entrances to dug-outs. The infantry reporting any they find and mount guard over the entrances until the charge is laid. M.G. Emplacements, even if found empty, should be similarly dealt with. This would also prove useful as it would prevent demoralized men from seeking shelter in these dug-outs when cleared & being lost to subsequent operations.	
		10.30am	On the report of Capt. SIM being wounded, Capt. PRESSEY reported to BDE. H.Q. and went up taking No 2 Section and an orderly, who had brought a wounded officer back. On the way up we met Lieut. CASSELS and the 2 Sections of the 222nd Company, R.E. Lieut. CASSELS reported he had received orders from Capt. SIM to move up and was in process of getting his Sections together. The orders for the work had been given to him personally & he knew what to do.	

2353 Wt. W2544/1454 700,000 5/15 D. D. & L. A.D.S.S./Forms/C. 2118.

Instructions regarding War Diaries and Intelligence Summaries are contained in F. S. Regs., Part II. and the Staff Manual respectively. Title pages will be prepared in manuscript.

WAR DIARY
or
INTELLIGENCE SUMMARY.
(Erase heading not required.)

Army Form C. 2118.

Place	Date	Hour	Summary of Events and Information	Remarks and references to Appendices
HIGH WOOD			On the way up the barrage proved very intensive and No. 2 Section was left in cover. On arrival at the wood the whole place was found in a very disorganized condition. No one could tell me exactly what had	
		11.30am	happened. This was about 11.30 am. The Officer in Command I could not find and the R.E. were holding the trenches with the infantry. The wood was reported full of snipers, an enemy M.G. was in action somewhere in the centre and the N corner seemed to be held by him. Our artillery were firing short on the E face about 12.30 pm. An order to leave the front trenches in the E face about 12.30 pm, emanating from an Officer, and to fall back to the support trench which had	
		12.30pm	been dug somewhere inside the wood. This was interpreted into a general order for retreat by many men. They were, however, rallied and sent back again firstly to the trenches in the W face of the wood and then they were moved back to the E face. Here the majority were killed largely by our own shell fire. By the evening this had accounted for every man in the S.W. face. On reconnoitring	

Instructions regarding War Diaries and Intelligence Summaries are contained in F. S. Regs., Part II. and the Staff Manual respectively. Title pages will be prepared in manuscript.

WAR DIARY
or
INTELLIGENCE SUMMARY.
(Erase heading not required.)

Army Form C. 2118.

Place	Date	Hour	Summary of Events and Information	Remarks and references to Appendices
HIGH WOOD			this, not a single live man was found and nearly all had shell wounds in the back.	
			At about 1 pm the 2nd. R.W.F. were seen advancing with parade precision under the most murderous barrage of shrapnel & 8" shells. On arrival, Major CRAWSHAY, commanding them, took over command. Capt. PRESSEY reported to him & told him the situation as far as he could make it out, and stayed with him during the majority of the rest of the time. The attack was then organized by Major CRAWSHAY and the R.W.F.	
		6.p.m.	cleared the wood, reporting it clear. The wood was then reconnoitred with 2Lieut. FRYER in order to take up a line & to find out positions for strong points. On the way, one prisoner was captured in a M.G. dug-out and another wounded one was taken in the wood. On advancing to the N face however, rifle fire was opened by the enemy ~~fr~~ from the N. corner, several of the R.W.F. were lying about dead, evidently sniped on their way back, and a report was made to the O.C. HIGH WOOD that the N face could not be held or work done	

2353 Wt. W2544/1454 700,000 5/15 D. D. & L. A.D.S.S./Forms/C. 2118.

Army Form C. 2118.

Instructions regarding War Diaries and Intelligence Summaries are contained in F. S. Regs., Part II. and the Staff Manual respectively. Title pages will be prepared in manuscript.

WAR DIARY
or
INTELLIGENCE SUMMARY.
(Erase heading not required.)

Place	Date	Hour	Summary of Events and Information	Remarks and references to Appendices
HIGH WOOD			until these were cleared out.	
			Plans were made for dealing with these people, but it was finally decided that, as the men in hand were very few, to leave these men in possession of the N corner and dig in as far forward as possible.	
			The wood was again reconnoitred & the O.C. 20th R.F. being found stated not much help could be given by him as his men were demoralized & tired. This was evident.	
		8.[illegible] pm	However, in moving up the west in the W face it was found that men could advance up to the N.W. face and a party of infantry, CAMERONIANS and 5 S.R. were moving in the open, both outside the wood on the N face where, half an hour earlier, no one could shew a hand. Apparently a party of troops, it was reported to me as CAMERONIANS, had, on their own initiative, cleared out the snipers, and 2nd Lieut. FRYER was brought up and ordered to take all the R.E. and dig a trench along the ride from S 3 b 81 to S 4 a 77. A report was made to Major	

2353 Wt. W2544/1454 700,000 5/15 D. D. & L. A.D.S.S./Forms/C. 2118.

Instructions regarding War Diaries and Intelligence Summaries are contained in F. S. Regs., Part II. and the Staff Manual respectively. Title pages will be prepared in manuscript.

WAR DIARY
or
INTELLIGENCE SUMMARY.
(Erase heading not required.)

Army Form C. 2118.

Place	Date	Hour	Summary of Events and Information	Remarks and references to Appendices
HIGH WOOD			CRAWSHAY who ordered up his sapping platoon to assist. This was about 8 p.m. A trench was started and was, in parts, taken down to a depth of four feet to four feet, six inches.	
		9 pm	On going out again to reconnoitre and having reached the position S4a40, a heavy machine gun & rifle fire broke out from the direction of the N corner. It was evident that the enemy had again obtained possession of that corner and were sweeping the wood. On the way back to report this, a Captain of the 20th R.F. reported that his front line had been broken through by a party of Germans (strength unknown) and his support line would soon go. This was reported to Major CRAWSHAY. However, time was taken up in rallying troops who, demoralized by having been exposed to a murderous shell fire throughout the day, were in no position to face or make an attack. Just then, the O.C. 212th Field Co. R.E. came up & told me he had come up to relieve me. At the time, about 9 p.m. and under the circumstances, it was not desirable to withdraw any men, so he was set to work making a	

T2134. Wt. W708—776. 500000. 4/15. Sir J. C. & S.

Army Form C.

Instructions regarding War Diaries and Intelligence Summaries are contained in F. S. Regs., Part II. and the Staff Manual respectively. Title pages will be prepared in manuscript.

WAR DIARY
or
INTELLIGENCE SUMMARY.
(Erase heading not required.)

Place	Date	Hour	Summary of Events and Information	Remarks and references to Appendices
HIGH WOOD			defensive flank & holding it along the road from S4c 80 southwards. Before this, however, when everything was quiet & the O.C. 11th Co. away reconnoitring the wood, he had found some men of the 11th Co. & told them he had come to relieve them. Their section commander had gathered them together and, not being able to find an R.E. Officer, had taken them home. The 18th Mdsx. (Pioneers) now arrived & were thrown in but, being short of Officers & being in a dis-organized condition, having been fetched up in a hurry after having been entrusted on a communication trench and were also thrown into confusion by other men, could not make any headway. The infantry were rallied and, it being found impossible in the dark to do much with them, were formed up in line along the road from S4c 80 to about S10a55.	
		10.30pm	The enemy chose this time to open a heavy fire with 8" guns, the shells dropping all over and through the wood and squares S3d, 4d and the three corners of the wood.	
			This was kept up until midnight when it stopped. During this	

T2134. Wt. W708–776. 500000. 4/15. Sir J. C. & S.

Instructions regarding War Diaries and Intelligence Summaries are contained in F. S. Regs., Part II. and the Staff Manual respectively. Title pages will be prepared in manuscript.

WAR DIARY
or
INTELLIGENCE SUMMARY.
(Erase heading not required.)

Army Form C. 2118.

Place	Date	Hour	Summary of Events and Information	Remarks and references to Appendices
HIGH WOOD			time the task of holding the line was not made any easier by a heavy gun of our own which persistently shelled our trenches with great accuracy. No infantry attack however developed and at about 12.15 am things quietened down and reliefs arriving for the infantry who could be found of the companies were gathered by Capt. PRESSEY and taken back. Many more men, however, who could not be found at the time and were thought to have been killed in the shelling, came back out of the wood where they had been holding, in about a quarter of an hour later. Casualties :- 4 Officers - wounded. 4 O.R. - killed 3 O.R. - missing (believed killed). 30 O.R. - wounded being exactly 50% of the Company who were in the action.	

T2134. Wt. W708—776. 500000. 4/15. Sir J. C. & S.

Instructions regarding War Diaries and Intelligence Summaries are contained in F. S. Regs., Part II. and the Staff Manual respectively. Title pages will be prepared in manuscript.

WAR DIARY
or
INTELLIGENCE SUMMARY.
(Erase heading not required.)

Army Form C. 2118.

Place	Date	Hour	Summary of Events and Information	Remarks and references to Appendices
HIGH WOOD			No. 1 Section,	
			Left billets at 12 mn. 1 Officer, 28 O.R.	
			Tools taken – 2 billhooks, 2 handaxes, 1 felling axe, 2 pairs wire-cutters and 2 mauls.	
			At the dump picked up picks & shovels, French wire & 10 sandbags per man.	
			Joined the Bde. behind 20th R.F. at S 9 d 0.0.	
			Moved off at 2.30 am in file under fairly heavy shell fire – 3 O.R. were wounded.	
			The Section moved up to the wood & up the S.E. face & commenced a strong point at S 4 a 3.0. Sketch attached. This was completed & wired at about 9 am, all the time under a heavy shell fire of both German & our own artillery & severe sniping. Lieut. CLIFTON was wounded almost immediately on reaching the job. Sergt. FIELD took charge of the Section & was killed about 15 minutes after Lieut. CLIFTON was wounded. Corpl HOUGH took charge of the section & completed the work.	

Army Form C. 2118.

Instructions regarding War Diaries and Intelligence Summaries are contained in F. S. Regs., Part II. and the Staff Manual respectively. Title pages will be prepared in manuscript.

WAR DIARY
or
INTELLIGENCE SUMMARY.
(Erase heading not required.)

Place	Date	Hour	Summary of Events and Information	Remarks and references to Appendices
			The work was completed about 9 am. When the work was completed, a Lieut. of the 20th R.F. called in the section to man the N.E. face of the wood as infantry; and the section dug itself in in a series of rifle pits. Here the section remained until ordered to retire by the same officer and it then retired to the support trench behind, in about the centre of the wood. Some of the section missed the support trench & came to the rear face of the wood. Here they remained till 8 pm. During the course of the afternoon Cpl HOUGH saw the O.C. Company & got orders to hold the trench until further orders. At about 8.30 pm the O.C. 212th Co. brought up some of his Company and, being relieved by him, the men of this section returned at 8.30 pm to their billets. Everything was very quiet at the time.	

T2134. Wt. W708—776. 500000. 4/15. Sir J. C. & S.

Instructions regarding War Diaries and Intelligence Summaries are contained in F. S. Regs., Part II. and the Staff Manual respectively. Title pages will be prepared in manuscript.

WAR DIARY
or
INTELLIGENCE SUMMARY.
(Erase heading not required.)

Army Form C. 2118.

Place	Date	Hour	Summary of Events and Information	Remarks and references to Appendices
HIGH WOOD			No. 2 Section. Was left behind in reserve under Capt. PRESSEY in the bivouac. On hearing that Capt. SIM had been wounded, they were ordered up and, taking 2 billhooks, 2 hatchets and 2 pairs of wire-cutters, picking up picks & shovels and French wire ~~oth~~ at the Dump & moved up. The German barrage, growing very thick, they were told on the way to take cover in shell holes & push on as opportunity offered. The N.C.O. in charge being wounded, the remainder of the section not knowing where to go, returned, not going into action at all.	

T2134. Wt. W708—776. 500000. 4/15. Sir J. C. & S.

Instructions regarding War Diaries and Intelligence Summaries are contained in F. S. Regs., Part II. and the Staff Manual respectively. Title pages will be prepared in manuscript.

WAR DIARY
or
INTELLIGENCE SUMMARY.
(Erase heading not required.)

Army Form C. 2118.

Place	Date	Hour	Summary of Events and Information	Remarks and references to Appendices
HIGH WOOD			No. 3 Section/.	

Paraded at 12 m.n. 1 Officer, 22 O.R.

Tools - 2 billhooks, 2 handaxes, 1 felling axe, 10 pairs wire-cutters and 2 mauls. At the dump picked up 18 picks & shovels, 10 sandbags per man & French wire & staples.

Joined up behind 20th R.F. and moved off at 2.30 a.m. & halted about 150 yards from the S.W. face of the wood & lay in the open.

Lieut. BALCOMBE was wounded but remained on. The section sergeant and 2 O.R. were wounded.

At about 3.30 a.m. the section advanced to the wood and dug in in the rear face of the wood with orders to await orders from Capt. SIM. There the section remained till 8 a.m. when Lieut. BALCOMBE was again wounded, this time severely, the artery in his arm being cut. He waited till Capt. SIM, who had gone off to make a reconnaissance of the wood returned. Capt. SIM, not returning for a long time, he handed over the section to Cpl DORRINGTON and started back when he found Capt. SIM on

Instructions regarding War Diaries and Intelligence Summaries are contained in F. S. Regs., Part II. and the Staff Manual respectively. Title pages will be prepared in manuscript.

WAR DIARY
or
INTELLIGENCE SUMMARY.
(Erase heading not required.)

Army Form C. 2118.

Place	Date	Hour	Summary of Events and Information	Remarks and references to Appendices
HIGH WOOD			the way & reported the state to him. Capt. SIM gave the N.C.O i/c orders to take the section into the wood when the N.C.O i/c was wounded. Lce. Cpl LAKE then took over the section. Orders were given by Capt. SIM to get all the wire and picks and shovels. Capt. SIM led the way partly down the S.W. face of the wood & into the wood. When about S 4 c 65 the enemy started shelling the wood heavily and the section was ordered to take cover. Then Capt. SIM was wounded, also Lce. Cpl LAKE & 3 O.R were wounded. Sapper WHEELER then took charge of the section. Capt. SIM gave the order to go back & report to No. 4 Section. There being 11 men left after that time, this section was absorbed into No. 4 Section. Capt. SIM was wounded at 9 am.	

Army Form C. 2118.

WAR DIARY
or
INTELLIGENCE SUMMARY.
(Erase heading not required.)

Instructions regarding War Diaries and Intelligence Summaries are contained in F. S. Regs., Part II. and the Staff Manual respectively. Title pages will be prepared in manuscript.

Place	Date	Hour	Summary of Events and Information	Remarks and references to Appendices
HIGH WOOD			No. 4 Section.	
			Left bivouac at 12 mn 1 Officer, 28 O.R.	
			Tools – 2 billhooks, 2 bundasers, 1 felling axe, 2 mauls & 9 pairs wire-cutters.	
			Trench wire, 10 sandbags per man and picks & shovels were gathered from the dump.	
			Joined up behind 20th R.F. at S 9 d 0.0.	
			Moved off from there at 2:30 am and remained in a small trench at S. 4 c 8 0. for a few minutes & then moved up a small trench on S.W. face of HIGH WOOD where it remained till 8 pm. At about 11 am the Germans bring to the N corner of the wood and a M.G at about S 3 b central. A trench running from S 4 a. 0.8. to where the left of our line ended to about S 3 d 7.7. This was done by Nos 3 & 4 Sections without the help from infantry. 1 Casualty. Machine Gun Emplacement at S. 4 a. 0.8.	
			At 6 pm Lieut. FRYER went out with O.C. to reconnoitre position for a strong point to be made in N.W. face of wood. It was found there	

T2134. Wt. W708–776. 500000. 4/15. Sir J. C. & S.

Instructions regarding War Diaries and Intelligence Summaries are contained in F. S. Regs., Part II. and the Staff Manual respectively. Title pages will be prepared in manuscript.

WAR DIARY
or
INTELLIGENCE SUMMARY.
(Erase heading not required.)

Army Form C. 2118.

Place	Date	Hour	Summary of Events and Information	Remarks and references to Appendices
HIGH WOOD			were many Germans in the N corner, about S.4a.65. with a M.G., so nothing was done.	
			About 7.45 pm, the wood being found clear of Germans, Lieut. FRYER was taken out by O.C. and a trench which the infantry were already starting, was marked on running up the side from S.3b 8.1. to S4a.7.6	
			From 8 pm. till 10.30 pm, all being quiet, this section worked in the trench from its N end to about S4a 3.3. Trench traversed & 4' deep.	
			At 10.30 pm the work was interrupted by a burst of M.G. fire & the sections "stood to" in the trench. After about 15 minutes, the order to retire was given by an Officer of the R.W.F. who was i/c of the work & who had his platoon extending the trench to the right. The section left the trench & opened into extended order through the wood & swinging back the right flank, and extending to 5 yards interval, lay in this position (S3a 3.1. to about S4a.5.0.) till about 11.30 pm. Some infantry, either CAMERONIANS or 5th S.R., extended the flank to the right. At about 11 pm the enemy opened a heavy fire with 8" H.E. and small	

Instructions regarding War Diaries and Intelligence Summaries are contained in F. S. Regs., Part II. and the Staff Manual respectively. Title pages will be prepared in manuscript.

WAR DIARY
or
INTELLIGENCE SUMMARY.
(Erase heading not required.)

Army Form C. 2118.

Place	Date	Hour	Summary of Events and Information	Remarks and references to Appendices
HIGH WOOD			H.E. and shrapnel. At about 11.30 p.m. an officer of the 5th S.R. of CAMERONIANS ordered us to retire to the S.W. face of the wood. Lieut. FRYER was wounded by a shell at this time. We lay in this trench till between 12.30 p.m. & 1 p.m. when the section was relieved. At about 12.30 p.m., Sapper McLAUGHLIN came in from the end of the trench at S.3 b.8.1. where he had remained till then. Reporting that ~~they~~ he had seen no Germans in the wood but that they seemed to be digging in about 50 yards from the N.W. face. Casualties in this section:- 2/Lieut. Fryer wounded (about 11.30 p.m.). 1 O.R. missing (believed killed). 5 O.R. wounded.	

T2134. Wt. W708—776. 500000. 4/15. Sir J. C. & S.

Army Form C. 2118.

Instructions regarding War Diaries and Intelligence Summaries are contained in F. S. Regs., Part II. and the Staff Manual respectively. Title pages will be prepared in manuscript.

WAR DIARY
or
INTELLIGENCE SUMMARY.
(Erase heading not required.)

Place	Date	Hour	Summary of Events and Information	Remarks and references to Appendices
HIGH WOOD.			Lieut. CASSELS and 2 Sections of the 222nd Company; R.E. were attached to the Company. They were left at the dump at S 14 b. 2.4. A copy of orders attached. Here they remained till ordered at about 10.30 am. to proceed to the wood and make a strong point. The order was given verbally to Lieut. CASSELS by Capt. SIM who was returning wounded. These 2 sections moved up but, on the way, the Officer i/c was killed and others, killed & wounded. The section returned probably because no one knew where they were to proceed to.	

2353 Wt. W2544/1454 700,000 5/15 D. D. & L. A.D.S.S./Forms/C. 2118.

Instructions regarding War Diaries and Intelligence Summaries are contained in F. S. Regs., Part II. and the Staff Manual respectively. Title Pages will be prepared in manuscript.

WAR DIARY
or
INTELLIGENCE SUMMARY
(Erase heading not required.)

Army Form C. 2118

Place	Date	Hour	Summary of Events and Information	Remarks and references to Appendices
MAMETZ WOOD.	21.	1pm	marched off and joined 19th Bde on road between BECORDEL & MEAULTE.	
			marched off again with Bde and arrived at BUIRE SUR L'ANCRE. 11.30 pm.	
			Lieut ANDERSON rejoined company.	
BUIRE	22		No work.	
SUR L'ANCRE	23.		Rifle & kit inspection. all tools & company equipment ~~inspected~~ checked. 2Lieut S. J. KIRBY R.E. (T.C) joined.	
	24.		Company drill for 2 hours. Lieut ANDERSON taken away from company to be adjutant. 2Lieut E. KAYLOR R.E.(T.C) joined.	
	25.		No 4 Section ~~[illegible]~~ Erected camp for Divisional H.Q.	
			No 1,2 & 3 sections infantry drill 8 to 10.	
			musketry 2 to 3	
	26.		Evolved a drill for the picking up of stores from a dump & carrying up road entering along & making a strong point so as to be able to carry on if officers & Senior N.C.O's are casualties trace as sketch.	
			MG · MG · 15' · 15' · 15' · 15' · arrows shew direction of fire	

Instructions regarding War Diaries and Intelligence Summaries are contained in F. S. Regs., Part II. and the Staff Manual respectively. Title Pages will be prepared in manuscript.

WAR DIARY
or
INTELLIGENCE SUMMARY
(Erase heading not required.)

Army Form C. 2118

Place	Date	Hour	Summary of Events and Information	Remarks and references to Appendices
	28	(cont)	No 3 Sect continued BULGE No 4 Sect " BRICKSTACKS KEEP. No Infantry parties available.	
	29		No 1 Sect ditto No 2 Sect finished repair of overhead railway & continued BERKSHIRE LANE with 50 Inf at night No 3 Sect with 20 Inf at night continued BULGE No 4 Sect with 20 " " " " BRICKSTACKS KEEP	
	30		No 1 Sect ditto No 2 Sect continued BERKSHIRE LANE Nos 3 & 4 Sect continued BRICKSTACKS KEEP. No Infantry available.	
	31		No 1 Sect ditto. No 2 Sect at night with 70 Inf continued BERKSHIRE LANE. Also repaired revetment of HERTFORD ST where sandbags were giving way	

1875 Wt. W593/826 1,000,000 4/15 J.B.C. & A. A.D.S.S./Forms/C. 2118.

Instructions regarding War Diaries and Intelligence Summaries are contained in F. S. Regs., Part II. and the Staff Manual respectively. Title Pages will be prepared in manuscript.

WAR DIARY
or
INTELLIGENCE SUMMARY
(Erase heading not required.)

Army Form C. 2118

Place	Date	Hour	Summary of Events and Information	Remarks and references to Appendices
BUIRE SUR L'ANCRE	27	8 to 10	practised making of strong points	
		11 to 1	infantry drill	
		2 to 4	washing clothes.	
			2 Lieuts H.R. CHANTER R.E. (T.C) W.H.E. GARROD R.E.(T.C) joined the Company.	
	28	8 to 10	practised strong points	
		10.30 to 1	packing & unpacking pontoons + trestle waggon	
		2 to 4	Company bathed in the ANCRE.	
	29.	8 to 2	company pontooned	
	30th		Sunday Church parades in the morning + bathing.	
	31st.	8 to 1	Drill + fieldworks Clothes of the company were sterilised.	
		2.15	Bathing.	

[illegible]
Capt RE.
O.C. 11th Fd Co R.E.

Trenches July 16

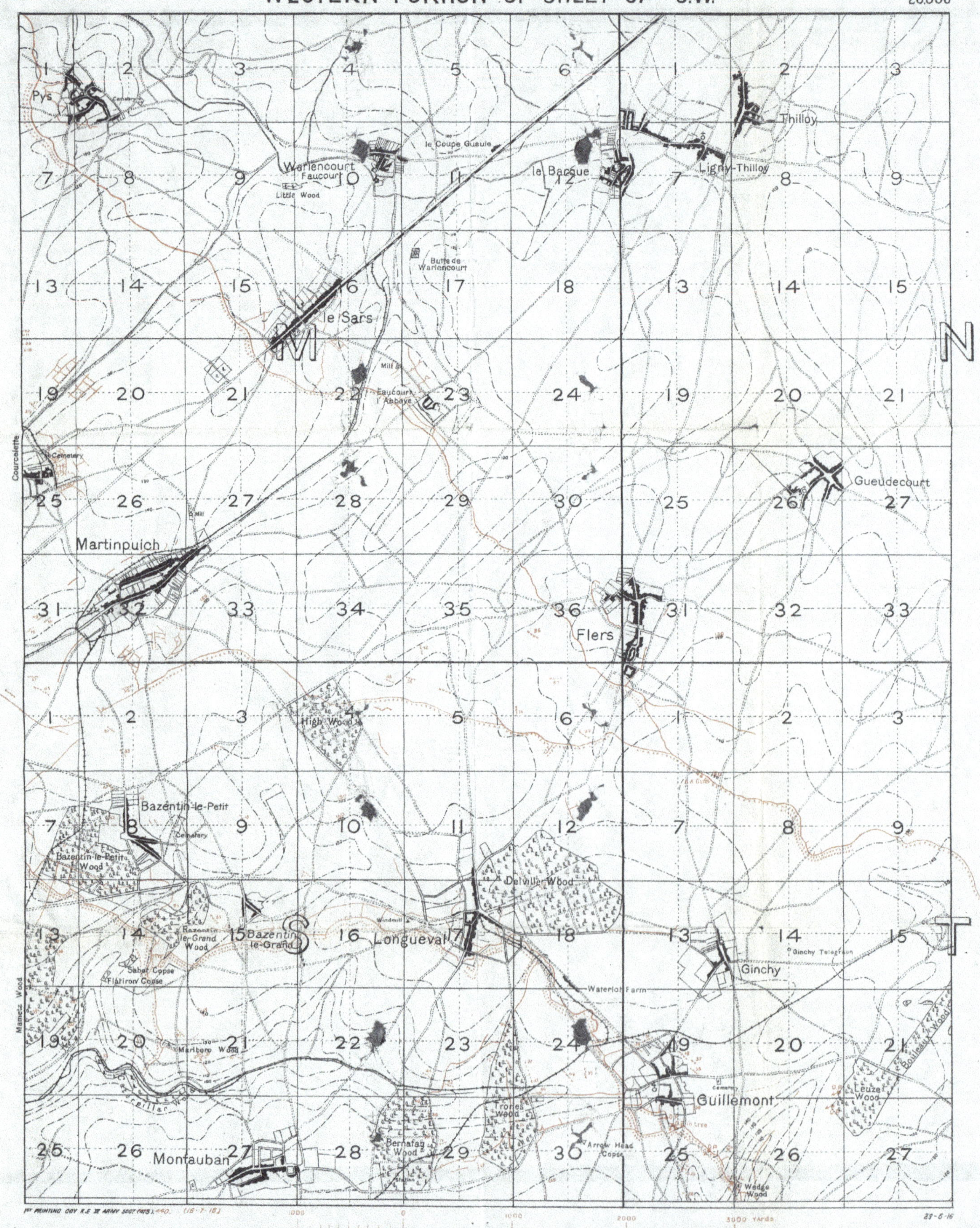
GERMAN TRENCHES according to latest information 16th JULY 1916.
WESTERN PORTION OF SHEET 57c S.W.
1/20,000
Pys
Warlencourt Faucourt
Little Wood
le Coupe Gueule
le Barque
Ligny-Thilloy
Thilloy
Butte de Warlencourt
le Sars
Eaucourt l'Abbaye
Courcelette
Gueudecourt
Martinpuich
Flers
High Wood
Bazentin-le-Petit
Bazentin-le-Petit Wood
Delville Wood
Bazentin-le-Grand Wood
Bazentin-le-Grand
Longueval
Ginchy
Waterloo Farm
Mametz Wood
Flatiron Copse
Marlboro Wood
Guillemont
Leuze Wood
Bouleaux Wood
Montauban
Bernafay Wood
Trones Wood
Arrow Head Copse
Wedge Wood
M
N
S
T
1000
0
1000
2000
3000 Yards

Trenches July 16

2

11 Fd Coy R.E

Vol XXI

33rd Divisional Engineers

11th FIELD COMPANY R. E.

AUGUST 1 9 1 6

33

Instructions regarding War Diaries and Intelligence Summaries are contained in F. S. Regs., Part II. and the Staff Manual respectively. Title Pages will be prepared in manuscript.

WAR DIARY
or
INTELLIGENCE SUMMARY
(Erase heading not required.)

Army Form C. 2118

11 FCRE

Vol 25

Place	Date	Hour	Summary of Events and Information	Remarks and references to Appendices
			CONFIDENTIAL	
			WAR DIARY	
			of	
			11th FIELD COMPANY R.E.	
			From 1/8/16 to 31/8/16	

1875 Wt. W593/826 1,000,000 4/15 J.B.C. & A. A.D.S.S./Forms/C. 2118.

Instructions regarding War Diaries and Intelligence Summaries are contained in F. S. Regs., Part II. and the Staff Manual respectively. Title Pages will be prepared in manuscript.

WAR DIARY or INTELLIGENCE SUMMARY

(Erase heading not required.)

Army Form C. 2118

11th Field Co RE
August 1916.

Place	Date	Hour	Summary of Events and Information	Remarks and references to Appendices
BUIRE SUR L'ANCRE	1st Aug	6 to 10.30	Pontooning	
		11.30 AM to 2.30 PM.	Erecting stage for 19th Bde Concert.	
		12 noon	Bathing parade	
	2	6 AM to 10 AM.	Pontooning	
		11.30 AM	Kit Inspection	
		12.30 PM.	Bathing parade.	
	3	6 AM to 10 AM.	Pontooning	
		11.30 AM	Kit Inspection No 4 Section moved to E.11. ~~d~~. Central	
		12.30 PM.	Bathing parade.	
	4	7 AM to 1.30 PM.	Sections 1 & 2. Pipe pushing	
		6 AM to 10 AM.	No 3 Section Field Works	
		12.30 PM.	Bathing parade.	
			No 4 Section at E.11.d. Central. 2 Mess Rooms completed with table & forms 3 do do do except one side. Tables & forms in one of these only. 2 Mess Rooms 14' x 10' commenced one with roof completed, other framework erected.	

1875 Wt. W593/826 1,000,000 4/15 J.B.C. & A. A.D.S.S./Forms/C. 2118.

Army Form C. 2118

Instructions regarding War Diaries and Intelligence Summaries are contained in F. S. Regs., Part II. and the Staff Manual respectively. Title Pages will be prepared in manuscript.

WAR DIARY
or
INTELLIGENCE SUMMARY
(Erase heading not required.)

Place	Date	Hour	Summary of Events and Information	Remarks and references to Appendices
BUIRE SUR L'ANCRE	5	7AM to 1PM	No 1 Section Musketry	II Lt H. Knight R.E. (T.C.) Joined the Company.
		2.30 PM	Rifle Inspection & bathing parade.	
		7AM.	No 2 Section Packing Pontoons	
		10.30AM to 2.30 PM	Musketry	
		7AM to 1.30PM	No 3 Section Pipe pushing	
		2.30PM	Swimming parade.	
			No 4 Section. Chairs fitted in 2 mess Rooms 3 Mess Rooms 14'x10' completed with exception of window panes. 2 Mess Rooms 16'x10' roof now on. Excavation for kitchens 9x7 completed Room 14'x8' Framework erected.	
	6		11th Field Company R.E. now moved to F.2 a.0.0. In front of Becourt Wood. No 1 Section on arrival commenced making baths for men out of tarpaulins. 3 commenced	

1875 Wt. W593/826 1,000,000 4/15 J.B.C. & A. A.D.S.S./Forms/C. 2118.

Army Form C. 2118

Instructions regarding War Diaries and Intelligence Summaries are contained in F. S. Regs., Part II. and the Staff Manual respectively. Title Pages will be prepared in manuscript.

WAR DIARY
or
INTELLIGENCE SUMMARY

(Erase heading not required.)

Place	Date	Hour	Summary of Events and Information	Remarks and references to Appendices
valley E of MAMETZ WOOD	7.		No 1 Section commenced a dug out for the dressing station in the QUARRY at S 14. c 5. 0. working in continuous reliefs.	
			No 2 Section were employed in two reliefs at the same place making splinter proof shelters.	
			No 3 Section with 2 reliefs of 100 Inf each, employed in making the road N of BAZENTIN LEGRAND wood passable for horse traffic.	
			Part of the section worked in erecting the baths at ALBERT – BECOURT Rd commenced the previous day.	
			Part employed making mining cases for deep dug outs.	
			No 4 Section continued work on Divl H.Q. at E 11 Central.	
	8.		Work as before ~~with [illegible]~~ 1 O.R. wounded.	

1875 Wt. W593/826 1,000,000 4/15 J.B.C. & A. A.D.S.S./Forms/C. 2118.

Army Form C. 2118

Instructions regarding War Diaries and Intelligence Summaries are contained in F. S. Regs., Part II. and the Staff Manual respectively. Title Pages will be prepared in manuscript.

WAR DIARY
or
INTELLIGENCE SUMMARY
(Erase heading not required.)

Place	Date	Hour	Summary of Events and Information	Remarks and references to Appendices
	9.		As before. for Nos 1 2 & 3 sections work of No 3 section on road much interrupted by shell fire. work done on road running up valley E of MAMETZ WOOD owing to shelling of the other part. No 4 Section rejoined the company. 7 men left behind to finish work at E.11. central	
	10.		Nos 1 2 & 3 sections as before. No 3 Section work much interrupted by shell fire. No 4 Section commenced work on House at in BAZENTIN LEGRAND making it into a strong point. half of the house undertaken by us, half by a section of the 212th Co R.E. Clearing and strutting the cellars. Sandbagging the walls & floors etc.	
	11.		as before	
	~~[illegible]~~		~~as before~~	
BAZENTIN LEGRAND	12 ~~[illegible]~~		Took over from 212th Co R.E. work on communication trenches and the Divisional line in front of BAZENTIN LEGRAND.	

1875 Wt. W593/826 1,000,000 4/15 J.B.C. & A. A.D.S.S./Forms/C. 2118.

Instructions regarding War Diaries and Intelligence Summaries are contained in F. S. Regs., Part II. and the Staff Manual respectively. Title Pages will be prepared in manuscript.

WAR DIARY
or
INTELLIGENCE SUMMARY
(Erase heading not required.)

Army Form C. 2118

Place	Date	Hour	Summary of Events and Information	Remarks and references to Appendices
	12		No 1 Section continued on the dug out in the Quarry. The two entrances were finished being driven into the hillside for a distance of 18 + 23 feet respectively. The dug out itself was commenced.	
			No 4 Section continued its work on the strong point.	
			The other two sections were employed in continuous reliefs of 6 hours superintending infantry working in continuous reliefs of 4 hours 200 men at a time in the communication trenches extending ~~[illegible]~~ HIGH ALLEY THISTLE ALLEY and ST GEORGES AVENUE back. Also digging Reserve line in front of BAZENTIN LE GRAND. The trenches were commenced and taken out to depth by infantry under R.E. supervision and were then levelled, trimmed, firestepped etc by 2 Coys of 18th Mx (Pioneers).	
			Work at night proved practically impossible owing to shell fire.	
			12 midnight shift was stopped on the way up due to shell fire.	

1875 Wt. W593/826 1,000,000 4/15 J.B.C. & A. A.D.S.S./Forms/C. 2118.

Army Form C. 2118

Instructions regarding War Diaries and Intelligence Summaries are contained in F. S. Regs., Part II. and the Staff Manual respectively. Title Pages will be prepared in manuscript.

WAR DIARY
or
INTELLIGENCE SUMMARY
(Erase heading not required.)

Place	Date	Hour	Summary of Events and Information	Remarks and references to Appendices
	13.		No 1 Section continued work in deep dug out	
			Infantry parties increase to 250 men. Work continued in communication trenches + divisional line. Much interrupted by shell fire.	
			No 4 Section in strong point as before.	
			Part of No 3 Section in making mine cases for deep dug outs.	
	14.		Work continued in deep dug out in Quarry by No 1 Section till 8 am when it was handed over to 222nd Co R.E.	
			10 men No 1 Section making "dogs leg" to ELGIN AVENUE.	
			10 men No 3 Section fire stepping + revetting parapets of fire trenches in divisional Reserve line.	
			Remainder superintended infantry. 750 men from 4 am to 8 am on communication trenches and fire trenches. 250 men in reliefs from 8 am to 8 pm. No night work. Communication trenches cut to depth need widening + deepening. St GEORGES AVENUE, not connected between St GEORGES TR + Divisional line.	

1875 Wt. W593/826 1,000,000 4/15 J.B.C. & A. A.D.S.S./Forms/C. 2118.

Instructions regarding War Diaries and Intelligence Summaries are contained in F. S. Regs., Part II. and the Staff Manual respectively. Title Pages will be prepared in manuscript.

WAR DIARY
or
INTELLIGENCE SUMMARY
(Erase heading not required.)

Army Form C. 2118

Place	Date	Hour	Summary of Events and Information	Remarks and references to Appendices
	~~14~~ 15		Infantry in continuous shifts 250 men 4 hours as before on Divisional line.	
			Nos 1 3 ~~& 4~~ Sections ~~commenced~~ commenced work on deep dugouts for Lewis gun emplacements.	
			Some infantry carrying wire and pickets to wire line.	
	16		Front edge of the wire was lined out by pickets and a single line of wire to ensure conjunction with Lewis gun & rifle fire from the trenches.	
			Nos 1 3 & 4 Sections continued as before on deep dugouts in continuous shifts. 3 other dugouts taken in hand by 222nd Co RE.	
			Infantry not on work at 8pm owing to shell fire.	
	17		No working party from 12 mn to 4 am. 4 am party not met owing to error it being the 4pm party that was cancelled by division. Only 8 to 12 noon & 12 to 4 parties of 250 men at work in carrying wire & pickets.	

1875 Wt. W593/826 1,000,000 4/15 J.B.C. & A. A.D.S.S./Forms/C. 2118.

Instructions regarding War Diaries and Intelligence Summaries are contained in F. S. Regs., Part II. and the Staff Manual respectively. Title Pages will be prepared in manuscript.

WAR DIARY
or
INTELLIGENCE SUMMARY
(Erase heading not required.)

Army Form C. 2118

Place	Date	Hour	Summary of Events and Information	Remarks and references to Appendices
1	17.		Nos 1 3 & 4 sections continued work in deep dug outs.	
			8pm party of infy stopped by shell fire.	
	18.		No party till 8 am. 250 men for 2 reliefs from 8am to 4pm in communication trenches and wire.	
			1 3 & 4 sections carried on work in deep dug outs.	
	19.		Company moved up to BAZENTIN LE GRAND. Sappers to take over from 212th Co	
			Rt. Officers & Sergts taken over the line. No work done.	
			1 OR killed 1 OR wounded.	
	20.		No 1 Section continued two deep dug outs commenced by previous company as Bn H.Q. one in BLACK WATCH TR near head of HIGH ALLEY the other in LEITH WALK by THISTLE [illegible] ALLEY.	
			No 4 Section & No 3 Section commenced making a series of "cubby holes" as shelters against shell fire in the left & right Bn fronts respectively	

1875 Wt. W593/826 1,000,000 4/15 J.B.C. & A. A.D.S.S./Forms/C. 2118.

Instructions regarding War Diaries and Intelligence Summaries are contained in F. S. Regs., Part II. and the Staff Manual respectively. Title Pages will be prepared in manuscript.

WAR DIARY
or
INTELLIGENCE SUMMARY
(Erase heading not required.)

Army Form C. 2118

Place	Date	Hour	Summary of Events and Information	Remarks and references to Appendices
			Consisting of 2 mining cases let in on their sides into the bottom of the trench to act as patterns for infantry to copy.	
			Section — trench — mine cases — undercut	
			These proved very popular and it became later a difficult matter to provide sufficient frames for the infantry. They certainly afforded a fair amount of shelter against anything less than 5·9 shells.	
			No 3 Section continued work on a Co H.Q. for Left front Co	
			No 2 Section was employed on sandbagging the walls & strutting the cellars of the billets and superintending 2 carrying parties of 100 men each carrying up sandbags wire & steel shelters & mine cases to the front line by night.	
			attempt made to report line from WORCESTER LANE to WOOD LANE given up owing to snipers in shell holes.	
	21.		As for 20th. No 3 commenced dugout for Co H.Q. Left Support Co.	
			attempt made by a party to tape out a trench to connect WORCESTER LANE & WOOD LANE frustrated by German patrol	
	22.		As for 21. No 2 Sec lent 1 N.C.O. & 8 men to No 3 Section	

Instructions regarding War Diaries and Intelligence Summaries are contained in F. S. Regs., Part II. and the Staff Manual respectively. Title Pages will be prepared in manuscript.

Army Form C. 2118

WAR DIARY
or
INTELLIGENCE SUMMARY
(Erase heading not required.)

Place	Date	Hour	Summary of Events and Information	Remarks and references to Appendices
	22		As for 21st. Position of Co H.Q. for left support Co ~~[illegible]~~ under construction by No 3 changed. 1 OR killed + 1 OR wounded in this work. It proved to be in a place that was incessantly shelled. A deep dug out started in BLACK WATCH TR in lieu.	
			also ~~[illegible]~~ shelters as first aid posts were started in near HIGH ALLEY BLACK WATCH TR + the head of ELGIN AVENUE.	
	~~23~~		No 3 Sec. A party were out trying to tape a line to connect A Sap in Right of WORCESTER TR a ~~[illegible]~~ German patrol was met + M.G. fire opened on the party. The party managed to ~~[illegible] 22~~nd get back to the trenches with 1 OR wounded + the Sergeant missing. 250 yards of the trench were taped before this happened.	
	23.		As for previous day. No carrying party infantry. 6 artillery boards were put out behind WORCESTER LANE.	

1875 Wt. W593/826 1,000,000 4/15 J.B.C. & A. A.D.S.S./Forms/C. 2118.

Instructions regarding War Diaries and Intelligence Summaries are contained in F. S. Regs., Part II. and the Staff Manual respectively. Title Pages will be prepared in manuscript.

WAR DIARY
or
INTELLIGENCE SUMMARY
(Erase heading not required.)

Army Form C. 2118

Place	Date	Hour	Summary of Events and Information	Remarks and references to Appendices
	24.		no work during day.	
			~~[illegible]~~ It being necessary to construct 4 saps, blinded with splinter proof cover for the installation of Flammenwerfer, the work to be completed on the 27th by 8 am the emplacements to be wired round. The work to be carried on regardless of casualties.	
			The emplacements to be made 3 & 4 60 feet long, No 6 70 feet long starting from the fire trench, direction as ordered by officer of the special company R.E. Places at Nos 3 4 5 + 6 Saps in ~~[illegible]~~ HIGH WOOD. No 5 sap was only to be 30' and the sap was already ~~[illegible]~~ completed only the overhead cover had to be put on.	
			Company paraded at 7 pm. orders were given to each officer & N.C.O so the work could be carried on in spite of casualties. The special Coy officer came up at the time. Journey to the wood rather hectic as the enemy had a barrage on owing to an attack further South. However	

1875 Wt. W593/826 1,000,000 4/15 J.B.C. & A. A.D.S.S./Forms/C. 2118.

Instructions regarding War Diaries and Intelligence Summaries are contained in F. S. Regs., Part II. and the Staff Manual respectively. Title Pages will be prepared in manuscript.

WAR DIARY
or
INTELLIGENCE SUMMARY
(Erase heading not required.)

Army Form C. 2118

Place	Date	Hour	Summary of Events and Information	Remarks and references to Appendices
			by choosing the moment the Company passed through with a loss of 1 O.R. killed & 3 wounded. 1 accidentally hurt.	
			Work was commenced covering parties being provided by the 1st Cameronians. Proceeded without interruption except for three very futile attempts of the enemy to bomb the party in No 3 sap. These were very easily repulsed by the covering party and no casualties were caused. The enemy being without [illegible] of bomb range.	
			Work was commenced in Nos. 3 5 & 6 saps. No 4 section being in hand to make up casualties or replace a section that was depleted. At 1 am all going well they were sent back to the billets. By daylight all the saps had been dug to an average depth of 4'6" to 5 feet. The sections returned to billets.	
	25	[illegible]	At 8 am the Pioneers commenced work deepening & widening but owing to rifle grenades they did not throw the earth out contenting themselves with sandbagging. The resulting progress was slow.	
			No 4 Section was employed during the day carrying up timber superintending and corrugated iron for the blindage. Carrying parties of 360 infantry	

1875 Wt. W593/826 1,000,000 4/15 J.B.C. & A. A.D.S.S./Forms/C. 2118.

Instructions regarding War Diaries and Intelligence Summaries are contained in F. S. Regs., Part II. and the Staff Manual respectively. Title Pages will be prepared in manuscript.

WAR DIARY
or
INTELLIGENCE SUMMARY
(Erase heading not required.)

Army Form C. 2118

Place	Date	Hour	Summary of Events and Information	Remarks and references to Appendices
			were employed. During the whole of this time the enemy were shelling the communication trenches, however the casualties were slight and all the material was carried to the spot.	
			~~The company from~~ The Company less No 4 Section paraded at 7pm and got to the work, casualties one O.R. missing believed killed by a direct hit from shell. No signs of the man could be found. Work was continued on	
	[illegible]		the saps deepening and widening by daylight they only needed trenching and trimming which was done by the pioneers.	
	26		On the night 26th 27th the emplacements were covered and wired all the sections working. Casualties 1 O.R. mortally wounded 3 OR wounded. Completed by 3 am 27th inst.	
	27		Company moved back to BECOURT E 2 a [illegible]	

1875 Wt. W593/826 1,000,000 4/15 J.B.C. & A. A.D.S.S./Forms/C. 2118.

Instructions regarding War Diaries and Intelligence Summaries are contained in F. S. Regs., Part II. and the Staff Manual respectively. Title Pages will be prepared in manuscript.

WAR DIARY
or
INTELLIGENCE SUMMARY
(Erase heading not required.)

Army Form C. 2118

Place	Date	Hour	Summary of Events and Information	Remarks and references to Appendices
	28		No work done by 2. 3 & 4 sections. No 1 Section went out at night to work on TEA LANE making shelters etc. No work done owing to shell fire. 1 O.R. wounded. 1 O.R. accidentally hurt (run over by wagon).	
	29		No 2 Section paraded 7am went out. Worked firestepping and improving TEA LANE. No 3 Section — 7 pm. Continued work No 2 Section put in shelter in same place. 1 O.R. wounded (at duty). No 4 Section paraded 7am and proceeded to erect water tanks under splinter proof cover at POMMIERES REDOUBT. Not quite completed.	
	30		No work done company standing by to move.	
	31		Company moved to RIBEMONT.	

H. A. Pursey
Capt R.E.
O.C. 11th Fd Co R.E.

1875 Wt. W593/826 1,000,000 4/15 J.B.C. & A. A.D.S.S./Forms/C. 2118.

Instructions regarding War Diaries and Intelligence Summaries are contained in F. S. Regs., Part II. and the Staff Manual respectively. Title Pages will be prepared in manuscript.

WAR DIARY
or
INTELLIGENCE SUMMARY
(Erase heading not required.)

Army Form C. 2118.

Vol 2

Place	Date	Hour	Summary of Events and Information	Remarks and references to Appendices
			War Diary of 11th Field Company R E for month of September 1916 [illegible] Henry Knight 2nd Lieut R E for OC 11th Fld Coy R.E	

2449 Wt. W14957/M90 750,000 1/16 J.B.C. & A. Forms/C.2118/12.

Confidential

Instructions regarding War Diaries and Intelligence Summaries are contained in F. S. Regs., Part II. and the Staff Manual respectively. Title Pages will be prepared in manuscript.

WAR DIARY

or

~~INTELLIGENCE~~ SUMMARY

(Erase heading not required.)

11th (Field) Co R.E.

Army Form C. 2118.

Place	Date	Hour	Summary of Events and Information	Remarks and references to Appendices
PIERREGOT	1/9/16		Company moved from RIBEMONT to PIERREGOT. (12 miles)	
BOISBERGUES	2/9		Company moved from PIERREGOT to BOISBERGUES (17 miles)	
do	3		Company rested.	
WAVANS	4		Company moved from ~~\#~~BOISBERGUES to WAVANS (7 miles)	
BLANGEVAL	5		Company moved from WAVANS to BLANGEVAL (12 miles).	
do	6		Company rested.	
do	7		Company rested.	
PETIT BOURET SUR CANCHE.	8		Company moved from BLANGEVAL to PETIT BOURET SUR CANCHE (7 miles)	
OPPY	9		Company moved from PETIT BOURET SUR CANCHE to OPPY. (5 miles)	

2449 Wt. W14957/M90 750,000 1/16 J.B.C. & A. Forms/C.2118/12.

Army Form C. 2118.

Instructions regarding War Diaries and Intelligence Summaries are contained in F. S. Regs., Part II. and the Staff Manual respectively. Title Pages will be prepared in manuscript.

WAR DIARY
or
INTELLIGENCE SUMMARY
(Erase heading not required.)

Place	Date	Hour	Summary of Events and Information	Remarks and references to Appendices
LA BAZÈQUE FARM	10		Company moved from ORPY to LA BAZÈQUE FARM (9 miles)	
do	11		Company rested. O.C. + 2 officers + 2 N.C.O.'s ~~took~~ went over line from HANNESCAMP to FONQUEVILLERS with officers 77th Co R.E. to take over from them.	
BIENVILLERS AND FONQUEVILLERS	12		Company moved from LA BAZÈQUE FARM. Two sections to BIENVILLERS and two sections to FONQUEVILLERS. Head Quarters section remained at LA BAZÈQUE FARM.	
	13			

2449 Wt. W14957/M90 750,000 1/16 J.B.C. & A. Forms/C.2118/12.

Army Form C. 2118.

Instructions regarding War Diaries and Intelligence Summaries are contained in F. S. Regs., Part II. and the Staff Manual respectively. Title Pages will be prepared in manuscript.

WAR DIARY
or
INTELLIGENCE SUMMARY
(Erase heading not required.)

Place	Date	Hour	Summary of Events and Information	Remarks and references to Appendices
FONQUEVILLERS	13		No 1 Section commenced work of revetting & repairing & draining CRAWLBOYS LANE communication trench.	
			No 3 Section commenced work of revetting etc ROBERTS AVENUE communication trench. Sappers working 8 hours. Infantry working in two reliefs of 4 hrs.	
HANNESCAMP	13		No 2 Section commenced work of revetting etc CHISWICK AVENUE also excavation of an Infantry Dugout in COLLINBOURNE AVENUE.	
			No 4 Section commenced work of revetting etc LULU LANE also completing dugouts in 74 STREET, KENDAL STREET and LIVERPOOL STREET.	
			Sappers working 8 hours. Infantry working in two reliefs of 4 hours.	
FONQUEVILLERS	14		Nos 1 & 3 Sections continued work on communication trenches. No 3 Section worked also a dugout in the BASTION.	
			Headquarters moved from BIENVILLERS to FONQUEVILLERS	
HANNESCAMP.			Nos 2 & 4 Sections continued work as before	
FONQUEVILLERS AND HANNESCAMP	15		All sections continued work as before. Nos 1 & 3 Sections commenced work on two dugouts in CRAWLBOYS AVENUE and SUPPORT LINE	
	16		Work continued as before. No 1 section commenced Co H.Q. dugout in SUPPORT LINE.	
			No 4 Section revetted front face of NO 75 STREET (firing line). Work done at night	

2449 Wt. W14957/M90 750,000 1/16 J.B.C. & A. Forms/C.2118/12.

Instructions regarding War Diaries and Intelligence Summaries are contained in F. S. Regs., Part II. and the Staff Manual respectively. Title Pages will be prepared in manuscript.

WAR DIARY
or
INTELLIGENCE SUMMARY
(Erase heading not required.)

Army Form C. 2118.

Place	Date	Hour	Summary of Events and Information	Remarks and references to Appendices
FONQUEVILLERS AND HANNESCAMP	17		Work continued as before by all Sections.	
do do / do do	18		do do do do. 1 O.R. wounded	
do do / do do	19		Work continued as before. No 4 Section revetting entrances to dugout in KENDAL ST	
do do / do do	20		do do do 1 O.R. wounded.	
do do / do do	21		do do do. Nos 2 + 4 Sections moved from HANNESCAMP to BIENVILLERS.	
do do / do do	22		Work continued as before. No 4 Section revetting entrances to dugout in LENS ST. Picket line + H. Q Section moved from LA BAZÈQUE FARM to HUMBERCAMP.	
do do / do do	23		Work continued as before.	
do do / do do	24		do do do	
do do / do do	25		Nos 2 + 4 Sections continued work as before. Nos 1 + 3 Sections did not work as they were detailed for baths + change of kit at FONQUEVILLERS.	
do do / do do	26		Nos 1 + 3 Sections continued work as before. Nos 2 + 4 Sections did not work as they were detailed for bath + change of kit at BIENVILLERS.	
do do / do do	27 / 28		All Sections worked as before.	
GAUDIEMPRÉ	29		Company moved to GAUDIEMPRÉ (6 miles)	
	30		Company moved to MILLY. (10 miles)	

[illegible signature]
Capt RE
O.C. 11th Field Co RE

2449 Wt. W14957/M90 750,000 1/16 J.B.C. & A. Forms/C.2118/12.

Instructions regarding War Diaries and Intelligence Summaries are contained in F. S. Regs., Part II. and the Staff Manual respectively. Title pages will be prepared in manuscript.

WAR DIARY
or
INTELLIGENCE SUMMARY.
(Erase heading not required.)

Army Form C. 2118.

Vol 22

Place	Date	Hour	Summary of Events and Information	Remarks and references to Appendices
			Confidential War Diary of 11th Field Coy R.E. From 1st Oct 1916 to 31st Oct 1916. [signature] Capt R.E OC 11th Fld Coy R.E	

A5834 Wt. W4973/M687 750,000 8/16 D. D. & L. Ltd. Forms/C.2118/13.

Instructions regarding War Diaries and Intelligence Summaries are contained in F. S. Regs., Part II. and the Staff Manual respectively. Title Pages will be prepared in manuscript.

Army Form C. 2118.

WAR DIARY
or
~~INTELLIGENCE SUMMARY~~
(Erase heading not required.)

Place	Date	Hour	Summary of Events and Information	Remarks and references to Appendices
MILLY	1/10.		Inspection of kit equipment and clothes.	
do	2/10		Company trained. Infantry drill, musketry & open order drill.	
DOULLENS	3/10		Company infantry drill in the morning. Moved to DOULLENS in the afternoon. (3 miles)	
do	4/10.		Infantry drill & preparing for inspection by G.O.C. 33rd Div.	
do	5/10.		Infantry drill. Open order training.	
do	6/10		Company inspected at 9 am by G.O.C. 33rd Div. Marched out at 2pm for BAYENCOURT. arrived at 6pm. (17 miles)	
BAYENCOURT	7/10.		Dismounted portion left BAYENCOURT for HEBUTERNE arriving in the evening. Horse lines at BAYENCOURT. Took over portion of the line opposite HEBUTERNE from 77th Co R.E. WHISKEY St incl to WARRIOR St excl.	
HEBUTERNE	8/10.		Line reconnoitred in daylight. Company started at night on making splinter proof shelters for magazines for Mills Grenades & Stokes mortar bombs. 4. Shelters for S.M & 20 shelters for Grenades being started. in B & C lines near the communication trenches & entrances to tunnels forward. All this being night work. Work interrupted by shell fire and bombs.	APPENDIX 1

2449 Wt. W14957/M90 750,000 1/16 J.B.C. & A. Forms/C.2118/12.

Army Form C. 2118.

Instructions regarding War Diaries and Intelligence Summaries are contained in F. S. Regs., Part II. and the Staff Manual respectively. Title Pages will be prepared in manuscript.

WAR DIARY
or
~~INTELLIGENCE SUMMARY~~
(Erase heading not required.)

Place	Date	Hour	Summary of Events and Information	Remarks and references to Appendices
HEBUTERNE	10/10		Continued on same work as previous	Ref map
			Started forming R.E. dump at entrance to WHISKEY ST at (6)	
	[illegible]		~~Continued on previous work~~ Also commenced making small trenches off top end of WHISKEY ST for forward R.E. dumps. ~~[illegible]~~	
	11/10		All grenade + T.M. stores completed by now with exception of 2 which had been blown in.	
			Carrying stores to stock forward R.E. dump ~~[illegible]~~ by ~~[illegible]~~ of 10 sappers 212th Co R.E. kept for this purpose.	
	12/10		No 1 section completed 2 T.M. emps + 2 Ammn shelters for same which had been started by 18th Mx Pioneers.	
			No 4 Section did the same.	
			No 3 Section started 3 new shelters for hand grenades in lieu of some blown in.	
			No 2 Section completed four new cuts for forward R.E. dump	
			Part of No 2 Section employed in labelling trenches.	
			25 Infantry employed clearing Blue of old mills grenades. 75 inf employed in carrying stores to forward R.E. dump.	

2449 Wt. W14957/M90 750,000 1/16 J.B.C. & A. Forms/C.2118/12.

Army Form C. 2118.

WAR DIARY
or
~~INTELLIGENCE SUMMARY~~

(Erase heading not required.)

Instructions regarding War Diaries and Intelligence Summaries are contained in F. S. Regs., Part II. and the Staff Manual respectively. Title Pages will be prepared in manuscript.

Place	Date	Hour	Summary of Events and Information	Remarks and references to Appendices
HEBUTERNE	13/10.		No1 Section revetting forward end of WHISKEY ST & left end of B line where damaged by fire. Repairing grenade D.Os. where damaged by fire. Work in both these cases interrupted by bombs & shelling.	
			No2 Section employed on cuts for forward R.E. dump.	
			No3 Section completed 2 stores for mills grenades & commenced 2 more.	
			No4 do framed & revetted sides of D.O. for stokes mortar bombs already completed.	
	14/10.		No1 Section revetting WHISKEY ST.	
			No 2 Section making a D.O. for T.M snipers.	
			Nos 3 & 4 Section moved back to SAILLY & made Bivouacs for themselves.	
	15/10.		No1 Section revetting WHISKEY ST. near C line.	
			No2 .. Continued D.O. for T.M.E.	
			No3 Section Commenced making 4 T.M. emps in a line just behind D line.	
			No4 Section completed Bivouacs at SAILLY.	

2449 Wt. W14957/M90 750,000 1/16 J.B.C. & A. Forms/C.2118/12.

Army Form C. 2118.

Instructions regarding War Diaries and Intelligence Summaries are contained in F. S. Regs., Part II. and the Staff Manual respectively. Title Pages will be prepared in manuscript.

WAR DIARY
or
~~INTELLIGENCE SUMMARY~~
(Erase heading not required.)

Place	Date	Hour	Summary of Events and Information	Remarks and references to Appendices
HEBUTERNE	16.		Nos 1 2 & 3 sections as before.	
			No 4 Section commenced a d.o. for M.G. emp. in welcome St.	
	17		Company handed over to 78th Co R.E. 17th Div. and left HEBUTERNE for MILLY (15 miles)	
MILLY.	18.		Company rested	
	19		Company left MILLY and proceed to VILLE-SOUS-CORBIE ~~[illegible]~~ in 'busses.	
VILLE SOUS CORBIE	20.		Stayed at VILLE SOUS CORBIE.	
	21		Marched from VILLE SOUS CORBIE to the CITADEL (8 miles) by cross country tracks very bad marching. Took over billets from 12th Field Co R.E. 6th Div.	
BRIQUETTERIE	22.		Marched from the CITADEL to bivouac ~~[illegible]~~ by the BRIQUETTERIE.	
do	23		Company lent to 4th Div. No 1 Section lent to 9th Field Co R.E.	
GUILLEMONT	24.		Company moved to bivouac taken over from 9th Co R.E. between TRONES WOOD & GUILLEMONT	

2449 Wt. W14957/M90 750,000 1/16 J.B.C. & A. Forms/C.2118/12.

Instructions regarding War Diaries and Intelligence Summaries are contained in F. S. Regs., Part II. and the Staff Manual respectively. Title Pages will be prepared in manuscript.

Army Form C. 2118.

WAR DIARY
or
~~INTELLIGENCE SUMMARY~~
(Erase heading not required.)

Place	Date	Hour	Summary of Events and Information	Remarks and references to Appendices
GUILLEMONT LESBOEUFS.	24		Company was to stay bivouaced in GUILLEMONT & work the line in front of LES BOEUFS. Officers reconnoitred the line with the help(?) of guides from the 9th Co R.E. O.C. reconnoitred line of Right battalion with C.O. right battalion (2nd R.W.F) incidentally losing the way and wandering up to the German line in front of 98th Bde area on the left of brigade. Company was working with (19th I.B). Also went into the French line and made acquaintance of French Battalion and Regimental commanders. 125th French regiment being on our right.	
	25th		By night whole company proceeded up to 25 Street to connect up with new front line (SNOW TRENCH) because just established by the 2nd Division before handing over and to improve 25 street. There was no R.E. work in the front line. The crying need was for communications back to GINCHY the fields being sodden & the GINCHY - LES BOEUFS road being so cut up by shells and traffic as to be impassable.	

Army Form C. 2118.

WAR DIARY
or
~~INTELLIGENCE SUMMARY~~
(Erase heading not required.)

Instructions regarding War Diaries and Intelligence Summaries are contained in F. S. Regs., Part II. and the Staff Manual respectively. Title Pages will be prepared in manuscript.

Place	Date	Hour	Summary of Events and Information	Remarks and references to Appendices
			A trench board track was arranged for by C.R.E. to be made under superintendance of 222nd Co R.E. who were in reserve.	
			The Coy undertook to try and improve the communication trenches. The infantry who were in the line having their hands full of their trenches they were holding and the battalions back requiring rest when they were not being used for carrying parties.	
	26th		~~[illegible]~~ Half Company worked for four hours in front line One section 25 STREET one section FLANK AVENUE. clearing and deepening	
	27th		do do	
	28th		do do	
	29th		do do	
	30th		Half company worked in FLANK AVENUE.	
	31st			

2449 Wt. W14957/M90 750,000 1/16 J.B.C. & A. Forms/C.2118/12.

Instructions regarding War Diaries and Intelligence Summaries are contained in F. S. Regs., Part II. and the Staff Manual respectively. Title Pages will be prepared in manuscript.

WAR DIARY
or
~~INTELLIGENCE SUMMARY~~
(Erase heading not required.)

Army Form C. 2118.

Place	Date	Hour	Summary of Events and Information	Remarks and references to Appendices
	31st		No 3 section with two platoons infantry taped and dug a new trench connecting ANTELOPE TRENCH to French advanced jumping off line. At the same time 150x of trench were taped from Southern gun pits to FLANK Av. but the working party was led astray by the guide and no work was done. H. A. L. Pusey Capt RE. O.C. 11th Field Co R.E.	

2449 Wt. W14957/M90 750,000 1/16 J.B.C. & A. Forms/C.2118/12.

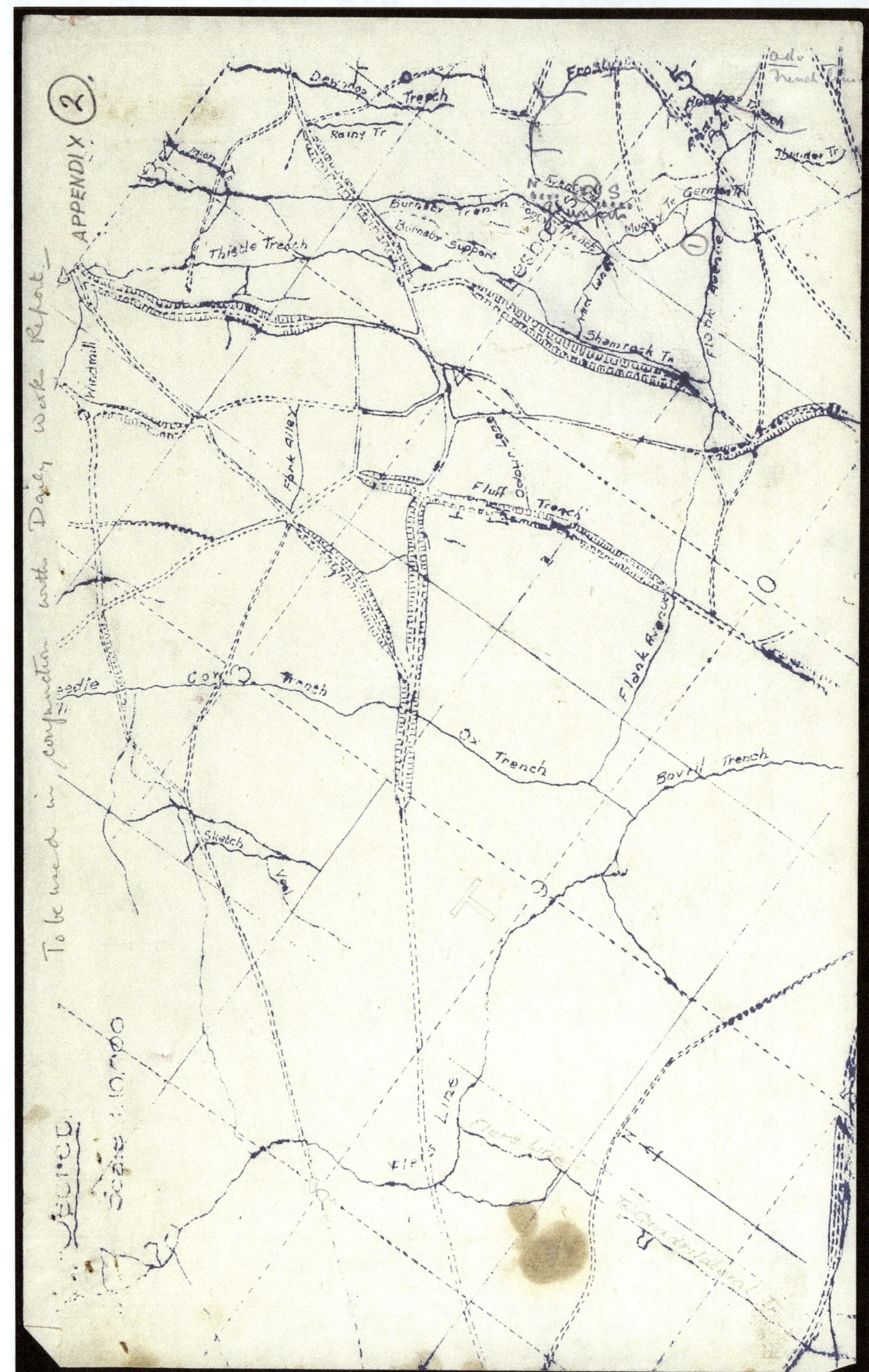
APPENDIX 2
To be used in conjunction with Daily Work Report
Scale 1:10,000
Frosty
Rainy Tr
Thunder Tr
Burnaby Trench
Burnaby Support
Thistle Trench
Mucky Tr
German Tr
Shamrock Tr
Flank Avenue
Windmill
Flank Alley
Fluff Trench
Cow Trench
Ox Trench
Bovril Trench
Sketch
Flank Avenue
Fir Line
Flers Line

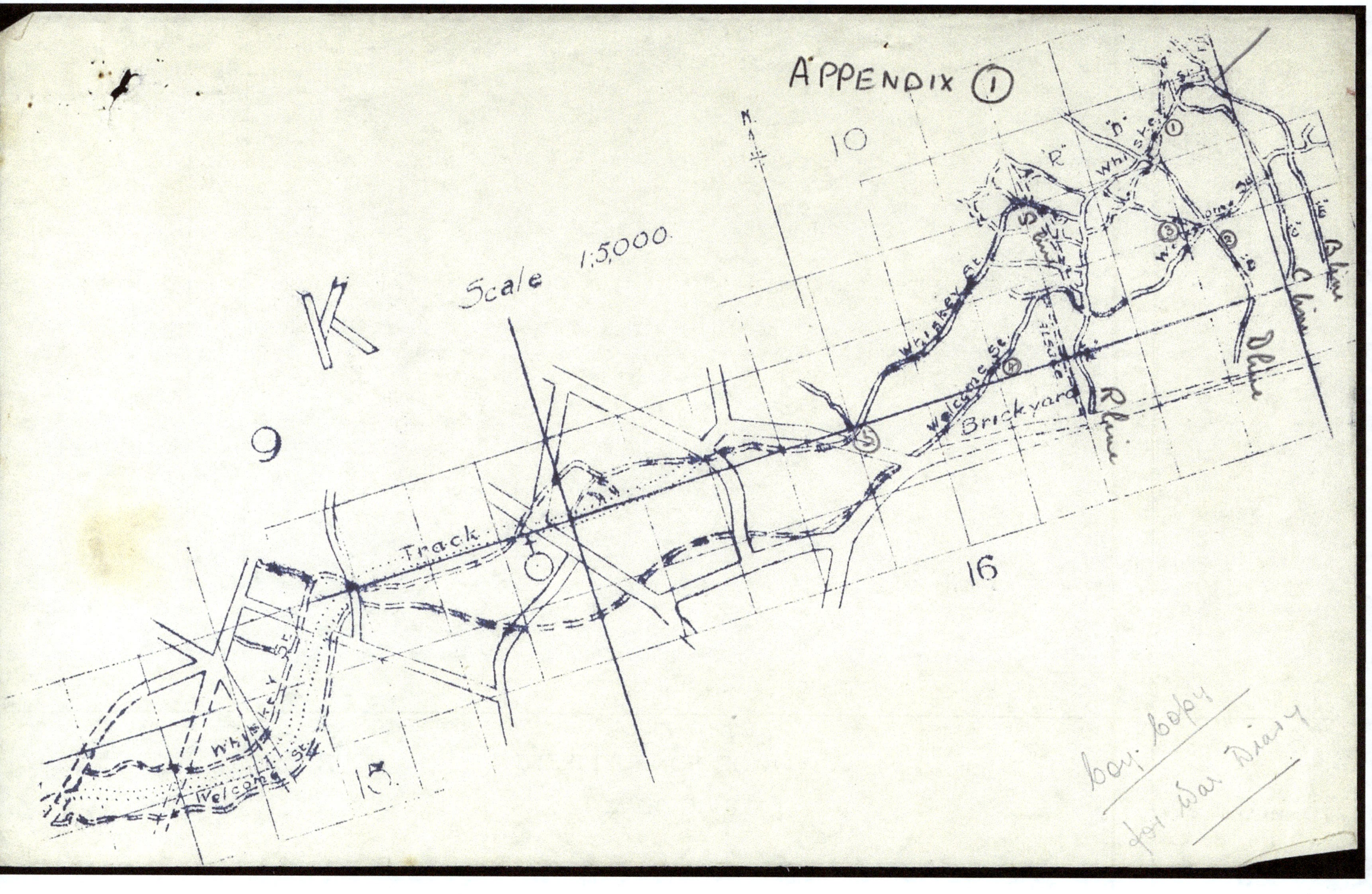
APPENDIX 1
Scale 1:5,000
K
9
10
15
16
N
B line
C line
D line
R line
S line
Whiskey St.
Welcome St.
Brickyard
Track
Whiskey St.
Welcome St.
Coy: copy for War Diary

Army Form C. 2118.

WAR DIARY
or
INTELLIGENCE SUMMARY
(Erase heading not required.)

Instructions regarding War Diaries and Intelligence Summaries are contained in F. S. Regs., Part II. and the Staff Manual respectively. Title Pages will be prepared in manuscript.

Place	Date	Hour	Summary of Events and Information	Remarks and references to Appendices
			Vol 23	
			Confidential War Diary of 11th Field Company Royal Engineers From 1st Nov 1916 to 30th Nov 1916 H a Russey [signature] Capt RE OC 11th Fld Coy RE.	

2449 Wt. W14957/M90 750,000 1/16 J.B.C. & A. Forms/C.2118/12.

Instructions regarding War Diaries and Intelligence Summaries are contained in F. S. Regs., Part II. and the Staff Manual respectively. Title Pages will be prepared in manuscript.

WAR DIARY
or
INTELLIGENCE SUMMARY
(Erase heading not required.)

Army Form C. 2118.

Place	Date	Hour	Summary of Events and Information	Remarks and references to Appendices
LESBOEUFS.	1.11.16		The Company paraded at 9 am and proceeded to HOGS BACK where it waited to consolidate in case attack made by 100th Bde succeeded. Attack reported successful on left flank and WORCESTERSHIRE Regt reported in possession of HAZY TR. (36 d 0.0 to 5 b 4.5) Two sections were sent forward each with carrying party of 25 men to consolidate flanks by making ~~s~~ strong points at these points. However the WORCESTERS had to fall back before the sections arrived and they returned to billets. The attack was unsuccessful on the right against BARITSKA but was ordered again for 1 am. No 3 section was ordered up to make a strong point on the immediate left of the French whose attack had succeeded when ours took place. Before arrival the attack was ~~postponed~~ countermanded. This were used in improving jumping off trench between ANTELOPE TR & FRENCH LEFT. (2 O.R. missing) Remaining sections returned to camp.	Sketch map appendix I
	2.11.16 ~~2.11.16~~.		No work done by Company. O.C. & 4 O.R. went out to tape a new jumping off line 80 to 120 yds from BARITSKA in front of ANTELOPE TR. After taping 90 yards the taping party were seen in the moonlight & forced to take cover in a shell hole for 1½ hours. Taking advantage of a cloud they regained Antelope trench and it was found the working party had returned home. So no work was done.	
	3.11.16		Company moved forward to BOX TRENCH to help in consolidation of position attacked by infantry. Attack a complete failure. Company returned home at 9 pm not being required	

2449 Wt. W14957/M90 750,000 1/16 J.B.C. & A. Forms/C.2118/12.

Army Form C. 2118.

Instructions regarding War Diaries and Intelligence Summaries are contained in F. S. Regs., Part II. and the Staff Manual respectively. Title Pages will be prepared in manuscript.

WAR DIARY
or
INTELLIGENCE SUMMARY
(Erase heading not required.)

Place	Date	Hour	Summary of Events and Information	Remarks and references to Appendices
LESBOEUFS	4.11.16		No 4 Section laid out track from Bn. H.Q. to ANDREWS POST & to Co H.Q. of support Co of Left Bn.	
			O.C. with 4 O.R. taped out assembly trenches and aligned 2nd WORCESTER REGT in them at 5 d. 9.2	
			in 4 lines facing N.W for attack on BARITSKA & mirage from the flank.	
			Remainder of company no work.	
	5.11.16.		Company moved forward to assist in attack with 100th Bde. being in OX TR. 4 sections each with	
			carrying party of 25 infantry.	
			The attack was successful.	
			No 4 Section moved off at about 3 pm. made a small strong point and wired it in at about	
			T. 6 a 0.5. It was garrisoned on completion by men of the 16th K.R.R. 1 M.G. + 1 Lewis gun.	
			Casualties 2 O.R. wounded. This point was about 40x in front of line infantry was holding.	
			No 3 Section moved forward soon after and made a similar point at about T 6 a 3.7 in the	
			gap between the British and French lines. Garrisoned by 2nd Worcesters (20 men) & 1 M.G. 1 Lewis gun.	
			Casualties 3 O R wounded.	
			No 2 Section moved forward at about 6 pm and constructed a strong point at about T 5 b 3.7	
			Garrison 20 men 2nd Worcesters, 1 M.G. 1 Lewis gun. This point was in a gap that	
			existed between the left of the 100th I.B and the right of the 19th I.B.	
			Casualties 1 O.R. wounded.	

2449 Wt. W14957/M90 750,000 1/16 J.B.C. & A. Forms/C.2118/12.

Army Form C. 2118.

Instructions regarding War Diaries and Intelligence Summaries are contained in F. S. Regs., Part II. and the Staff Manual respectively. Title Pages will be prepared in manuscript.

WAR DIARY
or
INTELLIGENCE SUMMARY

(Erase heading not required.)

Place	Date	Hour	Summary of Events and Information	Remarks and references to Appendices
			No 1 Section moved off at 6.30 pm made a strong point at T.N. 35 d 2.1. also in a gap between the two Bdes. garrisoned by 1st Queens & 16th KRR with 2 Lewis guns.	
			Casualties nil	
			A track to the new front line was taped out by an Officer & men of the 18th Mx Pioneers	
GUILLEMONT MEAULTE	6.11.16		Company ~~was relieved by the 15th Field Coy 8th Division and marched back~~ rested.	
			O.C. went to MEAULTE to take over work being done by 2nd Field Co R.E. 8th Division.	
MEAULTE.	7.11.16		Company moved to MEAULTE being relieved by 15th Field Co R.E. 8th Division. taking over billets of 2nd Field Co R.E. 8th Divn	
			Kit inspection and cleaning up. Inventory of tools etc taken.	
do	8.11.16		No 1 Section started work in Corps School at MEAULTE putting up Nissen huts washhouse	
	9.11.16.		& Cookhouses. Remainder of company awaiting orders	
	10.11.16.		ditto	
	11.11.16		No 1 Section as before.	
			3 Sections with O.C. moved to Huts in Carnoy Montauban Road.	

Instructions regarding War Diaries and Intelligence Summaries are contained in F. S. Regs., Part II. and the Staff Manual respectively. Title Pages will be prepared in manuscript.

WAR DIARY
or
INTELLIGENCE SUMMARY
(Erase heading not required.)

Army Form C. 2118.

Place	Date	Hour	Summary of Events and Information	Remarks and references to Appendices
CARNOY	12.11.16.		Company commenced work on hutting in camps on CARNOY MONTAUBAN RD. under C.E. XIV Corps. No 1 Section at MEAULTE as before.	
	13.11.16		ditto	
	14.11.16 15.11.16 16.11.16 17.11.16 18.11.16		From the 12th November till the 25th November as above No 1 Section being at MEAULTE Nos 2 3 & 4 on hutments on the CARNOY–MONTAUBAN road.	
			On the 20th 2/Lt KIRBY went on leave.	
			On the 20th 2/Lt GARROD proceeded to FLIXECOURT to an Officers School.	
	26th 19.11.16		Transport of company moved by road to MERICOURT.	
	20.11.16			
	27th.		Company moved by Bus to VAUX. ~~[illegible]~~ near OISEMONT to rest.	
			Transport by road to ARGOEUVES	
	28th		Dismounted portion cleaning up	
			Transport by road to VAUX.	

Instructions regarding War Diaries and Intelligence Summaries are contained in F. S. Regs., Part II. and the Staff Manual respectively. Title Pages will be prepared in manuscript.

WAR DIARY
or
INTELLIGENCE SUMMARY
(Erase heading not required.)

Army Form C. 2118.

Place	Date	Hour	Summary of Events and Information	Remarks and references to Appendices
VAUX.	29.		Kit inspection. Stock taking of stores + tools.	
	30.		Carpenters worked in Bde workshops making tables beds etc for billet improvements Remainder of company billet repairs + washing Vehicles	
			H. A. S. Prisley Capt R.E. O.C. 11th Field Co R.E.	

2449 Wt. W14957/M90 750,000 1/16 J.B.C. & A. Forms/C.2118/12.

Army Form C. 2118.

Instructions regarding War Diaries and Intelligence Summaries are contained in F. S. Regs., Part II. and the Staff Manual respectively. Title Pages will be prepared in manuscript.

WAR DIARY
or
INTELLIGENCE SUMMARY
(Erase heading not required.)

Vol 24

Place	Date	Hour	Summary of Events and Information	Remarks and references to Appendices
			Confidential War Diary of 11th Field Company. RE From. 1. 12. 16 to 31. 12. 16 W.H. Garrod 2nd Lieut RE for OC 11th Field Coy RE	

2449 Wt. W14957/M90 750,000 1/16 J.B.C. & A. Forms/C.2118/12.

Army Form C. 2118.

Instructions regarding War Diaries and Intelligence Summaries are contained in F. S. Regs., Part II. and the Staff Manual respectively. Title Pages will be prepared in manuscript.

WAR DIARY
or
INTELLIGENCE SUMMARY
(Erase heading not required.)

Place	Date	Hour	Summary of Events and Information	Remarks and references to Appendices
VAUX	1.12.16		Carpenters at Bde Hq making Tables etc for billet improvements of Bde No 3 Section billeted at ARAINES working billet improvements for R.A. Company drill for remainder. Skirmishing & musketry ½ Officers completing a reconnaissance of the district for materials etc.	
do	2		do do with exception of reconnaissance for materials	
do	3.		do do	
do	4		do do	
do	5.		do do	
do	6		do do 2/Lt KIRBY returned from leave	
do	7		Transport moved by road. to ARGOEUVES. No 3 Sec transport joined Co at ARAINES on march Company drill for dismounted men	
MORLANCOURT	8.		Dismounted men entrained at ARAINES train to MERICOURT. No 3 Section rejoined company at ARAINES. Then marched to ~~[illegible]~~ MORLANCOURT. Transport joined company there	

2449 Wt. W14957/M90 750,000 1/16 J.B.C. & A. Forms/C.2118/12.

Army Form C. 2118.

WAR DIARY
or
INTELLIGENCE SUMMARY
(Erase heading not required.)

Instructions regarding War Diaries and Intelligence Summaries are contained in F. S. Regs., Part II. and the Staff Manual respectively. Title Pages will be prepared in manuscript.

Place	Date	Hour	Summary of Events and Information	Remarks and references to Appendices
Camp III	9.		Company marched to Camp III N of BRAY	P
do	10		Company rested	P
MAUREPAS.	11		dismounted portion of company moved to R.E dump W of MAUREPAS. B 14 b 1.3 ALBERT Combined sheet 1/40000. Mounted portion moved to Horse lines at Camp 23 on the MARICOURT RD Eastwards dismounted men put up temporary shelters for themselves. No 4 Sec billeted in existing dug outs constructed by the French.	P
	12.		No 4 Section continued work on the 4th Div Hq a large cut & cover dug out started by the French. The other three sections started on cut & cover dug outs for billets for themselves. 2/Lt KIRBY went away sick.	P
	13		do for No 4 Section & 2½ sects. ½ No 3 Section marched to camp 21 on the MARICOURT — SUZANNE Road	P
	~~14~~		~~No 4 Sec continued~~	

2449 Wt. W14957/M90 750,000 1/16 J.B.C. & A. Forms/C.2118/12.

Army Form C. 2118.

WAR DIARY
or
INTELLIGENCE SUMMARY

(Erase heading not required.)

Instructions regarding War Diaries and Intelligence Summaries are contained in F. S. Regs., Part II. and the Staff Manual respectively. Title Pages will be prepared in manuscript.

Place	Date	Hour	Summary of Events and Information	Remarks and references to Appendices
	14		No 4 Section on Div Hq. No 1 Section constructing drying rooms for socks 4 at Camp 23 for 400 socks each in one long shed; and same at ~~Camp~~ MAUREPAS RAVINE (B14c 4.2.) No 2 Section commenced erection of 4 Nissen huts at FERME ROUGE. No 3 Section commenced erection huts for spray baths 1 at MAUREPAS RAVINE B20a1.5 1 at Camp 21	[initials]
	15		Work Seen do do	[initials]
	16		do do	[initials]
	17		do do 4 men No 2 Sec went to TOURBIÈRES - BRAY with 217 A.T. CoRE to make portable huts for Bde HQ.	[initials]
	18		do do	[initials]
	19		do do	[initials]
	20		do do	[initials]
	~~22~~21		[illegible] do do No 2 Sec completed 2 Nissen huts + foundations for 2 more. No more huts on site	

2449 Wt. W14957/M90 750,000 1/16 J.B.C. & A. Forms/C.2118/12.

Army Form C. 2118.

Instructions regarding War Diaries and Intelligence Summaries are contained in F. S. Regs., Part II. and the Staff Manual respectively. Title Pages will be prepared in manuscript.

WAR DIARY
or
INTELLIGENCE SUMMARY
(Erase heading not required.)

Place	Date	Hour	Summary of Events and Information	Remarks and references to Appendices
	22		Nos 1, 3, & 4 secs as before. No 2 sec on billet improvements	[illegible]
	23.		do do	[illegible]
	24.		Nos 1 3 & 4 as before No 2 raising screening on the roadside by FERME ROBBE to hide the huts erected by them. One block of drying sheds erected by No 1 section blown down by high wind owing to lack of diagonal bracing. One Bde Hqr Hut made by No 2 sec at TOURBIÈRES erected by No 1 at Camp 21.	[illegible]
	25		Company worked as before for half a day. afternoon packing up.	[illegible]
	26.		Company moved by road to Camp 12 near SAILLY LAURETTE.	[illegible]
	27.		Transport by road to ARGOEUVES. Remainder entrained at DERNANCOURT to PONT REMY by rail & then to BUIGNY L'ABBÉ. 2/Lt CHANTER went on leave	[illegible]

2449 Wt. W14957/M90 750,000 1/16 J.B.C. & A. Forms/C.2118/12.

Army Form C. 2118.

Instructions regarding War Diaries and Intelligence Summaries are contained in F. S. Regs., Part II. and the Staff Manual respectively. Title Pages will be prepared in manuscript.

WAR DIARY
or
INTELLIGENCE SUMMARY
(Erase heading not required.)

Place	Date	Hour	Summary of Events and Information	Remarks and references to Appendices
BUIGNY L'ABBY	28		Transport by road to BUIGNY L'ABBY. dismounted men rested.	[illegible]
	29.		Kit inspected. cleaning up etc.	[illegible]
	30.		Washing wagons. 2Lt P. MELHUISH joined Company from base.	[illegible]
	31		Major PRESSEY went away on leave. Section & Company Drill for Sappers. Drivers cleaning harness.	WHG.

W H Garrod
II Lt. R.E.
for O.C. 11th Field Co. R.E.

2449 Wt. W14957/M90 750,000 1/16 J.B.C. & A. Forms/C.2118/12.

Instructions regarding War Diaries and Intelligence Summaries are contained in F. S. Regs., Part II. and the Staff Manual respectively. Title pages will be prepared in manuscript.

WAR DIARY
or
INTELLIGENCE SUMMARY.
(Erase heading not required.)

Army Form C. 2118.

Place	Date	Hour	Summary of Events and Information	Remarks and references to Appendices
			Vol 25	
			CONFIDENTIAL	
			War Diary	Jan 1917
			of	May 1919
			11th (Field) Co., R.E.,	
			from January 1st 1917. to January 31st 1917	
			(Volume)	
			J. Anderson Lt, R.E. Commdg. 11th Coy. R.E	

A5834 Wt. W4973 M687 750,000 8/16 D. D. & L. Ltd. Forms/C.2118/13.

Instructions regarding War Diaries and Intelligence Summaries are contained in F. S. Regs., Part II. and the Staff Manual respectively. Title pages will be prepared in manuscript.

WAR DIARY
or
INTELLIGENCE SUMMARY.
(Erase heading not required.)

Army Form C. 2118.

Place	Date JANUARY	Hour	Summary of Events and Information	Remarks and references to Appendices
BUIGNY L'ABBE (ABBEVILLE 1:100,000)	1	–	Raining. Mounted portion exercising horses and cleaning harness Dismounted portion seven miles route march	J.E.A.
"	2	-	Raining at intervals. Mounted portion exercising. Dismounted portion, squad drill J.E. ANDERSON Temp. Lt ~~R.E~~ & Adjt RE assumed command of Company during absence in BRITAIN of H.R.S. PRESSEY Capt (a/MAJOR) R.E.	J.E.A.
"	3	-	Raining. Mounted portion as yesterday. Animals inspected by A.D.V.S, & found to be in bad condition Dismounted portion as yesterday. Football match Right Half v Left Half at 2.p.m 2/Lt. KAYLOR goes on leave.	J.E.A.
"	4	-	Raining at intervals. 5 horses evacuated on orders of A.D.V.S to M.V.S. at LONGUET. One animal shot. Clipping of all horses proceeded with. No 1. Section fixing up Soyers Stoves in an empty house for washing while in billets. No 2. Section Squad & Section Drill by N.C.Os. No 3 Section with transport draw one set spray baths from 19th Inf Bde. H.Q. at BALLENCOURT and convey same to EPAGNE where they commence erection of same No 4 Section same as No 2	J.E.A.

A5834 Wt. W4973 M687 750,000 8/16 D. D. & L. Ltd. Forms/C.2118/13.

Instructions regarding War Diaries and Intelligence Summaries are contained in F. S. Regs., Part II. and the Staff Manual respectively. Title pages will be prepared in manuscript.

WAR DIARY
or
INTELLIGENCE SUMMARY.
(Erase heading not required.)

Army Form C. 2118.

Place	Date	Hour	Summary of Events and Information	Remarks and references to Appendices
	JANUARY			
BUIGNY L'ABBE (ABBEVILLE 1:100,000)	5	–	Raining at intervals. One G.S. Waggon with six horses goes to FONTAINE saw-mill, met by M. MESNY (Interpreter to Divl R.E.) and loaded with firewood. No 3 Section and transport continue with spray baths at EPAGNE. Remaining Sections cleaning up billets Bicycles inspected at 9 am and six sent to workshops for overhaul	J.E.t.
" "	6	–	Raining at intervals One G.S. Wagon proceeds to BUSSUS - BUSSUEL (222nd Field Co RE) & borrows piano for concert. No 1 Section bathing No 2 Section constructing an oven for H.Q. Section & fixing up concert room in drivers' billet No 3 Section, 8 men continue with baths at EPAGNE, remainder dismissed for day after inspection at 9. a.m No 4 Section day off. Company paid between 9 am and 11 am ~~Football match in afternoon, N.Z. v. 222nd Co~~ ~~Concert in evening.~~ stet. J.E.t.	J.E.t.
" "	7	–	Forage Cart goes to ABBEVILLE for clipping machine Cpl. Matthews & Smith attend at SCHOOLHOUSE, LONG, for a lecture by A.D.V.S on skin diseases No 1. Section - Erecting latrines, oiling linen, preparing drivers' billet for concert room No 2 Section - Bathing No 3. Section - Flagging out manoeuvre-ground between BUIGNY L'ABBE & AILLY-LE-HAUT-CLOCHER under 2nd Lt. ROBERTS. A party of six detached to continue baths at EPAGNE. No 4 Section - Begins felling forest near 19th I.B refilling-point for wood for Brigade Group. x ~~Football match at 2.30 pm 11th Fd. Co. v. 222nd Fd. Co~~ x ~~Concert in evening~~ delete. J.E.t.	J.E.t.

A5834 Wt. W4973 M687 750,000 8/16 D. D. & L. Ltd. Forms/C.2118/13.

Instructions regarding War Diaries and Intelligence Summaries are contained in F. S. Regs., Part II. and the Staff Manual respectively. Title pages will be prepared in manuscript.

WAR DIARY
or
INTELLIGENCE SUMMARY.

(Erase heading not required.)

Army Form C. 2118.

Place	Date (January)	Hour	Summary of Events and Information	Remarks and references to Appendices
BUIGNY L'ABBE (ABBEVILLE 1:100,000)	8	–	Fine in morning, but very stormy in evening, snow & sleet & high wind.	
		–	Mounted section continues clipping with machine	
			No. 1 section proceeds to 4th ARMY INFANTRY SCHOOL at FLIXECOURT for work on billets etc	
			No. 2 Bathing	
			No. 3 Carry on with flagging-out MANOEUVRE GROUND.	
			No. 4 Carry on felling wood.	
			2/Lt GARROD goes on leave	[illegible]
	9	–	Cold day, rain and sleet	
			Mounted portion pushes on with clipping	
			No. 2 section } No. 3 section } proceed to PONT REMY for work in connection with the 4th Army Musketry School relieving 3 sections of the 29th Divl Engineers	
			No. 4 section Woodcutting	
			Majority of H.Q., 2, 3 & 4 sections inoculated.	[illegible]
			G.O.C., Division, visited the Coy.	
	10	–	Cold day, cloudy & inclined to snow	
			Extra grooming ordered for mounted portion	
			One rider drawn from C.R.E.'s Office, LONG	
			Nos. 1, 2 & 3 continue at ~~the~~ FLIXECOURT & PONT REMY.	
			No. 4. Cutting wood.	
			Football match at BUSSUS-BUSSUEL, 11th Co. v 222nd Co R.E.	
			Rifle match at same place between N.C.O's of these Companies.	[illegible]

A5834 Wt. W4073 M687 750,000 8/16 D. D. & L. Ltd. Forms/C.2118/13.

Instructions regarding War Diaries and Intelligence Summaries are contained in F. S. Regs., Part II. and the Staff Manual respectively. Title pages will be prepared in manuscript.

WAR DIARY
or
INTELLIGENCE SUMMARY.
(Erase heading not required.)

Army Form C. 2118.

Place	Date	Hour	Summary of Events and Information	Remarks and references to Appendices
	JANUARY	-		
BUIGNY L'ABBE" (ABBEVILLE 1:100,000)	11		Wet day. Company at work as yesterday	J.E.A.
"	12	-	Rain and sleet at intervals. Company as yesterday. 2/LT. CHANTER returns from leave.	J.E.A.
"	13	-	Wet day. Presentation of medal ribbons by G.O.C. Division to those men of the Coy who had won decorations in the SOMME and at CAMBRIN. Presented near Bde. H.Q at BELLANCOURT. G.O.C gives more than ordinary praise to the Company Preparations begun for move into forward area. Inspection of Transport by D.A.D.O.S.	J.E.A.
"	14		Raining Further preparations for move. No 1 Section returns from FLIXECOURT Mounted Portion paid. Nos 2. 3 & 4 Sections continue duties at PONT REMY & wood-chopping at Repling - ?	J.E.A.
"	15		Fine day. Transport under 2/LT. MELHUISH leaves for CAMP III via ARGOEUVES etc. at 8.15 am. Billet stores returned to 19th Inf. Bde at BELLANCOURT. Nos 2 & 3 ~~& 4~~ Sections return to BUIGNY L'ABBE. No 4 finishes up wood-cutting 2/LT CHANTER goes sick & is sent to rest station near ABBEVILLE Draw 12000 francs from Imprest and pay dismounted portion of Company	J.E.A.

A5834 Wt. W4973/M687 750,000 8/16 D. D. & L. Ltd. Forms/C.2118/13.

Army Form C. 2118.

Instructions regarding War Diaries and Intelligence Summaries are contained in F. S. Regs., Part II. and the Staff Manual respectively. Title pages will be prepared in manuscript.

WAR DIARY
or
INTELLIGENCE SUMMARY.

(*Erase heading not required.*)

Place	Date JANUARY	Hour	Summary of Events and Information	Remarks and references to Appendices
BUIGNY L'ABBÉ (ABBEVILLE 1:100000)	16	-	Fine day, cold Dismounted Section cleaning up billets Preparing to move ~~on the~~ to-morrow morning	J.E.A.
	17	-	Moved off in the snow at 6.30 am. Arrived at PONT REMY 7.40 am & had to wait till 1.00 PM before entraining. Arrived at BRAY TOURBIÈRES at 10.30, and at Camp 111 at 11.15 pm. Billetting party under 2/Lt ROBERTS had everything in readiness. Mounted portion already in.	J.E.A.
CAMP. 111 L.2.b.2.9 (ALBERT SHEET Combined 1:40000)	18	-	All day at Camp 111.	
G.8.C.6.6. (ALBERT SHEET)	19	-	Fine cold weather Moved to SUZANNE, leaving Camp 111 at 2.35 pm and arriving at 5 pm All in tents (horses in rough stables) for the night at G.8.C.6.6. Come under orders of C.R.E. to complete the move.	J.E.A.
P.C. OURCEL ~~[illegible]~~ H.5.6.7.3 (ALBERT SHEET).	20	-	O.C. & 2/Lt. KAYLOR go to meet a French guide at P.C. JEAN (CURLU) at 6 am and are conducted to French Cie du GENIE (9/51) which 11th C. is to relieve. 2/Lt. KAYLOR returns & brings up with 2/Lt ROBERTS, the dismounted portion of the Company. O.C. goes around line and takes over from French Company. 2/Lt. MELHUISH takes the mounted portion, & No. 1 section into good billets in FRISE BEND about G.18.b.4.5. Dismounted portion, less No. 1 section, arrives at P.C. OURCEL (H.5.C.7.3) about 7 pm	J.E.A.

A5834 Wt. W4973 M687 750,000 8/16 D. D. & L. Ltd. Forms/C.2118/13.

Army Form C. 2118.

Instructions regarding War Diaries and Intelligence Summaries are contained in F. S. Regs., Part II. and the Staff Manual respectively. Title pages will be prepared in manuscript.

WAR DIARY
or
INTELLIGENCE SUMMARY.
(Erase heading not required.)

Place	Date JANUARY	Hour	Summary of Events and Information	Remarks and references to Appendices
P.C. OURCEL H.S.C. 7.3 CALBERT COMD SHEET 1:40,000	21	–	Fine day very cold, snow freezing on ground. Men cleaning out billets. Take officers & N.C.O's over part of line. 2/Lt MELHUISH takes No 1 Section into new billet at P.C. JEAN (CURLU).	J.E.A.
"	22	–	Fine day, very cold. Nos 2 & 3 sections commence work on INT. LINE South of MAUD AVENUE. No. 4 section on billet improvements. Take officers & N.C.O's on further reconnaissance of line.	J.E.A.
"	23	–	Fine weather, very cold. Great aerial activity & several fights. Sent in report on Rt Bde Sector (copy attached) to C.R.E. 2/Lt Roberts with Nos 2 & 3 continue on INTERMEDIATE LINE.	J.E.A.
"	24	–	Fine, very cold weather. 2/Lt ROBERTS & N.C.O's explore INT. LINE and OMMIECOURT LOOP DEFENCES. No. 4 section on billet improvements. 2/Lt GARROD returns from leave. 4 platoons of infantry employed under R.E. supervision. 2/Lt MELHUISH & Cpl LAWES save a Frenchman from drowning in SOMME RIVER. As a result of his immersion in the cold water, the former collapses & goes into hospital for 24 hours.	J.E.A.
"	25	–	Fine, very cold as yesterday. No 2 Section with 1 platoon deepening & widening & revetting INT. LINE South of MAUD AVENUE. No 3 Section with 1 platoon retracing new fire-trench of INT. LINE north of MAUD AVE. No 4 Section with 1 platoon repairing mule track & bridging old trenches north of DOUBLE MAUD AVE. Two platoons carrying revetting material to INT. LINE. 2/Lt MELHUISH returns to No 1 Section from hospital.	J.E.A.

A5834 Wt. W4973 M687 750,000 8/16 D. D. & L. Ltd. Forms/C.2118/13.

Army Form C. 2118.

WAR DIARY
or
INTELLIGENCE SUMMARY.

(*Erase heading not required.*)

Instructions regarding War Diaries and Intelligence Summaries are contained in F. S. Regs., Part II. and the Staff Manual respectively. Title pages will be prepared in manuscript.

Place	Date January	Hour	Summary of Events and Information	Remarks and references to Appendices
P.C. OURCEL H.S.C.7.3 (ALBERT SHEET 1:40,000)	26	-	Freezing hard Work of Company as yesterday No 1 section still at P.C. JEAN working for C.R.E. on billet improvements etc	J.E.A.
"	27	.	Freezing hard No 2 with 3 platoons on INT. LINE south of MAUD. AVE No 3 with 3 platoons north of MAUD. AVENUE No 4 with 2 platoons north of WURZEL AVENUE No 1 at P.C. JEAN on same work	J.E.A.
"	28		Freezing hard No 1 on dugouts etc. at P.C. JEAN No 2 with 2 platoons on INTERMEDIATE LINE. No 3 with 2 platoons continue retracing of fire-trench N. of MAUD AVE No 4 with 2 platoons continue retracing of fire-trench N. of WURZEL AVE. A platoon of 'D' Coy, 18th MX Pioneers wiring INTERMEDIATE LINE N. of MAUD AVE.	J.E.A.
"	29		Same as yesterday No 4 has only one platoon 3 platoons of 18 MX Pioneers "D" Coy improving MAUD AVE. Go over INTERMEDIATE LINE with G.S.O.1 of Division	J.E.A.
"	30	-	Freezing hard Same work as yesterday	J.E.A.
"	31		Company ceases work on INTERMEDIATE LINE which is continued by Corps Lay out 40cm. decauville track up BERLIN VALLEY 98th Inf Bde comes in in relief of 19th Inf Bde from to-night No infantry parties	J.E.A.

A5834 Wt. W4973/M687 750,000 8/16 D. D. & L. Ltd. Forms/C.2118/13.

SECRET

War Diary

Copy. CRE 9th I.B.

Report on Right Bde Area 33rd Divl. Front.

A. FRONT LINE.

Held generally as single line, with occasionally a short parallel fire trench thrown out in front to act as Outpost Lines. General condition - fair - but worse on right battalion front. There are few traverses and in places trench is too shallow and generally too wide at top. What trench boards there are, are imbedded in the mud. Requires fire-stepping and revetting throughout, formation of traverses and trench-boarding with the trench-boards raised on trestles.

B. INTERMEDIATE LINE.

For convenience the line may be divided into five sections 'A' 'B' 'C' 'D' & 'E' respectively.

Sector 'A'. (from left of Brigade front to the communication trench Doublure d'Ordre). The trench has been partly dug and is about 2'0" wide x 3'0" deep. It is traversed at intervals of about 20'0" by 9'0" traverses. It is faced by H.W.E. (one line only about 8'0" in depth.)

Sector 'B' (from Doublure d'Ordre to Boyau d'Ordre).

Between the points B_1 & B_2 (see sketch) the line has been doubled, the easterly piece of line being on the ridge and the westerly on the reverse slope. The condition of the trench is as in Sector 'A', but there is no wire. There are 2 dugouts in this portion (see sketch)

Sector C (Between Boyau Olde and Boyau L'Elew.)

This trench is good but requires to be widened and fire stepped; it is about 5'0" deep and the Infantry are at present forming fire bays at intervals.

In the sub-sector C_1 (see sketch) posts have been erected for H.W.E. and in the sub-sector C_2 one or two strands of wire are already in position. For the remainder of this sector the wiring has been completed and is about 10'0" deep.

Sector D (from Boyau L'Elew to Road.)

As in Sector C.

Sector E.

The Chateau is being put in a state of defence by the Infantry who are constructing a strong point (see sketch.)

The cellars of the Chateau are good and have been strutted by 6"x6" timbers in a similar manner to deep dugouts. There is accommodation for about 60 men in these cellars.

North of point "A" (see sketch I) which is the intersection with boundary between Brigades the line is only traced out by a trench 2'x2'. The trace is practically straight and should be retraced to give deep traverses. About 30 yds in front of this trace, H.W.E. exists in 2 bays but require thickening.

The trace ends at present in a

little copse on a mound where Boyau ACARIES crosses its alignment. This copse (where proposed M.G.s are shown on the plan) have also two good one entrance deep dugouts and should make an excellent supporting point for the whole Intermediate Line.

On the whole, the line is well sited on the reverse side of MARNE SPUR and has an average field of fire of 200 yards.

C. OMMIECOURT LOOP DEFENCES.

The left bank of the river between the points 'A' & 'B' (see sketch) is lined by H.W.E. and this piece of front is patrolled during the night.

There are 2 Machine Guns and 1 Lewis Gun on either bank of the CANAL at points 'B' and 'C'.

D. SECOND LINE.

In fair condition, consisting of short lengths of fire bays with Machine & Lewis Gun positions and dugouts joined up by lengths of communication trenches.

E. COMMUNICATION TRENCHES.

Generally in good order and mostly cut in chalk, which should not give much trouble when thaw sets in, the parts cut in clay will be a source of trouble however, they require revetting, preferably with 'A' frames and draining to the sides at intervals by shafts.

trenches leading into sump pits. The French sump pits on this principle seem to answer this purpose.

They are practically trenchboarded throughout but the boards are laid on the ground.

It is essential that a permanent maintenance party of twenty five men should be detailed for each of three communication trenches. They should be instructed to gradually deepen the CTs remove the trenchboards and replace them on trestles.

F. ACCOMMODATION

On the whole good and sufficient for present ~~use~~ needs. The dugouts are deep but as a rule have only one entrance.

G. GENERAL

Roads. CURLU to CLERY. In good condition. French state they are not usually fired upon by enemy artillery from 6 am to 8 am and from 7 pm to 10 pm.

Road CLERY-BOUCHAVESNES good to DUMP at its intersection with BOYAU DOUBLURE D'ODDE. From that point to ROAD WOOD, there is a "piste" for pack animals. It is subjected to enemy artillery fire especially at points where it crosses trenches but is fairly safe between 6 & 8 am & between 7 & 10 pm.

J E Anderson Lt, R.E.
Commdg. 11th Coy. R.E

23/1/17

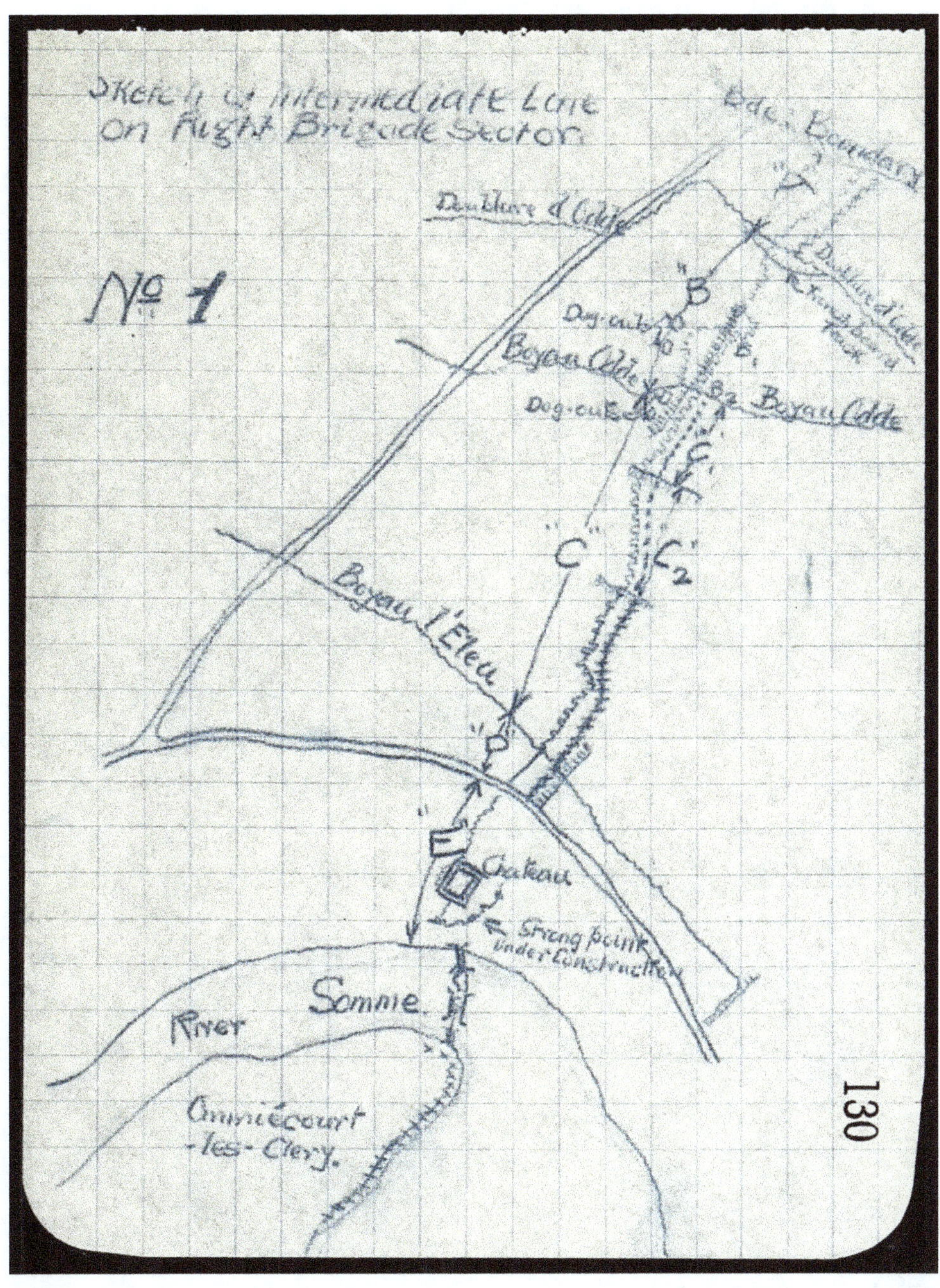
Sketch of Intermediate Line
on Right Brigade Sector.
No 1
Bde. Boundary
"A"
"B"
Dog-outs
Boyau
"C"
Chateau
Strong point
under Construction
Somme
River
130

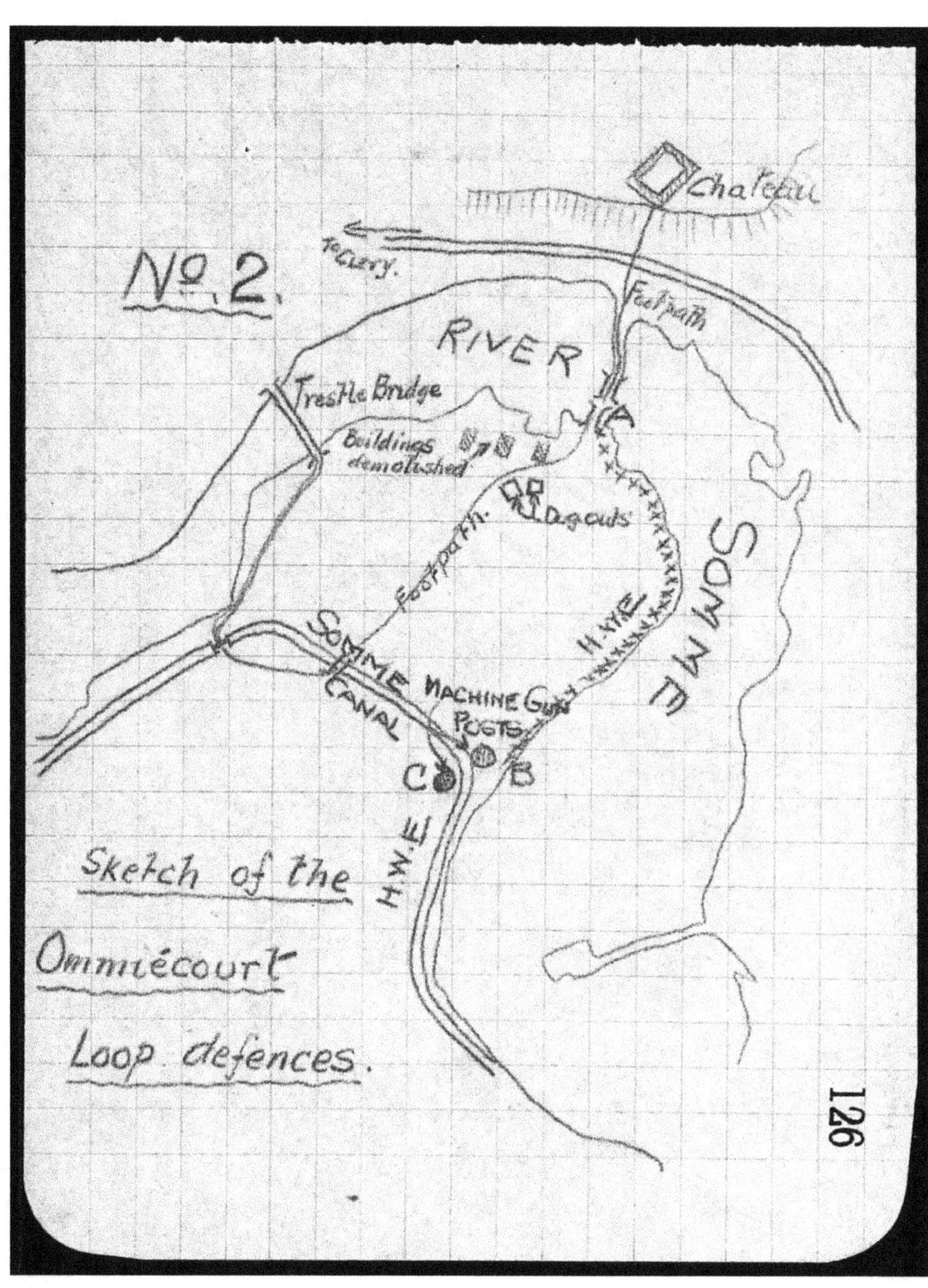
No. 2.
Chateau
to Clery.
Footpath
RIVER
A
Trestle Bridge
Buildings demolished
Dugouts
Footpath.
SOMME
H.W.E
SOMME
CANAL
MACHINE GUN
POSTS
C
B
H.W.E
Sketch of the
Ommiécourt
Loop defences.

4. [illegible] requiring [illegible]
[illegible] of [illegible] pictures.

I (a) INTERMEDIATE LINE. Will require to be [illegible] with assistance of a platoon of infantry daily. In front, the [illegible] trenches [illegible] parties and [illegible] entanglement to [illegible] will take [illegible] weeks' continuous work for each [illegible] party.

(b) [illegible] of [illegible] trenches throughout [illegible] (the [illegible] [illegible] picking [illegible] boards [illegible] for [illegible].)

(c) Provision of [illegible]

(d) Communication Trench [illegible] ROYAL [illegible] ROAD [illegible] the [illegible] [illegible] [illegible] [illegible], but it is [illegible] to [illegible] the [illegible] should [illegible] [illegible] it is [illegible] a new [illegible] should be [illegible].

II (a) SECOND LINE. To be [illegible].

(b) Provision of [illegible] [illegible] [illegible] of new men.

[illegible]

Lieut. R.E.
O.C. [illegible] R.E.

Instructions regarding War Diaries and Intelligence Summaries are contained in F. S. Regs., Part II. and the Staff Manual respectively. Title pages will be prepared in manuscript.

WAR DIARY
or
INTELLIGENCE SUMMARY.

(*Erase heading not required.*)

Army Form C. 2118.

Place	Date	Hour	Summary of Events and Information	Remarks and references to Appendices

A5834 Wt. W4973 M687 750,000 8/16 D. D. & L. Ltd. Forms/C.2118/13.

Instructions regarding War Diaries and Intelligence Summaries are contained in F. S. Regs., Part II. and the Staff Manual respectively. Title pages will be prepared in manuscript.

WAR DIARY
or
INTELLIGENCE SUMMARY.
(Erase heading not required.)

Army Form C. 2118.

Place	Date	Hour	Summary of Events and Information	Remarks and references to Appendices
			Vol 26	
			Confidential War Diary of 11th Field Company RE From 1/2/17 to 28/2/17	
			CRL Balcombe Capt RE O.C 11th Field Coy RE	

A5834 Wt. W4973 M687 750,000. 8/16 D. D. & L. Ltd. Forms/C.2118/13.

Army Form C. 2118.

Instructions regarding War Diaries and Intelligence Summaries are contained in F. S. Regs., Part II. and the Staff Manual respectively. Title pages will be prepared in manuscript.

WAR DIARY
or
INTELLIGENCE SUMMARY.
(Erase heading not required.)

Place	Date FEBRUARY	Hour	Summary of Events and Information	Remarks and references to Appendices
P.C. OURCEL H.S.C 7 3 (ALBERT COMB^D SHEET 1/40,000)	1	-	Fine morning, cold but some indication of a thaw. Visibility poor. Lt. Anderson & 2/Lt Kaylor went over proposed route of 40 cm. decauville track up BERLIN VALLEY. Decide that ground too hard to dig & all infantry parties will be used for carrying up stores ready to commence work when thaw sets in. Decide also that old existing C.T. in prolongation of MAUD AVENUE should be opened up. Company engaged in extending dug-outs for our own Company, Brigade Headquarters, Dressing Stations & Trench Mortar Battery; also as guides for conducting carrying parties and wagons to forward dumps. Front portion of No 2 Section Toolcart destroyed by shell fire last night.	J.E.A.
"	2.	-	Fine, cold day, & any sign of thaw has gone. Work same as yesterday. Quiet day. Make up Imprests & dispatch same. Have 4 platoons of Infantry at work laying trench-boards up BERLIN VALLEY. Establish R.E. storeman at *MARNE DUMP to look after our interests there.	J.E.A. * H.12. b. 9.5.
"	3	-	Fine, cold day as yesterday. Work as yesterday except 6 platoons work in BERLIN VALLEY. Reconnoitre to begin dug-outs for M.G. detachments near CLERY COPSE. 2/Lt. CHANTER returns from hospital (rest station) & takes over horses & transport line work.	J.E.A.

A5834 Wt. W4973 M687 750,000 8/16 D. D. & L. Ltd. Forms/C.2118/13.

Instructions regarding War Diaries and Intelligence Summaries are contained in F. S. Regs., Part II. and the Staff Manual respectively. Title pages will be prepared in manuscript.

WAR DIARY
or
INTELLIGENCE SUMMARY.
(Erase heading not required.)

Army Form C. 2118.

Place	Date	Hour	Summary of Events and Information	Remarks and references to Appendices
P.C. OURCEL H.5.C.7.3 (Ref ALBERT Combd Sheet 1:40,000)	4	-	Fine, cold morning; visibility poor during forenoon, but improves in afternoon. Heavy bombardment of enemy's trenches opposite LEFT BRIGADE FRONT commenced at 10 AM. and continued till about 7 pm. Not much retaliation though Brig Gen. MAITLAND considered it advisable to cancel working party of ~~a~~ platoons on trench board tracks up BERLIN VALLEY At 12.30 p.m. advised by C.R.E's message that wind was dangerous & "GAS ALERT" was ordered. Wind changed to "SAFE" about 7 PM Work as yesterday, except 5 men were taken off Coy H.Q. dug-outs and commenced a deep dugout for M.G.C. off MAOO AVENUE at I.1.a.5.2 C.R.E. sends part of No 1 Section (in Divl R.E. RESERVE) up to H.11.a.5.7 to dig themselves into accommodation along with rest of company. After working for 5½ hours, till midnight, they returned to sleep at P.C. JEAN Message from Lt BALCOMBE from BASE to say he has been posted to 77th Field Co. RE - probably in error.	J.E.A.
"	5	-	Fine, cold day Work as yesterday, but no infantry parties, except for two shifts for dugout for M.G.C. at I.1.a.5.2 also same for new M.G.C. dugout South of CLERY CORSE. No 1 Section comes up & commences to dig itself into accommodation at Coy H.Q. H.5.C.7.3, ~~returns at night to sleep at P.C. JEAN~~ & remains here	J.E.A.
"	6	-	Fine day, very cold, strong northerly wind. No 1. Section ~~continues~~ digging in Work same as yesterday, no infantry again, except as yesterday. Go round line (Front & Intermediate) with Brig. Gen. CROOKSHANK, C.E., & CRE. Informed by C.R.E. that 77th (Fd) Co. is willing to exchange Lt C.P.L. BALCOMBE	J.E.A.

A5834 Wt. W4973 M687 750,000 8/16 D. D. & L. Ltd. Forms/C.2118/13.

Army Form C. 2118.

WAR DIARY
or
INTELLIGENCE SUMMARY.
(Erase heading not required.)

Instructions regarding War Diaries and Intelligence Summaries are contained in F. S. Regs., Part II. and the Staff Manual respectively. Title pages will be prepared in manuscript.

Place	Date	Hour	Summary of Events and Information	Remarks and references to Appendices
P.C. BURGEL H.5.C.7.3 (ALBERT Com Sh 1:40,000).	FEBRUARY 7	–	Fine cold day; visibility good. Arrange to start new Battn. H.Q. (H.6.b.6.3) in INT. LINE. to-morrow. 2/Lt ROBERTS goes on leave Work as yesterday.	J.E.A.
	8	–	Fine, cold day Work as yesterday, but no infantry working-parties in afternoon. New Battn. H.Q. (H.6.b.6.3) commenced by No. 1 Sections. Telegram received from C.R.E. stating that Lt. C.P.L. BALCOMBE will rejoin the Company, transferred from 77th Field Co. (14th Corps).	J.E.A.
	9	–	Fine, very cold day. No infantry working parties to day & consequently very little progress shown. 5 men attached to Battalions in line to assist and supervise dug-out construction	J.E.A.
	10	–	Fine day, not so cold Infantry parties available to-day & work carried on as follows: C.26.c.0.0. Deep Dug-out for T.M. Batty H.5.c.7.3 Stores notice-boards etc. H.K.a.5.7 ~~(Coy H.Q.)~~ Dug-outs for No 1 section & Officers. Latter completed H.K.a.3.5 (Bde HQ) New Signals Office H.11.a.2.3 Dressing Station Bomb-proof shelters. H.12.b.9.5 (MARNE DUMP) Accommodation (bomb proof) for storeman I.1.a.7.3 Deep Dug-out for M.G.C I.1.c.0.8 Deep Dugout for M.G.C H.6.b.9.4 New Battn. H.Q. Also Gas-proofing of Battns & Coys in line's Dugouts.	J.E.A.

Instructions regarding War Diaries and Intelligence Summaries are contained in F. S. Regs., Part II. and the Staff Manual respectively. Title pages will be prepared in manuscript.

WAR DIARY
or
INTELLIGENCE SUMMARY.
(Erase heading not required.)

Army Form C. 2118.

Place	Date FEB	Hour	Summary of Events and Information	Remarks and references to Appendices
P.C. OORSEL H.5.c.7.3 (ALBERT COM. SHT 1:40,000)	11	-	Fine, cold day Work as yesterday. Commenced working continuous 6 hr reliefs on new Batt. H.Q. Dug out (H.6.b.9.4). Got warning to prepare for raid on 13th inst.	
	12.	-	Fine day, milder & inclined to thaw. Visibility poor Gas alert ordered at 3 pm. and cancelled at 5.30 pm. Work as yesterday. also making 6 knob-kerries & 4 explosive boxes for raid to-morrow night. Major H.A.S. PRESSEY M.C. R.E. returns from leave, & reassumes command of the Coy. from this evening.	
	13.		Fine day. Frosty. Gas alert off. work as yesterday 6 O.R. co-operated in a raid with infantry carrying explosives for demolitions, none used. Lt. OATES missing	
	14.		Fine day frosty. work as before No 3 Section with Lt DAVIS R.W.F. started two support points MARNE Sup point I 7.a.0.7 MAUD Support point I 1.d.3.8 commencing the dugouts first leaving the trenches until the dugout, M.G. emplacement and wiring be completed No 4 Section left the T.M. dugout they were engaged on and continued completion of a trench one on the bank of the SOMME at M 12 d 8.5 for T.M. officers 2Lt C.P.L. BALCOMBE joined the company assuming duties of 2nd in command and given acting rank of Capt.	

A5834 Wt. W4973 M687 750,000 8/16 D. D. & L. Ltd. Forms/C.2118/13.

Instructions regarding War Diaries and Intelligence Summaries are contained in F. S. Regs., Part II. and the Staff Manual respectively. Title pages will be prepared in manuscript.

WAR DIARY
or
INTELLIGENCE SUMMARY.
(Erase heading not required.)

Army Form C. 2118.

Place	Date	Hour	Summary of Events and Information	Remarks and references to Appendices
	15		Fine frosty work as before	Cs
	16		do do 98th Bde relieved by 100th Bde	Cs
	17		do Company rested. Kit and gas helmet etc inspection at 3 p.m.	Cs
	18		Thawing work as for 18	Cs
	19		Slight thaw do	Cs
	20		Thaw. do	Cs
	21		Thaw set in for good do Trenches getting very bad especially MAUD AVENUE & left Bn front.	Cs
	22		work as for 21st	
	23		No 4 section taken off dugouts and set on to clearing and revetting MAUD AVENUE with working parties coming to 200 infantry	Cs

A5834 Wt. W4973 M687 750,000 8/16 D. D. & L. Ltd. Forms/C.2118/13.

Instructions regarding War Diaries and Intelligence Summaries are contained in F. S. Regs., Part II. and the Staff Manual respectively. Title pages will be prepared in manuscript.

WAR DIARY
or
INTELLIGENCE SUMMARY.
(Erase heading not required.)

Army Form C. 2118.

Place	Date	Hour	Summary of Events and Information	Remarks and references to Appendices
P[illegible] H.5.c.7.7 [illegible] Sheet 1/40000	23		Work continued as yesterday Misty weather	CPLB
	24		Work continued as yesterday Misty weather	CPLB
	25		Work continued as yesterday. Weather clearing. From reliable information it appears that enemy contemplate a retirement to a line N.E. of Cambrai. The Coy. was ordered to prepare to move at short notice. All necessary measures were taken. The above was received at about 3 of p.m. Later it was learnt that farther N. (Butte de WARLENCOURT) & other places, our patrols had pushed 200 yds. behind German front line & were still going on.	CPLB
	26		Work continued as yesterday. Road Reconnaissances as follows were made. Ref. Trench Map Sheet 62c N.W. 4A. H.5.c.7.2 – H.12.b.5.8. – I.7.b.2.4. & H.11.a.6.4 – H.c.6.00 – I.7.c.4.3	[signature]

Army Form C. 2118.

Instructions regarding War Diaries and Intelligence Summaries are contained in F. S. Regs., Part II. and the Staff Manual respectively. Title pages will be prepared in manuscript.

WAR DIARY
or
INTELLIGENCE SUMMARY.
(Erase heading not required.)

Place	Date	Hour	Summary of Events and Information	Remarks and references to Appendices
P.C. Daniel H.S.C.7.2. Albert-Combles 1/20,000	27th		Work continued as yesterday. On the night of the 27th–28th a raid on the Enemy trenches was made by the 2nd Worcester Regt. at I.7.d.17. I.7.d 13.75. & I.7.b. 15.00 (Ref Map. Trench Map PERONNE 62°N.W. 4) The infantry were accompanied by 2/Lt GARROD & No 4 Sect. (230.R) The raid was in two phases. In the first 4 Sappers, with boxes containing toll's gun cotton, went over with the view of destroying enemy dug outs etc. This was successfully done. 2/Lt GARROD & 7 Sappers went over with 2 BANGALORE torpedoes to cut the wire for the Inf to use in the 2nd phase. This party was unsuccessful, both torpedoes being destroyed by trench mortars hand grenades as soon as the party came to the German wire. 2/Lt Garrod & 4 sappers were wounded in this. On the time for evacuating the enemy line having reached No 22989 Sgt HOLMES & No 37485 Spr Clunes observed a wounded Private & Sgt (respectively) who were unable to make their way back, they each carried their man safely into our lines. This act was noticed by the O.C Raid & reported to his C.O. In the 2nd phase 4 sappers went over with boxes & successfully destroyed enemy dug outs etc. Two O.R. were wounded in this. The raid was a great success 22 prisoners being taken from the 2nd Guard Divn, the prisoners were all of the Kaiser Franz Augusta Regt de Grenadier.	[initials]

A5834 Wt. W4973 M687 750,000 8/16 D. D. & L. Ltd. Forms/C.2118/13.

Instructions regarding War Diaries and Intelligence Summaries are contained in F. S. Regs., Part II. and the Staff Manual respectively. Title pages will be prepared in manuscript.

WAR DIARY
or
INTELLIGENCE SUMMARY.
(Erase heading not required.)

Army Form C. 2118.

Place	Date	Hour	Summary of Events and Information	Remarks and references to Appendices
P.C. Cursel 45.c.7.2. Albert (Combd) 1/40,000	27	Contd.	This formed a most valuable identification as the Div. opposing us in this sector was thought to be the 29th R.D. The Coy's work was much appreciated by the G.O.C. 100th Bgd (B.G. BAIRD) who expressed his thanks. The total Casualties to the Coy were 1 Officer 6 O.R. wounded, + 2 wounded (at duty).	CRB
	28th		Work as yesterday. No 4 Sect. had day off after their previous night's operations.	CRB

A5834 Wt. W4973 M687 750,000 8/16 D. D. & L. Ltd. Forms/C.2118/13.

Instructions regarding War Diaries and Intelligence Summaries are contained in F. S. Regs., Part II. and the Staff Manual respectively. Title pages will be prepared in manuscript.

WAR DIARY
or
INTELLIGENCE SUMMARY.
(Erase heading not required.)

Army Form C. 2118.

Vol 27

Place	Date	Hour	Summary of Events and Information	Remarks and references to Appendices
			CONFIDENTIAL	
			War Diary of 11th (Field) Co. R.E.	
			from March 1st 1917 to March 31st 1917	
			(Volume .)	

A5834 Wt. W4973/M687 750,000 8/16 D. D. & L. Ltd. Forms/C.2118/13.

Army Form C. 2118.

Instructions regarding War Diaries and Intelligence Summaries are contained in F. S. Regs., Part II. and the Staff Manual respectively. Title pages will be prepared in manuscript.

WAR DIARY
or
INTELLIGENCE SUMMARY.
(Erase heading not required.)

Place	Date	Hour	Summary of Events and Information	Remarks and references to Appendices
P.C. OURSEL H 11 a. 5. 9 Ref. Map. ALBERT. cont'd 1/40.000	March 1st		No 1 Sect. T.M. dug out on River Bank. M.G. dug out in MAUD Avenue No 2 Sect. M.G. dug out on MARNE Crest. Gas blankets for front line dug outs. No 3 Sect. M.G. dug out in MARNE St. Pt. do do MAUD St. Pt. No 4 Sect. Clearing & revetting etc MAUD avenue	CPLB
	2nd		Work as before. Major MILLAR of 224 Fd Coy R.E. came & stayed the night for purpose of looking round the line etc, preparatory to taking "over" in a few days'	CPLB
	3rd		Work as yesterday, except No 4 Sect. went to Camp 121 to load up our Bridging wagons to be ready to move when required. Pontoons etc brought back to Horse lines (G.18. c. 4. 5)	CPLB
	4th		Work as yesterday. Coy. Hq. heavily shelled all day.	CPLB

A5834 Wt. W4973 M687 750,000 8/16 D. D. & L. Ltd. Forms/C.2118/13.

Instructions regarding War Diaries and Intelligence Summaries are contained in F. S. Regs., Part II. and the Staff Manual respectively. Title pages will be prepared in manuscript.

WAR DIARY
or
INTELLIGENCE SUMMARY.
(Erase heading not required.)

Army Form C. 2118.

Place	Date	Hour	Summary of Events and Information	Remarks and references to Appendices
P.C. OURSEL H.11.a.5.9 Ref Map ALBERT (Comb) 1/40,000	5th		Work as yesterday, 2Lt. KAYLOR left to join 214th A.T. Co. R.E. + 2nd Lt. McINTYRE joined us from that unit.	CPLB
	6th		Whole Coy cleaning up Billets etc., preparatory to moving. Advance Party of 1 Officer (Lt. CLARK) and 10 OR arrived from 224th Field Coy R.E. to take over. Company Headquarters heavily shelled.	CPLB
SUXANNE	7th		Company moved off from P.C. OURSEL at 4.30 am, moved into Camp at SUXANNE arriving there 12 noon.	CPLB
Camp 13 K.22.c.4.7 Ref Map ALBERT (Comb.) 1/40,000	8th		Company moved from SUXANNE at 8.0 am, arriving at Camp 13 11 am.	CPLB

A5834 Wt. W4973/M687 750,000 8/16 D. D. & L. Ltd. Forms/C.2118/13.

Army Form C. 2118.

Instructions regarding War Diaries and Intelligence Summaries are contained in F. S. Regs., Part II. and the Staff Manual respectively. Title Pages will be prepared in manuscript.

WAR DIARY
or
INTELLIGENCE SUMMARY
(Erase heading not required.)

Place	Date	Hour	Summary of Events and Information	Remarks and references to Appendices
Camp 13	9th		Major H.A.S. PRESSEY returned from Course and took over command of the Company.	[illegible]
			Company checking equipment and cleaning up	
	10th		Squad drill, instruction in connecting charges. Issue of clothing etc	[illegible]
	11th		~~[illegible]~~ Sunday no work church parade (Voluntary).	[illegible]
	12th		Practising construction of strong points etc. Pattern of strong point to be constructed by a section altered to ~~[illegible]~~ sketch	
			This to be constructed by a standard section of 1 officer 28 men, 3 men to each fire bay. Work sections cutting off fire bays as necessary. Men to extend themselves in 3's in order on fire bays as numbered.	[illegible]

Instructions regarding War Diaries and Intelligence Summaries are contained in F. S. Regs., Part II. and the Staff Manual respectively. Title Pages will be prepared in manuscript.

WAR DIARY
or
INTELLIGENCE SUMMARY

(Erase heading not required.)

Army Form C. 2118.

Place	Date	Hour	Summary of Events and Information	Remarks and references to Appendices
Camp 13.	13.		Musketry skirmishing etc.	S.
	14.		~~Otway~~ Pontooning dry ground lecture	S.
	15.		Owing to thaw stables became uninhabitable. whole company digging away top mud to hard ground level.	S. S.
	16		do do	
	17.		Route march by dismounted portion.	S.
	18		~~[illegible]~~ Sunday no work.	S.
	19.		Washing vehicles	S.
	20		Pontooning	S.
	21		Company inspected by Maj General PINNEY. G.O.C. 33rd Divn.	S.
	22.		Packing up preparatory to move. Pontooning in the morning	S.
	23		Company marched to LAMOTTE—BREBIÈRE. Arrived at 5.30 pm. 18 miles. At 9 pm. the billet in which the 4 Sections were was burnt down ~~by fire~~. Practically all the kit & equipment of these men was burnt.	S.

2449 Wt. W14957/M90 750,000 1/16 J.B.C. & A. Forms/C.2118/12.

Army Form C. 2118.

Instructions regarding War Diaries and Intelligence Summaries are contained in F. S. Regs., Part II. and the Staff Manual respectively. Title Pages will be prepared in manuscript.

WAR DIARY
or
INTELLIGENCE SUMMARY

(Erase heading not required.)

Place	Date	Hour	Summary of Events and Information	Remarks and references to Appendices
LAMOTTE BREBIÈRE	24.		Checking clothes and equipment &c. Find practically a new fit out needed. We made a clean sweep.	[illegible]
	25.		Issuing clothes etc. Sunday.	[illegible]
	26.		Pontooning	[illegible]
	27.		do	[illegible]
	28		Skirmishing drill	[illegible]
	29		Pontooning	[illegible]
	30		Pontooning	[illegible]
	31		Pontooning	[illegible]

H. G. L. [illegible]
Maj RE.
O.C. 11th F. Co RE.

2449 Wt. W14957/M90 750,000 1/16 J.B.C. & A. Forms/C.2118/12.

33

Army Form C. 2118.

Instructions regarding War Diaries and Intelligence Summaries are contained in F. S. Regs., Part II. and the Staff Manual respectively. Title pages will be prepared in manuscript.

WAR DIARY
or
INTELLIGENCE SUMMARY.
(Erase heading not required.)

Vol 28

Place	Date	Hour	Summary of Events and Information	Remarks and references to Appendices

CONFIDENTIAL.

WAR DIARY

of

11th (Field) Company. R. E.

From April 1st. 1917 To. April 30th 1917.

(Volume)

[signature] Capt R.E.
for. O.C. 11th Field Co R.E.

A5834 Wt. W4973 M687 750,000 8/16 D. D. & L. Ltd. Forms/C.2118/13.

Instructions regarding War Diaries and Intelligence Summaries are contained in F. S. Regs., Part II. and the Staff Manual respectively. Title pages will be prepared in manuscript.

WAR DIARY
or
INTELLIGENCE SUMMARY.
(Erase heading not required.)

Army Form C. 2118.

Place	Date	Hour	Summary of Events and Information	Remarks and references to Appendices
LAMOTTE BREBIERES	1/4/17		Sunday. Mounted check parade & church helmet inspection. Bicycles inspected.	
do	2/4/17		Company cleaning up billets. Pontoon Equipment packed up and stored at DAOURS owing to lack of horses to move it.	
VILLERS BOCAGE	3/4/17		Company marched to VILLERS-BOCAGE. No casualties	
BEAUVAL	4/4/17		Company march to BEAUVAL do	
			Received 12 L.D. horses. These sent back under 2/Lt FORBES to DAOURS for 2 Pontoon wagons left there earlier	
GROUCHES	5.4.17		Company received orders to march to MILLY on arrival find MILLY occupied. Billeted for night at GROUCHES. No casualties.	
do	6.4.17		Company rested. All vehicles washed.	
~~[illegible]~~	~~[illegible]~~		~~[illegible] marched to ST AMAND [illegible]~~.	
ST AMAND	7.4.17		Company marched to ST AMAND. No Casualties	
BAILLEULMONT	8.4.17		Company marched to BAILLEULMONT No casualties	

A5834 Wt. W4973/M687 750,000 8/16 D. D. & L. Ltd. Forms/C.2118/13.

Instructions regarding War Diaries and Intelligence Summaries are contained in F. S. Regs., Part II. and the Staff Manual respectively. Title pages will be prepared in manuscript.

WAR DIARY
or
INTELLIGENCE SUMMARY.
(Erase heading not required.)

Army Form C. 2118.

Place	Date	Hour	Summary of Events and Information	Remarks and references to Appendices
BAILLEULMONT	9.4.17		Company stayed at BAILLEUL MONT ready to move off at short notice.	[initials]
	10.4.17		do do	[initials]
	11.4.17		Company marched at very short notice to dug outs on FICHEUX – AGNY Road about ½ mile N of FICHEUX. Wet march many checks arrived at 9.30 pm. No Casualties	[initials]
	12.4.17		Company rested.	
BOIRY BECQUERELLE	13.4.17		Marched off at 7.30 am to position in BOIRY BECQUERELLE to be in readiness. 62nd I.B attacked HINDENBURG LINE Bombing up trenches and also attacking N. of the line. 19th I.B (with 11th Field Co) Came under orders of 21st divn and replaced 62nd Bde as they moved out to attack. 2/Lts. GARROD & FORBES accompanied the 20th R.F and 1st Cameronians to report on work required. Attack only partially successful. Company not required. Later in day two sections moved up each with party of 25 Infantry from the 5th S.R. and made two strong points at N. 35.C 1.8 and at N 34 d 3 7. No 1 section at night started on bomb blocks at T5a 7.5 and T 5 a. 7 8. Company billeted at BOIRY BECQUERELLE.	See map Appendix I [initials]

A5834 Wt. W4973 M687 750,000 8/16 D. D. & L. Ltd. Forms/C.2118/13.

Army Form C. 2118.

WAR DIARY
or
INTELLIGENCE SUMMARY.
(Erase heading not required.)

Instructions regarding War Diaries and Intelligence Summaries are contained in F. S. Regs., Part II. and the Staff Manual respectively. Title pages will be prepared in manuscript.

Place	Date	Hour	Summary of Events and Information	Remarks and references to Appendices
BOIRY BECQUERELLE	14/4/17.		Company moved at 4 am. to take up position of readiness at Sunken road T 3. c. 8.7 near HENIN. 19th I.B still under 21st div. attacked from line N 35 c and a and from T 5.a in HINDENBURG LINE with objective Sunken road W of FONTAINE LES CROISILLES and road north of it. attack did not succeed. Bombing parties made no progress and 5th S.R attacking from N of HINDENBURG LINE only succeeded in reaching valley in N 35 d.	Map Trench map Sheet 57B S.W.
BOIRY BECQUERELLE			Nos 2 & 3 sections were occupied during day in improving Bde Hqs. Nos 1 & 4 sections moved up at night to help infantry consolidating the line but could not do anything owing to reliefs and delays. 20th R.F. relieved 5th S.R during night 14th 15th	
do	15.4.17.		No 2 section carried on improvements to Bde Hq dug outs. No 4 section 1 N.C.O [illegible] men with reliefs 16 inf started construction ado Hq for R.A. Group.	
	16.4.17		At evening Nos 1 & 3 sections moved up to HINDENBURG SUPPORT line and waited in dug out there to co operate in attack to take place on the 16th. ~~(Coy remained in [illegible] at BOIRY BECQUERELLE~~	

Instructions regarding War Diaries and Intelligence Summaries are contained in F. S. Regs., Part II. and the Staff Manual respectively. Title pages will be prepared in manuscript.

WAR DIARY
or
INTELLIGENCE SUMMARY.
(Erase heading not required.)

Army Form C. 2118.

Place	Date	Hour	Summary of Events and Information	Remarks and references to Appendices
BOIRY BECQUERELLE	16.4.17		At 3am 19th I.B. 20th R.F on left 1st Cameronians on right attacked the german positions. 20th R.F attacking with objective T.6.b.2.3 to O 31 c 3 6. 1st Cameronians to bomb up the HINDENBURG front & support lines. 1st Cameronians failed to make progress. 20th R.F. forced to dig in on line N 35 d 6.3. to N 36 central. R.E. were not used. During day 19th I.B. were relieved by 98th I.B. except 2 Companies of R.F. on the left who could not be got in.	
	17.4.17		Nos 1 & 2 sections worked on the road from BOIRY BECQUERELLE & MAISON ROUGE. No 3 section improved the strong point at N 35 c 2 8. No 4 section improved Bde Hq.	
	18.4.17		do do	

A5834 Wt. W4973 M687 750,000 8/16 D. D. & L. Ltd. Forms/C.2118/13.

Army Form C. 2118.

Instructions regarding War Diaries and Intelligence Summaries are contained in F. S. Regs., Part II. and the Staff Manual respectively. Title Pages will be prepared in manuscript.

WAR DIARY
or
INTELLIGENCE SUMMARY

(Erase heading not required.)

Place	Date	Hour	Summary of Events and Information	Remarks and references to Appendices
BOIRY BECQUERELLE	19.4.17.		As for 17th	B
do	20.4.17.		No 1 Section employed on improving wire round strong point at T 35 d 1.9. 1. O.R wounded.	
			No 2 Section making arrangement for lowering stretchers into HINDENBURG TUNNEL by a winch. 6 men remainder helping No 3 Section.	
			No 3 Section making arrangements for stopping mud flowing down entrances to tunnel	B
			No 4 Section making an infantry track from Bde Hq in T 9 b to HINDENBURG LINE in T 34 C.	
	21.4.17.		Nos 2 & 4 Sections as for 20th	
			No 1 Section made a strong point at T 10. b 3.5 to join up with strong point in T 10. d made by 100th Bde and wired in conjunction with these points to HINDENBURG LINE to make a check for safeguarding batteries ~~in~~ R.F.A in T 4. C. who were very exposed to raids from the ~~Left~~ Right.	B.
			No 3 Section assisted No 1 section in above wiring. also 12 O.R. R.F.A. & 12 men 18th Mx Pioneers	
	22.4.17.		No work. Nos 1 & 3 sections moved up during evening & reported to 98th Bde to cooperate in attack on 23rd.	B.

2449 Wt. W14957/M90 750,000 1/16 J.B.C. & A. Forms/C.2118/12.

Army Form C. 2118.

Instructions regarding War Diaries and Intelligence Summaries are contained in F. S. Regs., Part II. and the Staff Manual respectively. Title Pages will be prepared in manuscript.

WAR DIARY
or
INTELLIGENCE SUMMARY
(Erase heading not required.)

Place	Date	Hour	Summary of Events and Information	Remarks and references to Appendices
BOIRY BECQUERELLE	23.4.17.		The Company took part in the attack on the HINDENBURG LINE. Orders appended	Appendix II
			No 1 Section reported to O.C. 4th Suffolk Regt in HINDENBURG SUPPORT line	
			No 3 .. .. at Hq O.C. 4th Kings do do	
			Nos 2 & 4 in reserve in BOIRY BECQUERELLE. O.C. in reserve.	
		4.45am	Zero at 4.45 am.	
			The Middlesex & Argyle & Sutherland Highlanders moved forward and gained their objective as per programme.	
			The 4th Suffolks bombed up the trench and got to points U C 2.0 & U C 2.4.	
			One tank did not mature at all the other was 3 hours late.	
			30th Div on the left did not advance.	
			No1 Section:- 1 N.C.O & 4 men were sent to destroy the German barricade in the Support line at T 5 b 9.8. This they partially demolished with explosives immediately after the Infantry had cleared the enemy away from it and completely got rid of it with Shovels.	
			Remainder of the Section moved in after the infantry and made three small barricades in the trench after them with Sandbags. They then set to work to cut away 2 traverses at point T 6 d 5.8 in order to establish a good block. The	

2449 Wt. W14957/M90 750,000 1/16 J.B.C. & A. Forms/C.2118/12.

Instructions regarding War Diaries and Intelligence Summaries are contained in F. S. Regs., Part II. and the Staff Manual respectively. Title Pages will be prepared in manuscript.

WAR DIARY
or
INTELLIGENCE SUMMARY
(Erase heading not required.)

Army Form C. 2118.

Place	Date	Hour	Summary of Events and Information	Remarks and references to Appendices
		10 am	Traverses in this line are about 10x thick and the line is about 10' deep. Whilst employed on this the Germans attacked from our open flank on the left and bombed up the trench in great numbers. The Suffolks were forced back and about 11.30 a.m. were back in our original positions all along the line. 2Lt MELHUISH was wounded in the back & head by splinters but remained on. 4 O.R. were wounded.	
			2 Coys of Argyles & Middlesex on the left were cut off in their forward position and given up as captured. 2 Coys of Suffolks in Hindenburg front line were cut off by enemy coming down the communication trenches but got back by walking over the top by the wire.	
		10 am	No 3 Section were not used in the morning attack. at 10 am it was sent to report to C.O. 4th Suffolk regt to make bomb blocks but he wished to counter attack & did not want parties or blocks in the trench in the way. This was reported to Bde Hq. The existing Block in the Hindenburg front line was strengthened and a small barricade put up at T5b8.4	
		12 noon	at junction with a small communication trench. The enemy outflanked this barricade but was driven back by rifle fire & rifle grenades the section assisting in this	

2449 Wt. W14957/M90 750,000 1/16 J.B.C. & A. Forms/C.2118/12.

Army Form C. 2118.

Instructions regarding War Diaries and Intelligence Summaries are contained in F. S. Regs., Part II. and the Staff Manual respectively. Title Pages will be prepared in manuscript.

WAR DIARY
or
INTELLIGENCE SUMMARY

(Erase heading not required.)

Place	Date	Hour	Summary of Events and Information	Remarks and references to Appendices
		Afternoon	On things quieting down C.O. 4th Suffolk sent for the section and required work on the Hindenburg Support line. On reaching the spot No 1 Section was found at work and the O/C No 3 reported the section at liberty to the Bde. An attack was	
		6 p.m.	ordered by the Bde for 6.24 p.m. Zero. The same objectives being given as for the morning. 2 Coys of R.W.F. were used to supplement the Argylls & Middlesex. This attack failed and No 3 section was not required on the left. It proceeded to construct a good bomb block in the Hindenburg Support line. Cutting down two traverses thus arranging for a straight shoot of about 40 yards down the trench. No 1 Section joined in this work later it was completed at about 5.45 am on the 24th.	
		6 p.m.	No 1 Section 2nd attack. After the German counter attack time was spent collecting the section which had got mixed up with the other troops. Another barricade was built at T5 b 4.7. Orders were received from the O.C. 5th S.R. that in the second attack which would start at 6.24 p.m. the section were to follow up the second bombing party &	

2449 Wt. W14957/M90 750,000 1/16 J.B.C. & A. Forms/C.2118/12.

Instructions regarding War Diaries and Intelligence Summaries are contained in F. S. Regs., Part II. and the Staff Manual respectively. Title Pages will be prepared in manuscript.

WAR DIARY
or
INTELLIGENCE SUMMARY
(Erase heading not required.)

Army Form C. 2118.

Place	Date	Hour	Summary of Events and Information	Remarks and references to Appendices
			build barricades in their rear. However the attack did not succeed. The	
		7 pm	Section were ordered back 3 traverses & put under cover in the entrances to dugouts	
			At about this time Cpl McIlwraith who had been wounded in the morning was	
			relieved by Cpl FORBES. Shelling then grew heavy. The Sgt was killed. The	
			men were put under cover and some of them were used for policing the tunnel	
			which had got blocked by wounded etc finding their way down.	
			At about 7.30 pm the O.C. came up. No 1 Section then joined No 3 Sec	
			in making a bomb block.	
			On finishing this at 5.45 am, the Cameronians had by that time got up	
			to relieve the occupants of the trenches, the two sections returned to billets	
		5.30 pm	at BOIRY BECQUERELLE. Orders were received by O.C. at about 5.30 pm	
			to report to Hq 98th Bde and take up the other two sections. The O.C. went	
			up to report, the two sections going up to the Bde dump at T 34 c. On arrival	
			at Bde Hq it was found a scare was on that the Germans had rushed our	
			barricades and were bombing down the Hindenburg system. Nos 2 & 4 Sections were	
			sent for and put to make bomb blocks on the lines etc N 35 c & T 5 a.	
			However this proved a false alarm. Men were [illegible] by [illegible] and [illegible]	

2449 Wt. W14957/M90 750,000 1/16 J.B.C. & A. Forms/C.2118/12.

Instructions regarding War Diaries and Intelligence Summaries are contained in F. S. Regs., Part II. and the Staff Manual respectively. Title Pages will be prepared in manuscript.

WAR DIARY
or
INTELLIGENCE SUMMARY
(Erase heading not required.)

Army Form C. 2118.

Place	Date	Hour	Summary of Events and Information	Remarks and references to Appendices
	24.4.17		were wanted for the 4th Suffolk regt. The two sections relieved the Cameronians in T 4 a and T 10 b and this company was used in the relief. These two sections were relieved by the 5th S.R at about 11 am 24th.	
			Total Casualties in Company: 1 O.R killed; 2/Lt MELHUISH wounded; 4 O.R. wounded } all No 1 Sec.	
	25		At 6 am on the 24th it was found that the enemy had gone back and the division advanced and took up the position on the Green line in attached map. The 98th Bde thus securing all practically all their objectives. It was found the 2 Coys of the Argyles & Middlesex dug in beyond their objective quite happy.	Appendix I
	25.4.17		Company did no work.	
	26.4.17		Division relieved by 21st Div. Company marched to BLAIRVILLE. No casualties	
	27.4.17		Company marched to BALLEULMONT. No Casualties	

2449 Wt. W14957/M90 750,000 1/16 J.B.C. & A. Forms/C.2118/12.

Army Form C. 2118.

Instructions regarding War Diaries and Intelligence Summaries are contained in F. S. Regs., Part II. and the Staff Manual respectively. Title Pages will be prepared in manuscript.

WAR DIARY
or
INTELLIGENCE SUMMARY

(Erase heading not required.)

Place	Date	Hour	Summary of Events and Information	Remarks and references to Appendices
BAILLEULMONT	28.4.17		Company spent day cleaning up. Kit inspection at 3.30 pm.	
	29.4.17		Sunday. Church parade morning	
	30.4.17		Washing waggons in the morning. afternoon Baths	

C R E Balcombe Capt RE.
for Major RE
OC 11th Fd Co RE.

2449 Wt. W14957/M90 750,000 1/16 J.B.C. & A. Forms/C.2118/12.

REFERENCE.
T. Corps. Topo. Sec.
Scale 1 : 20,000.
HOSTILE ACTIVITY & SITUATION MAP
New Position from Air. Photos
Battery reported active
Locations
New Work.
British Front Line at 6.30 p.m. shewn.
For period of 24 hrs ending 6.30 p.m. 30.4.17.
No. 144.
Note—Magnetic Variation from Grid N. is 12° 16' W.
3rd Field Survey Co., R.E. April, 1917
Appendix I
Guémappe
Wancourt
Héninel
WANCOURT TOWER (RUINED)
British Front 13.4.17
Front 14.4.17
Front 21.4.17
Strong points Constructed 13.4.17
taken over from 21st Div.
Wired 21.4.17.
Strong point 21.4.17
100th Bde Str. point
114 G.R.
55 R.I.R.
99 R.I.R.
Dugouts
H.Q.
190

Appendix II

COMMANDING ROYAL ENGINEERS No. K326 21.4.17 33rd DIVISION. B.E.F.

S E C R E T

33 Div. Order No. 177.

Copy No. 17

21 April 1917.

1. The enemy probably intends to retire before long to the QUEANT - DROCOURT Line. The 220 Div. consisting of the 99th Reserve, 190th and 55th Reserve Regiments, is believed to be in front of us, but may have been relieved.

2. The Division is to take part on April 23 in a general attack by the First and Third Armies, and to capture the ridge overlooking the SENSEE Valley and also the HINDENBURG Line as far as the 80 Contour South of the River SENSEE.

3. 30 Div. attacks on the left of this Division and is to reach the line of the road in O.31.c., a. and b.

The V Corps is to co-operate on our right with Artillery fire, bombarding the HINDENBURG Line and villages and localities in rear.

4. The attack will be carried out as follows :-

100 Inf. Bde.	Against that portion of the HINDENBURG Line South of the SENSEE between the 80 Contour and the River.
98 Inf. Bde. (with 2 Cos. 19 Inf.Bde.)	From its present front to the general line T.6.central - road junction in O.31.c., and further to capture the HINDENBURG Line as far as the SENSEE.

5. These objectives and the inter-brigade boundary are shown on the attached map (issued to certain recipients of this order only, vide distribution).

6. The advance will commence at Zero at which hour barrages will be formed along the portions of the hostile front to be attacked, while heavy artillery bombards places of importance in rear and the HINDENBURG Line on both flanks of the 100 Inf. Bde. attack.

7. Artillery will co-operate as follows :-

100 Inf. Bde. attack -

21 Div. Art.
150 Army F. A. Bde.
Detachment 62 Div. Art.

98 Inf. Bde. attack -

37 Div. Art.

8. No.8 H.A. Group is affiliated to this Division during the operations.

P. T. O.

9. 100 M. G. Co. and three Sections 19 Inf. M. G. Co., will, under the orders of the 100 Inf. Bde., assist in the operations in the SENSEE Valley.

10. Tanks will co-operate as follows :-

<u>100 Inf. Bde.</u>	One pair to advance from CROISILLES and return by same route.
<u>98 Inf. Bde.</u>	One pair to move down HINDENBURG Line and return via CROISILLES.

11. Engineers will be at the disposal of attacking Brigades as follows :-

<u>100 Inf. Bde.</u>	2 Sections 222 F. Co. R.E.
<u>98 Inf. Bde.</u>	2 Sections 11 F. Co. R.E.

12. Two Cos. Pioneers, will be ready to move from their billets at any time after Zero for work on Communication trenches, one Co. in the area of each attacking Inf. Bde.

13. 19 Inf. Bde. (less two Cos.)
Div. Eng. (less 2 Sects. of 11 and 222 F. Cos. R.E.)
Pioneers (less 2 Cos.)

will be in Divl. Reserve.

14. The two Bns. 19 Inf. Bde. between HENIN and NEUVILLE-VITASSE must be prepared to move at 10 minutes notice from Zero onwards.

15. When the left of the 98 Inf. Bde. reaches its objective, a continuous front trench is to be made between the HINDENBURG Line and the road junction in O.31.c. by joining up existing trenches, etc.

The present German front line in N.36. will be consolidated and wired as a second position.

16. 100 Inf. Bde. will consolidate a line from the captured HINDENBURG trenches to the Fifth Army boundary, to connect with the 62 Div. who will advance their left if necessary.

17. <u>After Zero + 90</u> the S.O.S. barrage will be on the line U.13.b.3.9 - U.8.c.4.7 - U.8.a.2.5 - U.1.d.3.5 - U.1.a.2.2 - O.31.c.8.5, unless modifications are notified.

18. Should the enemy evacuate FONTAINE, it will be occupied in the first instance by the 100 Inf. Bde. and the 98 Inf. Bde. will secure FONTAINE Wood.

19. The Artillery must be prepared for this move and will be ready to protect FONTAINE when occupied. Arrangements to this end are being made with the Artillery of flank Divisions, and Corps.

20. Contact aeroplanes will call for flares at Zero plus $1\frac{1}{2}$ hours and Zero plus $8\frac{1}{2}$ hours.

21. Signal flags will be waved by Infantry on reaching objectives but will not be stuck in the ground.

22. Other details have been dealt with in G.S. Ins. Series B, which will be carefully followed.

23. Prisoners will be taken over from Inf. Bdes. at T.2.d.9.2 (near HENIN Cemetery) and at ST. LEGER (T.28.b.9.3).

24. Watches will be synchronized at 10.3 p.m. on April 22.

25. The hour of Zero will be notified later.

26. Div. H. Q. will remain at HAMELINCOURT, with a Report Centre at T.16.b.9.4 (on CROISILLES - HENIN road).

D Foster

Issued at 9 p.m. Lieut. Colonel, G.S.,

33rd Division.

Distribution :-

1 - 6	Div. H. Q.	(3 maps)
8 - 10	Inf. Bdes.	(3 maps)
11	33 Div. Art.	(1 map)
12	21 Div. Art.	(1 map)
13	37 Div. Art.	(1 map)
16 - 19	33 Div. Eng.	(1 map)
20	Pioneers	(1 map)
22	10 Co.,D Bn. (H.B) M.G.C.	(1 map)
23	VII Corps	
24	30 Div.	
25	62 Div.	
26	"B" Sqn. North'd Hussars.	
27	M Section, Special Co. R.E.	

==========

S E C R E T.   Copy No. 8

98th INFANTRY BRIGADE ORDER NO. 132.

22nd April 1917.

Ref. Map.
51b. S.W.
Edition 4A.
1/20,000.

1. The enemy probably intends to retire before long to the QUEANT-DROCOURT Line. The 220th Division consisting of the 190th, 99th Reserve Regiment and 55th Reserve Regiment is believed to be in front of us. It may have been relieved.

2. The 33rd Division is to take part on April 23rd in a general attack by the First and Third Armies and to capture the Ridge overlooking the SENSEE Valley and also the HINDERBURG Line as far as the 80 contour South of the River SENSEE.

3. The 30th Division attacks on the Left of the 33rd Division, and is to reach the line of the road in O.31.a. and b.

4. The 98th Infantry Brigade (with two companies 19th Infantry Brigade) will attack from its present front to the general line T.6.central - road junction in O.31.c., and further to capture the HINDENBURG Line as far as the SENSEE.

5. The 100th Infantry Brigade is to attack that portion of the HINDENBURG Line South of the SENSEE between the 80 Contour and the River.

6. The attack of the 98th Infantry Brigade will be carried out as follows :-

(a) 4th Suff. Regt. and 2 companies 19th Infantry Brigade on right.
2nd Arg. & Suth'd. High'rs. in centre.
1st Midd'x. Regt. on left.
1 Section 11th Field Coy. R.E.,
4th King's (L'pool) Regt. (less 1 company.)
No 98 M.G.Coy., (less 2 Sections.) } In Brigade Reserve.

(b) Dividing lines will be Between 4th Suff. Regt. and 2nd Arg. & Suth'd. High'rs, HINDENBURG Support Line (inclusive to 4th Suff. Regt.)

Between 2nd Arg. & Suth'd. High'rs. and 1st Midd'x. Regt:- S.W. corner of hedge N.35.d.65.85. (inclusive to 1st Midd'x. Regt.) - North edge of Copse N.36.c.7.4 (inclusive to 2nd Arg. & Suth'd. High'rs.) - T.6.?.6.6

(c) The objectives will be :-
First objective:- COPSE Line from T.6.a.6.3. to N.36.b.0.2.

Final objective for left and Centre Battalions, General Line T.6.Central - Road Junction in O.31.c.

Final objective for Right Battalion, to capture the HINDENBURG Line as far as the River SENSEE.

7. The Brigade Boundaries will be :-

Southern Line drawn through T.5.d.8.2. - U.7.a.0.7. - U.7.b.15.70.

Northern Line drawn through N.36.a.2.3. - Road junction O.31.c.35.65. - U.2.a.5.7. (North corner of wood.)

8. Assembly positions will be :-

4th Suff. Regt. and 2 Companies 19th Infantry Brigade, HINDENBURG Front and Support Lines.
2nd Arg. & Suth'd. High'rs. Trench from N.35.d.55.00. - N.36.c.0.7. and Trench from N.35.d.35.75. - S.W. corner of hedge (N.35.d.65.85.)
1st Midd'x. Regt. remainder of trenches from N.36.c.0.7. and S.W. corner of hedge.
4th King's (L'pool) Regt. (less one company) HINDENBURG Support Line in T.5.a.

9. The advance will commence at Zero at which hour barrages will be formed along the portions of the hostile front to be attacked, while heavy artillery, bombards places of importance in rear.

10. The 37th Divisional Artillery will co-operate with the attack of this Brigade.

11. One pair of Tanks are co-operating in the attack of this Brigade. They are to move down the HINDENBURG Line and return via CROISILLES.

12. 2 Sections 11th Field Coy. R.E., are at the disposal of the Brigade.

One Section will be in Brigade Reserve: This will repor at 4th King's (L'pool) Regt. Headquarters at 7-30 p.m to-day.

One Section is placed under the orders of O.C. 4th Suff. Regt. They will report to O.C. 4th Suff. Regt. at HENIN Cross Roads at 2-30 p.m. to-day.

13. Battalions will be in their Assembly positions by 2 hours before Zero. Arrival there will be reported to Brigade Headquarters.

14. When the Left of the Brigade reaches its objectives a con continuous front trench is to be made between the HINDENBURG Line and the Road junction in O.31.c. by joining up existing trenches, etc.

The present German front line in N.36. will be consolidat and wired as a second position by the occupants thereof.

15. Should the enemy evacuate FONTAINE, the 98th Infantry Brigade is in the first instance to secure FONTAINE WOOD; the 100th Infantry Brigade are at the same time occupying FONTAINE.

16. A Section of M. Detachment Special Coy. R.E., will assist in the attack. Mortars will be placed as follows

2 in the HINDENBURG Front Line to fire on block in German Front Line.

2 in the HINDENBURG Support Line to fire on block in German Support Line.

2 in trench about T.5.b.8.9. to fire on Copse N.36.c.7.3.

They will fire from Zero + 1 to Zero + 3.

17. No 98 M.G.Coy., will be prepared to cover the consolidation of the final objective of the Left and Centre Battalions with two sections.

Remainder will be in Brigade Reserve, less one detachment, which will remain in the Strong Point in T.10.b.

18. 98th T.M.Battery will be under the orders of O.C. 4th Suff. Regt. O.C. 98th T.M.Battery will report at 4th Suff. Regt. Headquarters at 7-0 p.m. to-day.

19. One company 4th King's (L'pool) Regt. will remain in position in Trench T.5.c. and Strong Point T.10.b. and cover the Right flank of the Brigade.

20. Contact Aeroplanes will call for flares at Zero + 1½ hours and Zero + 8½ hours.

21. Signal flags will be waved by infantry on reaching objectives but will not be stuck in the ground.

22. All details laid down in 33rd Divisional Instructions, Series B. will be complied with.

23. Prisoners will be sent to Brigade Headquarters.

24. Watches will be synchronized at 11-32 p.m. to-night.

25. Tools will be taken forward by the attacking troops in the following proportions :-

50% will carry no tools.
35% " " shovels.
15% " " picks.

26. All box respirators will be worn in the "Alert" position.

27. S.A.A., Bombs and Rifle Grenades will be carried in accordance with instructions issued yesterday.

28. The Tunnel under the HINDENBURG Support Line is to be clear of all troops by 2 hours before Zero. It is being policed. Traffic up to the front line, i.e. from West to East will be allowed for small parties. Only Officers, Runners and Signallers will be allowed to go against the traffic i.e. from East to West.

29. The hour of Zero will be notified later.

30. Brigade Headquarters will close at T.9.b. at 9-0 p.m. and open at 1st Midd'x. Headquarters in HINDENBURG Support Line at 10-0 p.m. The nearest staircases to this Headquarters will be marked :-

"FOOTBALL. H. Q.,"

Major,
Brigade Major,
98th Infantry Brigade.

(4)

Issued through
Signals at 8-0 a.m.
to:-

Copy No.
1. G.O.C.,
2. 1st Midd'x. Regt.
3. 2nd Arg. & Suth'd. High'rs.
4. 4th King's (L'pool) Regt.
5. 4th Suff. Regt.
6. No 98 M.G.Coy.,
7. 98th T.M.Battery.
8. 11th Field Coy. R.E.,
9. No 2 Coy. Train.
10. 99th Field Ambulance.
11. Brigade Signals.
12. 13. } B Battalion -H.B.-M.G.Coy.
14. M. Detachment Special Coy. R.E.
15. 16. } 37th Divisional Artillery.
17. 33rd Division. "G".
18. 33rd Division. "Q".
19. 20. } 19th Infantry Brigade.
21. 90th Infantry Brigade.
22. 100th Infantry Brigade.
23. A.D.M.S.
24. Senior Supply Officer.
25. Staff Captain.
26. O. C. File.
27. 28. } War Diary.

SECRET

Copy No 8

19th Infantry Brigade – Order No. 228

Map Ref Sheet 51 B. S.W 1/20,000.

22nd April 1917.

1. The enemy probably intends to retire before long to the QUEANT – DROCOURT Line. The 220th Divⁿ consisting of the 99th Reserve, 190th and 55th Reserve Regiments is believed to be in front of us, but may have been relieved.

2. The Division is to take part on April 23rd. in a general attack by the First and Third Armies, and to capture the Ridge overlooking the SENSEE VALLEY and also the HINDENBURG LINE as far as the 80 CONTOUR South of the River SENSEE.

3. 30th Division attacks on the Left of the Division and is to reach the line of the Road in O. 31. c. a and b.

4. The attack will be carried out as follows:–

   100th Infy. Bde. against that portion of the HINDENBURG LINE South of the SENSEE between the 80 CONTOUR and the River.

   98th Infy. Bde. with 2 Coys. 19th Infy. Bde, from its present front to the general line T. 6. CENTRAL – Road Junction in O. 31. c., and further to capture the HINDENBURG LINE as far as the SENSEE.

5. The advance will commence at ZERO, at which hour barrages will be formed along the positions of the hostile front to be attacked, while Heavy Artillery will bombard important points in the Rear, and the HINDENBURG LINE on both flanks of the 100th Bde. attack.

6. 3 Sections of the 19th M. G. Coy. will assist in the operations in the SENSEE VALLEY, under the orders of the 100th Bde.

7. 19th Inf. Bde. (less 2 Coys)
   Div. Eng. (less 2 Sects. of 11th and 222nd Field Coys. R.E.)
   Pioneers (less 2 Coys).
   will be in Divisional Reserve.

8. The 1/5th Scottish Rifles and The Cameronians between HENIN and NEUVILLE – VITASSE will be prepared to move at 10 minutes notice from ZERO onwards.

9. (a). The 2 Coys mentioned in para. 4. will be detailed from the 2nd Royal Welsh Fusiliers.

   (b). These 2 Coys will be attached to the 4th Suffolks and will come under the orders of the 98th Bde.

   (c) Packs will be carried and arrangements will be made for the storage of these in the HINDENBURG FRONT and SUPPORT LINES.

   (d) 2 Days rations will be carried on the man.

9. (continued).

(e) All tools, grenades, extra S.A.A. will be found by the 98th Bde.

(f) Guides will be at 19th Bde. Headquarters at 4.30pm today, 22nd inst, to take these Coys. to their destination.

(g) The following distances will be maintained during the march :-

Between Coys.... 500 yards.
Between Platoons.. 200 yards.

10. When the Left of the 98th Bde. reaches its objective, a continuous front trench will be made between the HINDENBURG LINE and the Road junction in O.31.c. by joining up existing trenches.

The present German front line in N.36 is to be consolidated and wired as a second position.

11. The 100th Bde. are to consolidate a line from the captured HINDENBURG Trenches to the Fifth Army boundary to connect with the 62nd Divn who will advance their Left if necessary.

12. Should the enemy evacuate FONTAINE, it will be occupied in the first instance by the 100th Bde, and the 98th Bde. are to secure FONTAINE WOOD.

13. Signal Flags will be waved by Infantry on reaching objectives, but will not be stuck in the ground.

14. Prisoners will be taken over from Inf. Bdes. at T.2.d.9.2 (near HENIN CEMETERY) and at ST. LEDGER (T.28.b.9.8.)

15. Watches will be synchronised at 10.15pm and 10.30pm to-night through the Signals. Battalions will detail an officer to attend Battalion Signal Offices at these times.

16. The ZERO hour will be notified later.

17. Div. H.Q. will remain at HAMELINCOURT with a report centre at T.16.b.9.4 (on CROISILLES-HENIN Rd). All units will send Runners today to ascertain exactly where the Report Centre is.

18. 19th Bde. H.Q. will remain at T.3.a.5.1.

19. ACKNOWLEDGE.

A. Miller
Captain,
Bde Major,
19th Infantry Bde.

Issued through Signals at

Copies Nos. 1-9. Units of 19th Infy Bde.
10. 98th Infy. Bde.
11. 100th Infy. Bde.
12. 33rd Divn (G).
13. 33rd Divn (Q).
14. C.R.A. 33rd DIVN.
15. S.O. 19th Infy Bde.
16. Staff Captain
17. Signals.
18. Office.
19. File.
20. War Diary.

Instructions regarding War Diaries and Intelligence Summaries are contained in F. S. Regs., Part II. and the Staff Manual respectively. Title pages will be prepared in manuscript.

WAR DIARY
or
INTELLIGENCE SUMMARY.

(Erase heading not required.)

Army Form C. 2118.

Vol 29

Place	Date	Hour	Summary of Events and Information	Remarks and references to Appendices

CONFIDENTIAL

War Diary of

11th (Field) Co RE

From May 1st 1917 To May 31st 1917.

(Volume)

[illegible] Maj RE
O.C. 11th Fd Co RE

A5834 Wt. W4973 M687 750,000 8/16 D. D. & L. Ltd. Forms/C.2118/13.

Army Form C. 2118.

Instructions regarding War Diaries and Intelligence Summaries are contained in F. S. Regs., Part II. and the Staff Manual respectively. Title Pages will be prepared in manuscript.

WAR DIARY
or
INTELLIGENCE SUMMARY
(Erase heading not required.)

Place	Date	Hour	Summary of Events and Information	Remarks and references to Appendices
BAILLEULMONT	1.5.17.		Whole company salving material from old British & German front lines in the neighbourhood of RANSART.	
MONCHY-AU-BOIS	2.5.17.		Company moved with 19th I.B. to bivouac in MONCHY. No casualties.	
	3.5.17.		Work on billets.	
	4.5.17.		Company drill musketry etc. [illegible]	
	5.5.17		Nos 1 & 2 Sections putting up baths. 1 at ADINFER and 1 at MONCHY Nos 3 & 4 Sections worked on clearing a track between MONCHY and BERLES AU-BOIS.	
	6.5.17		Church for company. Parade Services.	
	7.5.17.		Whole company worked on track between MONCHY & BERLES during morning. Afternoon Divl Races 2Lieut ROBERTS went to	
	8.5.17		Company on track between MONCHY & BERLES.	
	9.5.17		do do	
	10.5.17.		do do	
	11.5.17		Company packed up ready to move.	

Army Form C. 2118.

Instructions regarding War Diaries and Intelligence Summaries are contained in F. S. Regs., Part II. and the Staff Manual respectively. Title Pages will be prepared in manuscript.

WAR DIARY
or
INTELLIGENCE SUMMARY
(Erase heading not required.)

Place	Date	Hour	Summary of Events and Information	Remarks and references to Appendices
HAMELINCOURT	12.5.17		Company moved to HAMELINCOURT No Casualties	P.
do	13.5.17		No 2 Section started work on tracks	
			(1) from FERME ROUGE to Right Bde Hq	
			(2) BOYELLES to HAMELINCOURT.	
			(3) BOYELLES to Right Bde Hq	
			(4) BOYELLES to Left Bde Area	
			(5) BOISLEUX AU MONT to BOYELLES.	
			(6) MOYENNEVILLE Round HAMELINCOURT to join up with other tracks.	
			These existing tracks were taken round villages.	
			No 1 Section. Started clearing 2 wells in MOYENNEVILLE.	
			No 3 Section worked in reliefs on a well in CRE's yard at HAMELINCOURT.	
			No 4 Section ~~[illegible]~~ started work on salving pickets from old German barbed wire entanglements.	
			A workshops & painters shop was started with 8 carpenters from the company & 4 painters 1 tinsmith & 2 fitters.	P

2449 Wt. W14957/M90 750,000 1/16 J.B.C. & A. Forms/C.2118/12.

Instructions regarding War Diaries and Intelligence Summaries are contained in F. S. Regs., Part II. and the Staff Manual respectively. Title pages will be prepared in manuscript.

WAR DIARY
or
INTELLIGENCE SUMMARY.

(*Erase heading not required.*)

Army Form C. 2118.

Place	Date	Hour	Summary of Events and Information	Remarks and references to Appendices
M.D.H.Q. HAMELINCOURT	14.5.17		Work as for 13th. 2 officers + 85 infantry were employed assisting Nos 2 & 4 Sections.	[illegible]
	15.5.17		do do	[illegible]
	16.5.17.		Nos 1 & 2 Sections as before. No 2 Sec with 2 officers 60 inf. No 3 Section improved waterpoint in HAMELINCOURT. No 4 Section employed in erecting foundations for Nissen huts for inf camps in neighbourhood of HAMELINCOURT.	[illegible]
	17.5.17		do do	[illegible]
	18.5.17		No 1 Section erecting Nissen huts at JUDAS COPSE and on the HAMELINCOURT–CROISILLES Road past FERME Rouge. No 2 Section continued on tracks. No 3 Section continued on work in [illegible] yard. No 4 Section went to St LEGER to practise an attack in conjunction with the 5th [illegible]	[illegible]
	19.5.17		Nos 1, 2 & 3 as before. No 4 Section went up at 6pm to the Quarry at U 19 a 1.2 whence they were to move forward in the 20th [illegible]	[illegible]

A5834 Wt. W4973 M687 750,000 8/16 D. D. & L. Ltd. Forms/C.2118/13.

Army Form C. 2118.

Instructions regarding War Diaries and Intelligence Summaries are contained in F. S. Regs., Part II. and the Staff Manual respectively. Title pages will be prepared in manuscript.

WAR DIARY
or
INTELLIGENCE SUMMARY.
(Erase heading not required.)

Place	Date	Hour	Summary of Events and Information	Remarks and references to Appendices
HAMELINCOURT	20.5.17.		Nos 1 2 & 3 Sections as before.	
			No 4 Section took part in an attack on the HINDENBURG LINE orders attached	Appendix A (1) (2) (3) (4)
			Following arrangements were made.	
			(1) Lieut CRAIG with 10 R.E. & a carrying party of 8 infantry were to make a bomb block in the HINDENBURG LINE at U 14 c 5.4.	
			(2) Sgt HAMPSHERE 13 R.E. & 7 infantry to make a bomb block at about U 14 c 3.5 in the communication trench leading to the support line.	
			Both these parties remained in the assembly positions	
		5.15am	Zero hour the infantry went over.	
		6.15am	Lt Col CRAYTON ordered the R.E. forward to consolidate stating he believed his men in position	
			The party proceeded forward on reaching the front line were they came under heavy M.G. & rifle fire from the right. The RE advanced by man by man by rushes from one shell hole to another. The infantry carrying parties could not get forward. Casualties at this point were 3 O.R. The HINDENBURG Line was entered at the point U13 b 7.9 the parties then moved to the right till about the point U 14 a 1.1. where they found a party of about 20 S.R with 2 officers engaged in a bombing attack on the enemy who were holding the	
		7.15am	trench E. from that point	

A5834 Wt. W4973 M687 750,000 8/16 D. D. & L. Ltd. Forms/C.2118/13.

Instructions regarding War Diaries and Intelligence Summaries are contained in F. S. Regs., Part II. and the Staff Manual respectively. Title pages will be prepared in manuscript.

WAR DIARY
or
INTELLIGENCE SUMMARY.
(Erase heading not required.)

Army Form C. 2118.

Place	Date	Hour	Summary of Events and Information	Remarks and references to Appendices
	20.5.17	7.15am	Lieut CRAIG kept Sgt HAMSHERES party in reserve and proceeded to make a bomb block a	
			traverse behind the covering party. within a few minutes of reaching the spot both infantry	
			officers were casualties so Lieut CRAIG took charge of the infantry parties.	
			fighting fluctuated between [when] the bomb block was being constructed and the point we were	
			first holding, for 3 to 4 hours. Several times the covering party was driven back past	
			the bomb block but they ~~original position~~ were rallied and the original position taken	
			till the block was completed at about 12 noon to 1pm. The casualties during this	
		12 noon	time were severe in the infantry about 30 to 40 in all. The party was kept up to	
			strength by keeping all men of carrying parties who came up.	
		1pm.	about 1pm a party of enemy tried to work round the flanks over the top but were	
			driven back by rifle fire.	
		5.30pm	at 5.30pm Lieut CRAIG was relieved by an officer of the 2nd Worcesters, he stayed	
			in with his section till 7pm when things being quiet he fell back about 100 yards to	
			the right of the Worcesters and helped them to dig in	
			At 7.30pm a second attack was made by the 19th I.B. against the German support	
			line. The section stood to for this. about 2am the section received orders to come back at which	

A5834 Wt. W4973 M687 750,000 8/16 D. D. & L. Ltd. Forms/C.2118/13.

Instructions regarding War Diaries and Intelligence Summaries are contained in F. S. Regs., Part II. and the Staff Manual respectively. Title pages will be prepared in manuscript.

WAR DIARY
or
INTELLIGENCE SUMMARY.

(Erase heading not required.)

Army Form C. 2118.

Place	Date	Hour	Summary of Events and Information	Remarks and references to Appendices
			here they returned to their billets. Casualties 1 O.R. killed 3 O.R. wounded 2 O.R. missing	
		20.5.17	At 4 pm. orders were received from C.R.E. 1 section was required to cooperate with the 19th I.B in an attack on the HINDENBURG SUPPORT LINE zero being about 7 pm.	
			All the sections being out at work men from those handy were gathered in and a section of 27 O.R under 2/Lt FORBES was made up and proceeded forward to report to HQ Cameronians in the Quarry at T. 18 b.	orders Appendix B
			O.C. went forward and arranged with C.O.s of the 1st Cameronians & the 20th R.F for 3 parties of 10 men one for each block. The two from the Cameronians were obtained but it was too late to obtain the parties from the 20th R.F.	
		10.30 pm	The Hindenburg Support line was captured and the two parties from the 1st Cameronians went forward. However in getting forward they found the infantry had not reached their objective. They spent their time digging & connecting a series of shell holes which the infantry had gained.	
		1.30 am	At 1.30 am no reports being received back the remainder went forward to help the former parties. However there was no R.E. work so they carried on connecting shell holes. They were then ordered back by the O.C. infantry in the line and came back at dawn. Some were caught by daylight and had to stop till the next night. Casualties 3 O.R. wounded.	

A5834 Wt. W4973 M687 750,000 8/16 D. D. & L. Ltd. Forms/C.2118/13.

Army Form C. 2118.

WAR DIARY
or
INTELLIGENCE SUMMARY.
(Erase heading not required.)

Instructions regarding War Diaries and Intelligence Summaries are contained in F. S. Regs., Part II. and the Staff Manual respectively. Title pages will be prepared in manuscript.

Place	Date	Hour	Summary of Events and Information	Remarks and references to Appendices
HAMELINCOURT	21.5.17		No 1 Section continued Nissen huts in CROISILLES Road. No 2 Section continued tracks Nos 3 & 4 Sections no work.	P
	22.5.17		No 2 Sections as previous. No 1 Section no work. No 3 Section continued well in CRE's yard No 4 Section Helped No 2 Section	P
	23.5.17		As previous. No 1 Section continued on Nissen huts	P
	24.5.17		No 1 Section made Signal shelter in Hindenburg Line. No 2 Section continuing on the tracks No 3 Section on well in CRE's yard. No 4 Section on with No 2 Section.	P
	25.5.17		No 1 Section commenced work on installing a canvas belt pump at the well [illegible] MOYENNEVILLE [illegible] No 2 Section collected [illegible] for foundations of Nissen huts. No 3 Section continued well in CRE's Camp. No 4 Section started work in [illegible] of VII Corps huts in area of MOYENNEVILLE	P

A5834 Wt. W4973 M687 750,000 8/16 D. D. & L. Ltd. Forms/C.2118/13.

Instructions regarding War Diaries and Intelligence Summaries are contained in F. S. Regs., Part II. and the Staff Manual respectively. Title pages will be prepared in manuscript.

WAR DIARY
or
INTELLIGENCE SUMMARY.
(Erase heading not required.)

Army Form C. 2118.

Place	Date	Hour	Summary of Events and Information	Remarks and references to Appendices
	26.5.17		No 2 Sec worked between 2nd R.W.F & 1st Cameronians to co-operate in attack on the HINDENBURG Support line. No 1 Section continued on the erection of the pump at MOYENNEVILLE. Nos 3 & 4 Sections worked on the erection of the huts in the MOYENNEVILLE area.	[illegible]
	27.5.17		No 1 Section stood by in case they were wanted. Also No 3 section. No 2 Section moved forward & stopped in the Quarry in T 18 b to cooperate in the attack on the HINDENBURG Line. The attack failed and they were not used returning to billets that night. Nos 3 & 4 Sections continued on the huts.	orders Appendix D [illegible]
	28.5.17		No 1 Section continued on the erection of the pump. Nos 3 & 4 Sections on the erection of the huts. No 2 Section having only returned at 5 a.m. rested.	[illegible]
	29.5.17		Nos 1 2 & 4 Sections worked on the erection of the huts. No 1 Section improved the water supply system at the western point of MOYENNEVILLE from troughs etc across the road.	
	30.5.17		As before. The huts were completed and the water point completed with the exception of erecting a standard for water carts.	[illegible]

Army Form C. 2118.

WAR DIARY
or
INTELLIGENCE SUMMARY.
(Erase heading not required.)

Instructions regarding War Diaries and Intelligence Summaries are contained in F. S. Regs., Part II. and the Staff Manual respectively. Title pages will be prepared in manuscript.

Place	Date	Hour	Summary of Events and Information	Remarks and references to Appendices
BAILLEULMONT	31.5.17		Company relieved by 95th Co of 21st Divn marched to BAILLEULMONT where it billeted. Casualties 1. O.R fell out	
			[illegible] Maj RE. O.C. 11th? Co RE.	

A5834 Wt. W4973 M687 750,000 8/16 D. D. & L. Ltd. Forms/C.2118/13.

Appendix A (1)

SECRET

33 Div. Order No. 185.

Copy No. 17

16 May 1917.

1. (a) The enemy's retirement to a line of defences further in rear is reported to be imminent.

(b) In front of us is believed to be the 49th Res. Div. consisting of the 225, 226 and 228 R. Inf. Regts., composed largely of Poles, whose morale is probably not very good.

2. 33 Div. is to capture the HINDENBURG line as far as the CROISILLES - HENDECOURT road, on May 17.

3. The V Corps on our right, and the remainder of the VII Corps on our left, will co-operate with artillery fire.

4. The attack will be carried out as follows :-

(a) 19 Inf. Bde.

One Bn. to attack THE HUMP from a position on the right of the CROISILLES - HENDECOURT road, and to form a defensive flank from about U.14.c.1.3 to cross roads at U.14.c.2.9.

(b) 100 Inf. Bde. to attack from the South-West that portion of the HINDENBURG line between the CROISILLES - HENDECOURT and CROISILLES - FONTAINE roads.

(c) 98 Inf. Bde. to attack South-East down the HINDENBURG line from present blocks as far as the CROISILLES - FONTAINE Road.

These objectives are shewn on the attached map.

5. The Division will assemble for attack before daylight on May 17, in accordance with G.S. Instructions D.7.

6. The advance of the 19th and 100 Inf. Bdes., covered by normal H.A. bombardment of HINDENBURG system, will be timed to reach the HINDENBURG front trench at Zero, at which time the artillery barrage programme given in G.S. Instructions D.3, will commence.

7. The advance of 98 Inf. Bde. will also commence at Zero, at which hour the mine under the HINDENBURG support trench, will be fired, if sufficiently advanced.

8. Special measures are being taken by the R.F.C. to keep off hostile aeroplanes, and deal with enemy observation balloons between dawn and Zero on May 17.

P. T. O.

9. Arrangements are also being made to attract the attention of enemy sentries for some minutes before Zero by some of our aeroplanes performing various evolutions over FONTAINE.

10. In order to blind hostile machine guns, smoke barrages will be formed as follows, if the wind is suitable :-

(a) By Detachment, No.1 Special Co. R.E. between the SENSEE and River road in the vicinity of the HINDENBURG system for five minutes after Zero.

(b) By Field Artillery along the Western side of FONTAINE for half an hour after Zero.

11 Artillery will support the attack as follows :-

19 Inf. Bde. Two F.A. Bdes. 7 Div.

100 Inf. Bde. (21 Div. Art.)
(124 & 150 F.A.Bdes.)

98 Inf. Bde. 123 F.A.Bde.

12. Machine guns will co-operate in the attack as ordered in G.S. Instructions D.4.

13. Engineers will be at the disposal of attacking Inf. Bdes. as follows :-

19 Inf. Bde. 1 Sect. 222 F. Co. R.E.

100 Inf. Bde. 2 Sects. 222 F.Co. R.E.

98 Inf. Bde. 2 Sects. 212 F.Co. R.E.

14. The Divl. Reserve will consist of :-

2 Bns. 19 Inf. Bde.

Div. Eng. (less 5 Sects.)

18 Middx. R. (Pioneers.)

15. The objective when gained will be consolidated as laid down in G.S. Instructions D.8

16. After Zero + 120 the S.O.S. Field Artillery barrage will be on the line :-

The KNUCKLE - U.14.c.6.2 - U.14.d.1.4 - U.14.d.8½.9 - Junction of CRUMB LANE and BULLECOURT - FONTAINE road - along latter to U.8.central, thence to YORK trench at U.1.d.0.8.

(3)

17. Should the enemy's retirement be found to be in progress, the Bns. 19 Inf. Bde. in Divl. Reserve will be prepared to advance in the first instance to the general line - cross roads at U.15.a.9.7 to FONTAINE Village.

18. Artillery must be prepared to move forward to support the Infantry in this position.

19. Contact aeroplanes will call for flares at Zero plus one hour.

20. Blue and white signalling flags will be waved by Infantry on reaching objectives, but will not be stuck in the ground.

21. Prisoners will be taken over from Inf. Bdes. at the cross roads at T.22.c.4.5 and at HENIN CEMETERY (T.2.d.8.2).

22. Watches will be synchronized at 10.3 p.m. on May 16.

23. The hour of Zero will be notified later.

24. Div.H.Q. will remain at HAMELINCOURT

D Forster

16/5/17. Lieut. Colonel, G.S.,

Issued at 1.50 a.m. 33rd Division.

Distribution :-

Div. H.Q.

1 - 6	Div. H.Q.
8 - 10	Inf. Bdes.
11	33 Div. Art.
12	21 Div. Art.
13	37 Div. Art.
16 - 19	Div. Eng.
20	Pioneers.
22	VII Corps.
23	18 Div.
24	62 Div.
25	21 Div.
26	Corps H.A.
27	No.1 Sect. Spl.Co. R.E.
28	181 TunnellingCo. R.E.

=======

Appendix A (2)

S E C R E T

Copy No. 16

33 Div. Order No. 189.

18 May 1917.

1. The attack ordered in 33 Div. Order 185 will probably take place about 5 a.m. on the 20th.

2. The following amendments are made to G.S.Instructions D.3.(Artillery Barrage Programme):-

(a) Field Artillery Barrage 1.b.(ii) on HINDENBURG Support line from U.7.d.8.1 to CROISILLES - FONTAINE road, will lift at Zero + 15, instead of at Zero + 20, that is, the barrage all along HINDENBURG Support trench from the right of the attack as far as the CROISILLES - FONTAINE road, lifts at the same time.

(b) Normal Heavy Artillery bombardment of HINDENBURG system will continue on both front and support lines North of R. SENSEE up to Zero.

(c) Heavy Artillery barrage 2 (ii) will extend Northwards from road junction at U.1.d.7½.9½ to include junction of YORK trench and ROTTEN ROW.

3. After Zero + 120 Artillery support will be afforded as follows:-

19 Inf. Bde.	...	293 F. A. Bde.
100 Inf. Bde.	...	21 Div. Art. and 293 F.A. Bde.
98 Inf. Bde.		37 Div. Art. and 150 F.A.Bde.

4. 149 Inf. Bde. will be assembled West of ST. LEGER on May 20 by 8 a.m.

5. With reference to para 17 of 33 Div. Order 185, 19 Inf. Bde. will be prepared to send forward patrols at Zero + 120 to the line mentioned. Definite orders as to this will be issued as soon as it is known that the objective of the Division has been captured.

6. Should a hostile counter-attack meet with any measure of success, 149 Inf. Bde. must be prepared to attack South of the SENSEE, probably about sunset.

7 For this purpose, the following barrages would be required :-

At Zero

(a) 18 Pdr. barrage on hostile front line whereever that may be.

(b) 4.5 Hows. in rear of 18 Pdr. barrage.

(c) Heavy Artillery barrage on approaches further in rear.

P. T. O.

At Zero + 5.

18 Pdr. barrages to commence to creep at 50 yards per minute, other barrages to conform.

6. Smoke barrages would probably be required again similar to those used in the first attack.

D Forster

Lieut. Colonel, G.S.,

Issued at 9.15 p.m. 33rd Division.

Distribution :-

1 - 6	Div. H.Q.
7	149 Inf. Bde.
8 - 10	Inf. Bdes.
11	33 Div. Art.
12	21 Div. Art.
13	37 Div. Art.
16 - 19	33 Div. Eng.
20	Pioneers.
22	VII Corps.
23	18 Div.
24	62 Div.
25	21 Div.
26	VII Corps H.A.
27	No. 1 Section, Spl.Co. R.E.
28	181 Tunn. Co. R.E

=====

Appendix A

"A" Form.

MESSAGES AND SIGNALS.

Army Form C.2121
(in pads of 100).
No. of Message (3)

Prefix ......Code......m.	Words	Charge	This message is on a/c of:	Recd. at......m.
Office of Origin and Service Instructions.	Sent		......Service.	Date......
	At......m.			From......
	To......			
	By......		(Signature of "Franking Officer.")	By......

TO { O.C. 11th Field Co R.E.

Sender's Number.	Day of Month.	In reply to Number.	AAA
* R.E. 315	16		

Refce Para 13 Div OO No. 185 the 1 Section 222 Fd Co RE is not available for 19th Inf Bde as it is working tonight AAA 1 Section of 11th Field Co RE will assist 19th Inf Bde and they should, unless there is special work for them, be near Bde HQ till required AAA G Staff are seeing B.G.C. about this and I will let you know where they are to go later.
I have informed 'G' that they are not available for work till tomorrow morning

From
Place
Time

The above may be forwarded as now corrected. (Z)

Censor. Signature of Addressor or person authorised to telegraph in his name.

* This line should be erased if not required.

750,000. W 2183–M509. H. W. & V., Ld. 6/16.

S E C R E T

33 Div.
G.83.

1. Reference 33 Div. Orders Nos. 185 and 189 -

ZERO hour will be 5.15 a.m. on the 20 May.

2. ACKNOWLEDGE.

19/5/17.

Issued at 1 p.m.

B. L. Montgomery.

Captain, G.S.,

33rd Division.

Distribution :-

1 - 6	Div. H.Q.
7	149 Inf. Bde.
8 - 10	Inf. Bdes.
11	33 Div. Art.
12	21 Div. Art.
13	37 Div. Art.
16 - 19	33 Div. Eng.
20	Pioneers.
22	VII Corps.
23	18 Div.
24	62 Div
25	21 Div.
26	VII Corps H.A.
27	No. 1 Sect. Special Co.R.E.
28	181 Tunn. Co. R.E.

=======

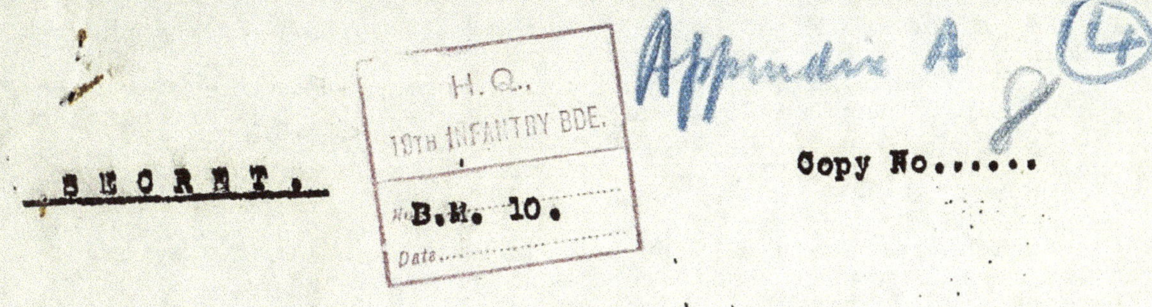

H.Q.
19TH INFANTRY BDE.
B.M. 10.
Date........

Appendix A

8 (4)

SECRET.

Copy No......

1. Reference 19th Inf.Bde. Order No.238 and amendment -

ZERO hour will be 5.15 a.m. on the 20 May.

2. ACKNOWLEDGE.

Awalker

Captain,
Brigade Major,
19th Infantry Brigade.

19/5/17.
To all recipients of
19th Inf.Bde. Order No.238.

SECRET.

May 19th.1917.

Ref.Map. Sheet 51.B.S.W.
1/20,000

19TH INFANTRY BRIGADE INSTRUCTIONS No.2.

1. Relief of the Right Brigade Sector will be carried out as follows:-
Officer Commanding 1st Queens will arrange to relieve the posts now held by the 2nd Royal Welch Fusiliers, with the exception of Nos.1 and 2 posts, as soon after dark as possible, under arrangements to be made direct between the Commanding Officers concerned.

Nucleus garrisons will be left in posts Nos.1 and 2 by the Officers Commanding 2nd Worcestershire Regt. and 16th K.R.R.C. respectively when the advance takes place. Their present garrisons being relieved by those units on their arrival at their assembly positions. The garrisons of these posts will be at once withdrawn and rejoin their unit at SUNKEN ROADS South of CROISILLES in Squares T.29.B., T.24.C., and T.30.A.

2. Rations for the 20th May will be issued tonight 19th/20th May for all Infantry Brigade units and carried by the man. Water bottles must be filled over night and must be very sparingly used.

3. Two pigeons will be sent to the 5th Scottish Rifles on the evening of the 19th instant.

4. 20th Royal Fusiliers will detail a liaison officer to report to 100th Inf.Bde H.Q. at SUNKEN ROAD T.22.D.90.95. one hour before Zero.
A liaison officer of 7th Div.Artillery will report to Officer Commanding 5th Scottish Rifles at U.19.A.1.2 at 3.30 am, 20th May.
A liaison officer of 186th Inf.Bde will report to 19th Inf.Bde H.Q. at 12 midnight night of 19th/20th May.

5. Should a hostile counter attack meet with any success, the 149th Inf.Bde. (50th Division) placed under the orders of 33rd Division will be prepared to attack South of the SENSEE River, probably about sunset.

6. ACKNOWLEDGE.

C Walker
Captain.
Brigade Major.
19th Infantry Brigade.

To all recipients of 19th Inf. Bde.Order No.238.

SECRET. Copy No....8.

AMENDMENTS to 19th INF. BDE INS. No.1.

Ref.Map Sheet
51b S.W. 1/20,000.

19th May 1917.

The following amendments are made to 19th Inf.Bde. Ins. No.1:-

Para. 5. (a) Patrols of 2nd Royal Welsh Fusiliers will move from their Battalion bivouacs in the SUNKEN Roads to the QUARRY in U.19.a.1.2. between ZERO and ZERO + 60 minutes. This margin of time is given to allow the patrols to take advantage of any break in the enemy's barrage should he put one down in this neighbourhood.

Para. 6. After U.19.a.1.2 read "or any other Signal Office". Message carriers of The Cameronians will also use the Signal Office in U.19.a.1.2. or any other Signal Office, and not as previously stated.

Should the Headquarters of the 1/5th Scottish Rifles move forward, they will arrange to leave an operator in the QUARRY Signal Office to receive these messages until other arrangements can be made.

ACKNOWLEDGE.

[signature]
Captain,
Brigade Major,
19th Infantry Brigade.

Copies to all Recepients of
19th Inf.Bde.Order
No.238.

SECRET.

Copy No. 8

19th INFANTRY BRIGADE - INS. No.1.

Ref Map 51b S.W. 1/20,000, Edn. 4a.

19/5/1917.

With reference to the forthcoming operations :-

1. When the result of the attack on the HINDENBURG Line on May 20th is known, the 19th Inf.Bde. will be prepared to send patrols forward to the line, Cross Roads U.15.b.4.4. - line of trenches running thence to N.E. edge of FONTAINE Village - thence to APPLE BRIDGE (U.2.b.2.1.) which will be the point of junction with the 18 Div.

2. These patrols will be found by the

2nd Royal Welsh Fusiliers on the Right, and
The Cameronians on the Left.

3. The objective of the 2nd Royal Welsh Fusiliers will be from Cross Roads, U.15.b.4.4. to trench junction U.9.a.2.4.; that of The Cameronians, the trench junction U.9.a.2.4. to APPLE BRIDGE, U.2.b.2.1.

4. Each of the above mentioned Battalions will detail four patrols composed of one leader (specially selected) and 8 O.R. The leader to be an Officer or selected N.C.O..

5. (a) The patrols of the 2nd Royal Welsh Fusiliers will pass the North Eastern Edge of ST. LEGER WOOD at ZERO on the 20th May, and proceed to the QUARRY in U.19.a.1.2., using the ground between 85 and 95 Contour.

On arrival at the QUARRY, the senior Officer or N.C.O. will report on the telephone to Brigade H.Q. by means of the telephone of the 1/5th Scottish Rifles at U.19.a.1.2. and await further instructions.

(b) The patrols of The Cameronians will arrive at the Headquarters 20th Royal Fusiliers, T.17.a.4.4. at ZERO - 15 minutes, report their arrival there by telephone to 19th Inf Bde. H.Q., and await further instructions.

If ordered to advance they will do so by Cross Roads at T.11.d.8.1. thence to their objective.

6. Reports will be sent back as follows :-

In writing and in duplicate by two men, each carrying a copy of the message.

Those of the 2nd Royal Welsh Fusiliers will be sent to the QUARRY at U.19.a.1.2. for transmission by telephone to 19th Inf.Bde. H.Q.

Those of The Cameronians to one of the Battalions of the 100th Inf.Bde. at the QUARRY in T.18.d.9.8. for transmission to Brigade H.Q.

7. Should the patrols reach their final objective, it is their duty to remain there, reporting their arrival as described above.

8. Rations for the day (20th) must be carried, and all water bottles must be filled before starting.

The hour of ZERO will probably allow for breakfast before starting.

9. ACKNOWLEDGE

A Walker

Captain,
Brigade Major, 19th Inf.Bde.

DISTRIBUTION.

~~1 - 6. All Units of Bde.~~
7- 10. Bde.H.Q.
11- 14. Group Commdrs.Artly.

To all recipients of B.O. 238.

SECRET. Copy No. 8.......

AMENDMENTS TO Brigade Order No.238.

Ref. Map Sheet 51b S.W., 1/20,000.

19th May 1917.

The following amendments and additions are made to Brigade Order No.238.

1. Para.2 For "May 17th" read "May 20th".

Para.5. do. do.

Para.13 For "1 Section 222nd Coy.R.E." read " 1 Section 11th Fld. Coy.R.E."

Para 17 For "The Cameronians" read "2nd Royal Welsh Fusiliers".
For "Cross Roads at U.15.a.9.7." read " U.15.b.4.4"
For "Trench Junction at U.9.b.2.4." read " U.9.a.2.4."
For "2nd Royal Welsh Fusiliers from etc" read " The Cameronians from U.9.a.2.4. to APPLE BRIDGE at U.2.b.2.1."

Para.26 For "Cameronians" read "2nd Royal Welsh Fusiliers on relief by the 100th Inf.Bde. will withdraw to the SUNKEN Roads S.of CROISILLES in Squares T.29.b., T.24.c. and T.30.a.
"The battalion will be concealed in these Sunken Roads as much as possible, and there will be no movement to give away their position after 3.30 a.m."

2. Close touch must be made by the 1/5th Scottish Rifles with the 2nd Worcershire Regt. on their Left.

C Macken

Captain,
Brigade Major,
19th Infantry Brigade.

Issued at 5 30 P.M.

Copies Nos.1 - 10. Units of 19th Inf.Bde.
11. 101st F.A.
12. 98th Inf.Bde.
13. 100th Inf.Bde.
14. 186th Inf.Bde.
15. 33rd Divn (G).
16. 33rd Divn (Q).
17. 21 Divl.Artly.
18. S.O. 19th Inf.Bde.
19. Signals.
20. Staff Captain.
21. Intelligence Officer
22. Bombing Officer.
23. Office.
24. File.
25. War Diary.
26. 7th Divl.Artly.
27. 94th Bde.R.F.A.
28. 95th Bde.R.F.A.
29. 48th H.A.G.

S E C R E T.   Copy No. 8....

19th INFANTRY BRIGADE - ORDER No.238.

Ref.Map Sheet 51 b S.W. Edition 4a.

16th May 1917.

1. (a) The enemy's retirement to a line of defences further in rear is reported to be imminent.
(b) In front of us is believed to be the 49th Reserve Divn. consisting of the 225, 226 and 228 R. Inf. Regts., composed largely of Poles, whose morale is probably not very good.

2. 33rd Div. is to capture the HINDENBURG Line as far as the CROISILLES - HENDECOURT Road, on May 17th.

3. The V Corps on our right and the remainder of the VII Corps on our left, will co-operate with artillery fire.

4. The attack will be carried out as follows :-

(a) 19 Inf.Bde.

One Bn., 1/5th Scottish Rifles, will attack THE HUMP from a position on the Right of the CROISILLES-HENDECOURT Road, and to form a defensive flank, from about U.14.c.1.3. to Cross Roads at U.14.c.2.9.

(b) 100 Inf.Bde. to attack from the South-West that portion of the HINDENBURG Line between the CROISILLES-HENDECOURT and CROISILLES- FONTAINE Roads.

(c) 98 Inf Bde. to attack South-East down the HINDENBURG Line from present blocks as far as the CROISILLES-FONTAINE Road.

5. The Div. will assemble for attack before daylight on May 17th, in accordance with G.S. Ins. D.7.
The 1/5th Scottish Rifles will be assembled as follows, by 3.30 a.m., 17th May :-

2 Coys in QUARRY at U.19.a.1.2.
2 Coys. along Road from T.24.d.9.5. to T.24.b.5.3.

2 Guns 19th T.M.Bty. will be assembled in QUARRY at U.19.a.1.2. by 3.30 a.m., 17th May. These guns will be prepared to move up to the new line at the request of O.C., 1/5th Scottish Rifles.
After 3.30 a.m. no movement of any sort is to take place in the open prior to the advance.

6. The advance of the 19 and 100 Inf.Bdes. covered by normal H.A. bombardment of HINDENBURG System will be timed to reach the HINDENBURG Front trench at ZERO, at which time, the artillery barrage programme given in G.S. Ins. D.3. will commence.

7. The advance of 98 Inf.Bde. will also commence at ZERO, at which hour the mine under the HINDENBURG Support Trench, will be fired, if sufficiently advanced.

8. Special measures are being taken by the R.F.C. to keep off hostile aeroplanes, and deal with enemy observation balloons between dawn and ZERO on May 17th.

9. Arrangements are also being made to attract the attention of enemy sentries for some minutes before ZERO by some of our aeroplanes performing various evolutions over FONTAINE.

10. In order to blind hostle Machine Guns, smoke barrages will be formed as follows, if the wind is suitable :-

(a) By Detachment, No.1 Special Coy. R.E. between the SENSEE and River Road in the vicinity of the HINDENBURG System for 5 mins after ZERO.

(b) By Field Artillery, along the Western side of FONTAINE for half an hour after ZERO.

11. The artillery supporting the attack of the 19 Inf.Bde. will consist of two F.A.Bdes. 7th Div.

12. Machine Guns will cooperate in the attack as ordered in G.S. Ins. D.4.

13. One Section, 222 F. Co R.E. will be at the disposal of the 1/5th Scottish Rifles.

14. The Divisional Reserve will consist of :-

The Cameronians and 2nd Royal Welsh Fusiliers 19th Inf Bde.

Div. Eng. less 5 Sections.

18 Middlesex Pioneers.

15. The objective when gained will be consolidated as laid down in G.S. Ins. D.8.

16. After ZERO plus 120 the S.O.S. Filed Artillery barrage will be on the line :-

The KNUCKLE - U.14.c.6.2. - U.14.d.1.4. - U.14.d.8½.9.-

Junction of CRUMB LANE and BULLECOURT - FONTAINE Road -

along latter to U.8.CENTRAL, thence to YORK TRENCH

at U.1.d.0.8.

17. Should the enemy's retirement be found in progress, the Bns. 19 Inf.Bde. in Divl. Reserve will be prepared to advance in the first instance to the general Line - Cross Roads at U.15.a.9.7. to FONTAINE Village.

The general line of The Cameronians will be from Cross Roads at U.15.a.9.7. to Trench Junction at U.9.b.2.4. inclusive.

2nd Royal Welsh Fusiliers from U.9.b.2.4. to U.2.b.2.2.

18. The advance of the 1/5th Scottish Rifles will be made at ZERO minus 13 and in accordance with instructions given verbally to C.O., 1/5th Scottish Rifles.
Each man will carry two sandbags and each man of the two supporting Coys. a pick or shovel.
The left of the advance will rest on the CROISILLES-HENDECOURT Road.

19. Contact aeroplanes will call for flares at ZERO plus one hour.

20. Blue and white signalling flags will be waved by Infantry on reaching objectives, but will not be stuck in the ground.

21. Prisoners will be taken over from Inf Bdes. at the Cross-Roads at T.22.c.4.5. and at HENIN CEMETERY (T.2.d.8.2.).

22. ~~Watches will be synchronized at 10.3 p.m. on May 16th.~~

23. The hour of ZERO will be notified later.

24. Wounded will be evacuated from the Regimental Aid Posts to the Advanced Dressing Station at ST. LEGER, U.28.a.4.0.

25. No maps, orders, or secret documents likely to be of use to the enemy will be taken forward by the attacking Bn.

26. The Cameronians on relief by the 100 Inf.Bde. will return to the bivouacs at present occupied by 1/5th Scottish Rifles in ST. LEGER.

27. An advanced Dump of S.A.A., Bombs, Trench Mortar Ammn. and R.E. material is being formed at U.13.c.9.4.

28. Div. H.Q. will remain at HAMELINCOURT.

Brigade H.Q. will remain at T.21.d.6.5.

29. ACKNOWLEDGE.

[signature]
Captain,
Brigade Major,
19th Infantry Brigade.

Issued at 4.30 pm.

Copies Nos. 1 - 10. Units of 19th Inf.Bde.
11. 101st F.A.
12. 98th Inf.Bde.
13. 100th Inf.Bde.
14. 186 Inf.Bde.
15. 222nd Co R.E.
16. 33rd Div. G.
16. 33rd Div. (Q).
17. 21 Div.Artly.
18. S.O. 19th Inf.Bde.
19. Signals.
20. Staff Captain.
21. Intelligence Officer.
22. Bombing Officer.
23. Office.
24. File.
25. War Diary.
26. 33 Div Artillery

SECRET. Appendix B Copy No.....26.....

19TH INFANTRY BRIGADE INSTRUCTIONS NO. 4.

With reference to Brigade Order No.241 of 20/5/17.

1. The 100th Infantry Brigade who carried out the attack this morning state that the tape marking the centre of the H.L.I. advance will be a useful guide for the right of the Cameronians to advance by; that marking the centre of the K.R.R.C. should mark the left of the Cameronians adva nce and ~~left~~ right of the 20th Royal Fusiliers.

2. On reaching the HINDENBURG support line posts should be pushed out a little way in front, thus making the support line the second line of defence.

3. On reaching the support line each battalion must ensure that the underground tunnel is blocked so as to prevent the escape of prisoners. Blocks will be immediately placed at each flank. The exits from the dug-outs must also picquetted.

4. One sect. 100th M.G.Coy will be in the QUARRY near Post 2.
   Each battalion can call on 2 guns to go up to the HINDENBURG Support Line after capture should they desire to utilise them.
   One Sect.19th M.G.Coy will proceed to the QUARRY after dark.

5. Two Stokes Mortars will be sent up to the QUARRY if time permits; each battalion can call on one gun after capture of the position.

6. One Sect. 11th Field Coy.R.E. will report to Officer Commanding 20th Royal Fusiliers at QUARRY at 7 pm. These will be divided to assist the Cameronians in forming three blocks (two above and one underground) and the 20th Royal Fusiliers, two blocks (one above and one underground). In the event of the Sect. not arriving in time, battalions will make their own arrangements for the blocking.

7. The 100th Inf.Bde who have carefully worked out the plan for this attack calculate that it should take each battalion 15 minutes to reach the line of the barrage from their positions of deployment.
   It should be noted that the barrage does not lift off the HINDENBURG Support trench until Zero + 10.

Issued at 5.15 pm.

20/5/17.

A Walker
Captain.
Brigade Major.
19th Infantry Brigade.

To all recipients of 19th Inf.Bde Order No.241.

Recd 6.45 pm

Appendix C

33 DIV.

OPERATIONS - 20 MAY 1917.

1. The plan of attack was as follows :-

98 Inf. Bde. to attack Southwards down the HINDENBURG system as far as the FONTAINE - CROISILLES Road.

100 Inf. Bde. to attack the HINDENBURG front and support lines between the FONTAINE - CROISILLES and HENDECOURT - CROISILLES Roads.

19 Inf. Bde. to attack the HUMP, and form a defensive flank on the right of the 100 Inf. Bde.

2. A bombardment of the HINDENBURG system with all natures of artillery had commenced on the 7 May, and was carried on day and night up till Zero. It was not increased in any way before Zero.

For the attack it was arranged that the H.A. should lift off the HINDENBURG front line South of the SENSEE River on to the support line at Zero - 5, and at Zero should lift on to a line about 1000 yards to the East.

The F.A. Barrage was to come down on the HINDENBURG support line South of the River at Zero, and was to commence to creep Eastwards at Zero plus 15.

3. Zero hour was 5.15 a.m. on 20 May.

4. The attack of the 19 Inf. Bde. was carried out by the 5 Sco. Rif., and the attack of the 100 Inf. Bde. by the 2 Worc. R., 9 H.L.I. and 16 K.R.R.C., in that order from right to left.

These Bns. assembled under cover of darkness on night 19/20 May. Their advance on the morning of the 20 May was timed so that they should reach the HINDENBURG front line at Zero.

It was foreseen that the left Bn. (16 K.R.R.C) of the 100 Inf. Bde., and part of the centre Bn. (9 H.L.I.) would come under view from the HINDENBURG line North of the River SENSEE, about RIVER ROAD. It was, therefore, arranged that this portion of the enemy line should be blinded by smoke; this was done by a Detachment of the Special Bde. R.E., firing smoke bombs from 4" Stokes Mortars.

The attack of the 98 Inf. Bde. was carried out by the 4 King's R. Their advance was to commence at Zero at which hour the mine under the enemy's block in the HINDENBURG support trench was to be fired.

5. The advance of the 100th and 19 Inf. Bdes. from their assembly positions commenced at Zero - 12 minutes.

The morning was very misty and attacking troops were not perceived until within a short distance of the HINDENBURG front line. This line was entered and captured without any difficulty.

The advance to the support line was continued almost immediately, and at 5.40 a.m. it was reported that the attacking Bns. of the 100 Inf. Bde. had captured the HINDENBURG support line, and were in touch with each other.

This report soon proved to be unfounded.

The HINDENBURG support line was very strongly held by large numbers of the enemy, with many machine guns, and there appears no doubt only elements of the 100 Inf. Bde. ever succeeded in reaching it.

P.T.O.

These elements were forced back by weight of numbers, and at 8 a.m. the 100 Inf. Bde. held the whole of the HINDENBURG front line between the HENDECOURT - CROISILLES and FONTAINE - CROISILLES Roads, with posts pushed out towards the HINDENBURG support line. They were in touch with the 19 Inf. Bde. on the right and with the 98 Inf.Bde. on the left.

6. The advance of the 4 King's, 98 Inf.Bde., commenced at Zero, at which time the mine under the HINDENBURG support line was successfully blown.

A charge of 300 lbs. Ammonal in rubber bags, and 100 lbs guncotton in wooden boxes, was used for the mine. This charge completely demolished the German block, making a crater about 40 feet in diameter and throwing a considerable amount of earth down the German side of the trench, and burying any garrison of the enemy block. After the attack a German electric listening instrument was captured from the vicinity of their block, showing that the enemy were guarding against underground attack.

The 4 King's made good progress down the HINDENBURG front line and reached the FONTAINE - CROISILLES Road, where they gained touch with the 100 Inf. Bde. at about 7 a.m.

In the HINDENBURG support line they were only able to advance to a point about 30 yards North of RIVER ROAD, where they were held up by machine guns.

7. When the situation of all attacking troops was definitely ascertained (about 10.30 a.m.) it was decided to hold and consolidate the ground gained and to prepare for a fresh advance in the evening to capture the HINDENBURG support line.

Orders for this attack were issued at 2 p.m; Zero hour was fixed for 7.30 p.m.

The 19 Inf. Bde. were to attack through the 100 Inf. Bde. and to capture the HINDENBURG support line between NELLY LANE and the FONTAINE - CROISILLES Road.

The 98 Inf.Bde. were to attack down the HINDENBURG support line and join up with the 19 Inf. Bde. on the FONTAINE - CROISILLES Road.

8. The attack of the 19 Inf. Bde. was carried out by the Cameronians and the 20 R.Fus. in that order from the right, and of the 98 Inf. Bde. by the 2 A. & S.H.

A mixed barrage of Howitzers and 18 Pdrs. was arranged for this attack, to come down at Zero on the HINDENBURG support trench between CRUMB LANE and the SENSEE River, and at Zero plus 10 to creep at 100 yards per 2 minutes to a line about 300 yards to the East.

At Zero - 15 the attacking Bns.of the 19 Inf. Bde. commenced to advance from their assembly positions in U.13.c.

They were unable to reach the HINDENBURG support line and took up a position in old shell holes and trenches about 150 yards West of it.

The 98 Inf.Bde. advanced successfully to a point in the HINDENBURG Support line about 100 yards North of the SENSEE River.

9. Further advance was found to be impossible owing to the strength of the enemy opposition, and the night was spent in reorganizing the fighting troops and in carrying up supplies of water and ammunition.

(3)

10. On the morning of the 21 May the 2 A. & S.H. discovered that a number of wounded Germans were in the tunnel between RIVER ROAD and the SENSEE River: these were rounded up and brought in during the night 21/22 May.

11. The total number of prisoners taken in the operations described above amount to 220.

B. L. Montgomery.

22/5/17.

Captain, G.S.,
33rd Division.

Distribution :-

	Copies	
Div. H.Q.	12	
149 Inf.Bde.	5	
Inf. Bdes.	25	each
Div. Arts.	75	
33 Div.Eng.	4	
Pioneers	5	
Train	5	
Div.Gas Offr.	I	
Depot Bn.	5	
14, 18, 21, 50 & 62 Divs.	1	each.

========

Aeroplane Reconnaissance.

3·30 pm. May 23 1917.

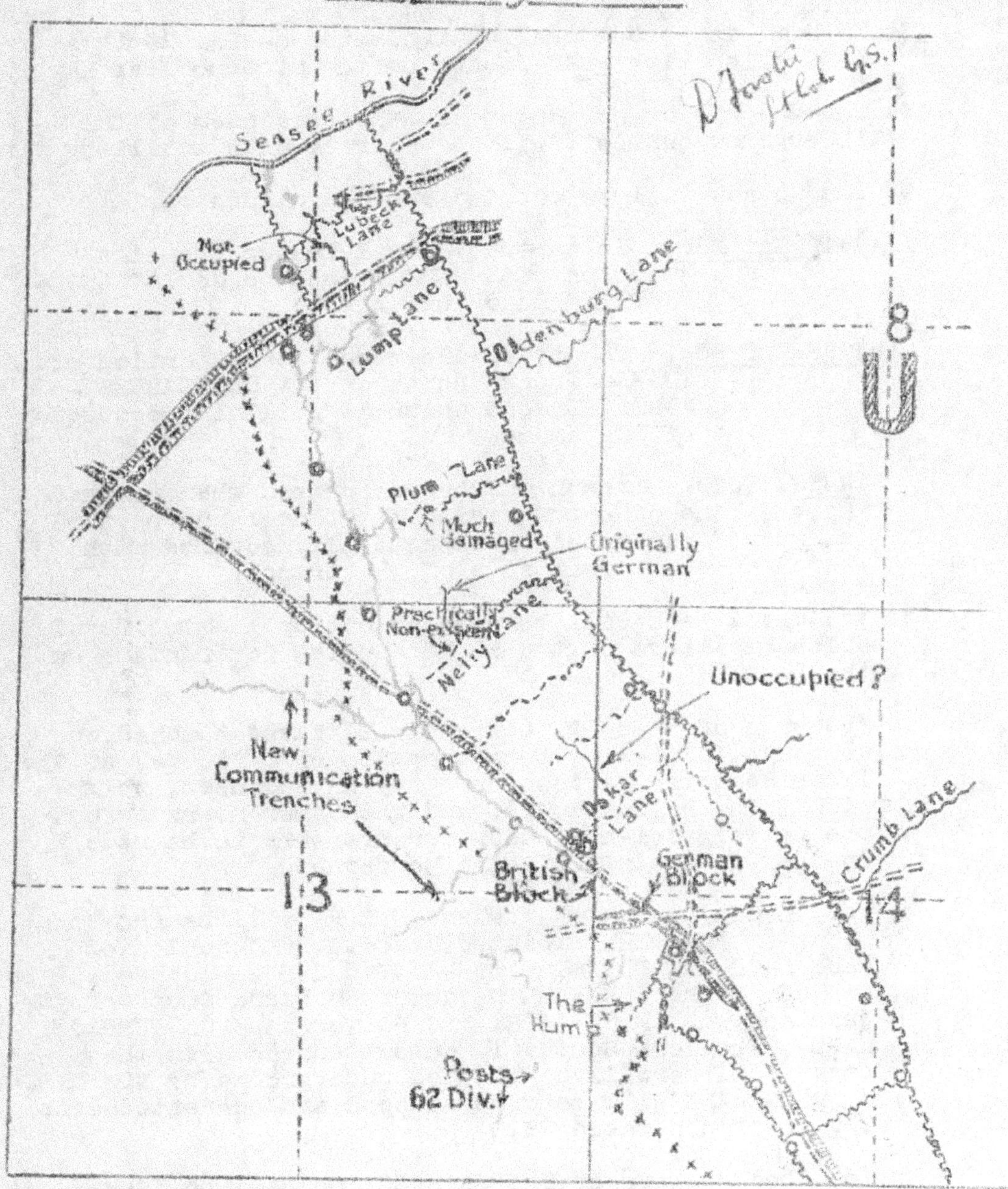

Ref: 7 Corps Map 'Fontaine-lez-Croisilles' 1/10,000.

Appendix D.

SECRET. Copy No....8

19th Infantry Brigade - ORDER No.246.

Ref Map Sheet
51 B S.W., 1/20,000.

26th May 1917.

1. The German 49th Res Div. which suffered severely in our attack on May 20th appears to have been relieved, partially at any rate, by the 220 Div. The 55th Regt. of the latter Div. is believed to be in our immediate front.

2. 33 Div. is to capture TUNNEL Trench as far South as its junction with PLUM Trench on the afternoon of May 27th.

3. The V Corps on our Right and the remainder of the VII Corps on our left will co-operate with artillery fire.

4. The attack will be carried out as follows :-

(a) 19 Inf Bde. To capture Tunnel Trench from its junction with PLUM Trench to CROISILLES - FONTAINE Road inclusive.

(b) 98 Inf Bde. To attack and secure that portion of TUNNEL Trench North of the CROISILLES - FONTAINE Road which is still in possession of the enemy.

NOTE. TUNNEL Trench can be recognised when reached by the line of entrances to the tunnel and by the mounds of excavated chalk partially covered with earth on the German side of the trench.

5. (a) The attack will be carried out by the 2nd Royal Welsh Fusiliers on the Right and The Cameronians on the Left.

(b) Each of these Battalions will have attached one Company (100 O.R. with proportion of Officers) of the 1/5th Scottish Rifles for carrying purposes, which will join the 2nd R.W.F. and The Cameronians before the relief tonight, under arrangements to be made by the Commanding Officers concerned.

(c) The objective of the 2nd R.W.F. will be from the block in PLUM LANE about U.7.d.4.4. - junction of PLUM LANE and TUNNEL Line - U.7.d.6.8 . Blocks will be formed in the TUNNEL Line about 60 yards South of its junction with PLUM LANE, and 60 yards up OLDENBURG LANE. The most Southerly dugout entrance in the captured line will be blocked underground by the R.E.
PLUM LANE will be fire-stepped and converted into a fire trench facing S.E.

(d) Theobjective of The Cameronians will be from U.7.d.6.8 to the FONTAINE Road with a block on the FONTAINE Road, and the underground Tunnel blocked by the R.E.

(e) All other dug-out entrances must be at once picquetted.

6. (a) Three sappers 11th Field Coy.R.E. will be at the disposal of 2nd R.W.F. and three sappers 11th Field Coy.R.E. at the disposal of the Cameronians, for purposes of forming blocks in the tunnel itself, on the right and left flanks of the objective.

(b) The objective being obtained, one section 11th Field Coy. R.E. will make a bomb block in the TUNNEL Line about 60 yards South of its junction with PLUM LANE, and one section of 222 Field Coy.R.E. will make a bomb block 60 yards up OLDENBURG LANE.

7. Instructions regarding attack formations have been issued separately to units concerned.

8. Machine Gun barrages will be formed as laid down in 19th Inf. Bde Instructions A.3.
In addition, four guns will be placed in the BURG LINE tonight, two under 2nd R.W.F. and 2 under The Cameronians.
These guns can be moved forward to the TUNNEL LINE if desirable.
A Mobile section will be in position in Square U.19.C.by 3.30 am 27th May. This section will not move without orders from the Brigade.

9. Two guns of the 19th T.M.Bty will move up to the BURG LINE tonight under orders of 2nd R.W.F, and one gun under orders of The Cameronians.
These guns will be employed to cover the blocks mentioned in para.5 (C. &. D) and to assist the initial advance up PLUM LANE.
One gun will be in Brigade Reserve at U.19.C. and will be in position not later than 3.30 am, 27th May.

10. As soon as the TUNNEL Trench has been secured as far as PLUM LANE and the TUNNEL in that portion "mopped up", the 2nd R.W.F. will continue the advance along TUNNEL Trench Southwards in conjunction with a bombing attack up NELLY LANE by the Left Company of the 9th H.L.I.

11. From Zero onwards, all Companies of the 9th H.L.I. and the Company of the 20th F.F. under the orders of the 9th H.L.I., will keep a good look-out for targets for Lewis gun and rifle fire. These may present themselves in the form of small parties of the enemy moving over the open, either retiring or advancing to reinforce.

12. From Zero onwards all Companies of the 9th H.L.I. and the Company of the 20th R.F. attached to 9th H.L.I. will endeavour to send out patrols to ascertain the situation in their immediate front. Should the TUNNEL Line be found evacuated or very lightly held, these Companies are to push forward to the line U.14.C.3.8 - U.14.A.3.7 - U.7.D.9.1, which should be consolidated. No further advance is to be made beyond this line withoutborders from the Brigade, except small patrols pushed out in front.

13. If the wind is suitable a smoke barrage will be formed from Zero to Zero plus 30 on the West side of FONTAINE and ROTTEN ROW as far North as YORK TRENCH.

14. When the original objective has been captured posts will be pushed out at least 100 yards in front of TUNNEL Trench which will then be held as a Support Line.

15. The artillery barrage as published in 19th Inf.Bde Instr.No.6 will fall at Zero and be the Signal for the Infantry to advance.

16. 100th Inf.Bde (less one battalion) and 149th Inf.Bde will be in Div.Reserve. One battalion of the former will be in the vicinity of CROISILLES by daylight on May 27th.

17. After Zero plus 30 the S.O.S.Barrage will be on the line, TUNNEL Trench from U.14.D.1.4 to U.14.A.3.6, to U.8.C.4.3, thence parallel to TUNNEL Trench as far as the SENSEE RIVER, along it to LEMON BRIDGE and thence along ROTTEN ROW to YORK TRENCH.

18. One battalion 100th Inf.Bde will be in position between CROISILLES and the HINDENBURG System by Zero plus 1½ hours ready to act if a German counter attack should meet with any success.

19. Flares will be lit at Zero plus 1 hour and when called for by the contact aeroplane.

20. Blue and white signalling flags will be waved by Infantry on reaching objectives, but will not be stuck in the ground.

21. Visual and liaison as in 19th Inf.Bde instructions No.4.

22. A Company of Pioneers will report at Brigade H.Q. at 9 pm. 27th instant, for work in opening up Communication trenches in LUMP LANE and PLUM LANE.

23. Watches will be synchronised at 8.37 am. and 12.23 pm, 27th May, by the same method as adopted for the attack on the 20th May.

24. Zero hour will be notified later. Zero hour 1.55 pm

25. Prisoners will be sent to Brigade H.Q. at T.22.B.8.0, thence to Prisoners cage at T.22.C.4.5.

26. Div.H.Q. will remain at HAMELINCOURT.
Brigade H.Q. will remain at T.22.B.8.0.

27. ACKNOWLEDGE.

A Walker
Captain.
Brigade Major.
19th Infantry Brigade.

Issued at

Copies Nos.1 to 8. Units 19th Inf.Bde.
9. 9th H.L.I.
10. 222nd Coy.R.E.
11. 101st Field Amb.
12. 149 Inf.Bde.
13. 187 Inf.Bde.
14. 98 Inf.Bde.
15. 100 Inf.Bde.
16. 33rd Div. "G"
17. do "Q"
18. Div.Artillery.
19.
20. 95th F.A.Bde.
21. Staff Captain.
22. Signals.
23. Intelligence Off.
24. Bombing Off.
25. Office.
26. File.
27. War Diary.

Instructions regarding War Diaries and Intelligence Summaries are contained in F. S. Regs., Part II. and the Staff Manual respectively. Title pages will be prepared in manuscript.

WAR DIARY
or
INTELLIGENCE SUMMARY.
(Erase heading not required.)

Army Form C. 2118.

Vol 30

Place	Date	Hour	Summary of Events and Information	Remarks and references to Appendices
			CONFIDENTIAL WAR DIARY of 11th (FIELD) Co. R.E. from June 1st 1917 to June 30th 1917. (VOLUME —)	

A5834 Wt. W4973/M687 750,000 8/16 D. D. & L. Ltd. Forms/C.2118/13.

Army Form C. 2118.

Instructions regarding War Diaries and Intelligence Summaries are contained in F. S. Regs., Part II. and the Staff Manual respectively. Title pages will be prepared in manuscript.

WAR DIARY
or
INTELLIGENCE SUMMARY.
(Erase heading not required.)

Place	Date	Hour	Summary of Events and Information	Remarks and references to Appendices
BAILLEULMONT	1/6/17		Kit inspection etc. cleaning up generally	
	2/6/17		Cleaning and washing up wagons.	
	3/6/17		Sunday no work. Church parade in morning	
	4/6/17		1 Section worked at LA CAUCHIE in erection VII Corps huts under direction of A.T. Co R.E. Company employed in putting up water troughs at BASSEUX, BAILLEULVAL + BAILLEULMONT Major H.A.G. PRESSEY went on leave	
	5/6/17		No 1 Sec erecting huts at LA CAUCHIE No 2 Sec employed salving R.E. material in neighbourhood of BAILLEULMONT. No 3 Sec employed in improvements to billets No 4 Sec completed erecting water point at BASSEUX	
	6/6/17		No 1 Sec LA CAUCHIE as before. No 2 Sec were making portable experimental wire entanglements and erecting a stage for a boxing tournament No 4 Sec were employed in making sample meat safes canvas targets + round billets	
	7/6/17		No 1 Sec as before. Nos 2 + 3 Secs proceeded to MOYENNEVILLE for work under C.R.E. 21st Div No 4 Sec were employed in making corrugated iron water troughs and sample meat safes	

A5834 Wt. W4973 M687 750,000 8/16 D. D. & L. Ltd. Forms/C.2118/13.

Instructions regarding War Diaries and Intelligence Summaries are contained in F. S. Regs., Part II. and the Staff Manual respectively. Title pages will be prepared in manuscript.

WAR DIARY
or
INTELLIGENCE SUMMARY.
(Erase heading not required.)

Army Form C. 2118.

Place	Date	Hour	Summary of Events and Information	Remarks and references to Appendices
BAILLEULMONT	8		No 1 Sec as before ditto No 4 Sec.	
			Nos 2 & 3 at MOYENNEVILLE Erecting an emergency Batt HQ for Divn	
	9		No 1 Sec as before	
			No 4 Sec Erected 3 C.I. water troughs in place of Canvas ones at BAILLEULVAL and went on with construction of more	
			Nos 2 & 3 as before	
	10		No work	
	11		No 1 Sec as before	
			Nos 2 & 3 Secs under Lt Garrod returned on completion of their work	
			No 4 Section on construction and erection of C.I. troughs	
			Water points completed at BELLACOURT BASSEUX BAILLEULVAL	
	12		No 1 Sec. as before	
			Nos 2 & 3 Secs infantry training	
			No 4 Sec employed in work round billets	
			In addition waggons were painted and instruction given in use of Lewis Guns by 4 men of 2 RWF	
	13		do do	

A5834 Wt. W4973 M687 750,000 8/16 D. D. & L. Ltd. Forms/C.2118/13.

Army Form C. 2118.

Instructions regarding War Diaries and Intelligence Summaries are contained in F. S. Regs., Part II. and the Staff Manual respectively. Title pages will be prepared in manuscript.

WAR DIARY
or
INTELLIGENCE SUMMARY.
(Erase heading not required.)

Place	Date	Hour	Summary of Events and Information	Remarks and references to Appendices
BAILLEULMONT	14.		Nos 2 & 3 Sections supplied 25 men for the work at LA CAUCHIE	
			Remainder 33 men innoculated. Instruction in loading & firing Lewis Gun & German M.G. Painting wagons.	
	15		Nos 2 & 3 as before	
			Remainder of company as before 33 men excused duty owing to innoculation	
			Painting wagons & Construction of sample portable meat safes.	
	16.		No work except on meat safes. Maj PRESSEY returned from leave.	
	17		No 2 Sec at LA CAUCHIE.	
			Nos 1 & 3 Secs Infantry drill etc.	
			No 4 Sec on meat safes Painting wagons etc.	
	18.		do do Capt BALCOMBE went on leave.	
			OC Co & "Lt" Garrod went up to BOIRY BECQUERELLE to take over from 126 Fd Co REs	
	19		No 2 Sec at LA CAUCHIE Remainder of company packing & Cleaning up.	
	20.		Company marched to Billets S.E. of BOIRY BECQUERELLE took over left Brigade sector of Divn front on relief of 21st Divn by 33rd Divn.	

A5834 Wt. W4973 M687 750,000 8/16 D. D. & L. Ltd. Forms/C.2118/13.

Instructions regarding War Diaries and Intelligence Summaries are contained in F. S. Regs., Part II. and the Staff Manual respectively. Title pages will be prepared in manuscript.

WAR DIARY
or
INTELLIGENCE SUMMARY.
(Erase heading not required.)

Army Form C. 2118.

Place	Date	Hour	Summary of Events and Information	Remarks and references to Appendices
BOIRY-BECQUERELLE	21		No 1 Sec took over and carried on with construction of 2 men shelters in HIND TR also construction of shelters for bombs.	Ref map Sheet 51c S.W.
			No 2 Sec ~~took~~ added to accommodation at Co Hq to house infantry who were to be attached to the Company during time of duty in the line.	
			No 3 Sec Undertook the repair + clearing up of the tunnel and entrances in SHAFT TR U.1.c	
	~~22~~		Today 4 officers and 100 infantry from 1st Middlesex 2nd A.&S.H 4th Kings + 4th Suffolk ~~[illegible]~~ arrived for attachment and work in the line.	
	22		Nos 1 + 2 Secs as before. No 1 Sec in addition took on superintending of construction of post C.11. (T 4 b 9.8) with infantry garrison.	
			No 4 Section ~~[illegible]~~ made good a track along RIVER ROAD from T 16 b to U 7 a making ramps + laying down bridges for mule traffic.	
			No 3 Sec as before in addition with 6 platoons (about 70 men) 4th Kings continued digging out KARL LANE.	
	24		attached infantry 2nd A&S.H working with No 3 Sec.	
			4th Kings working with No 2 Sec.	
			1st Middlesex + 4th Suffolks were digging out a siding off HIND TR for a forward R.E. battle dump.	

A5834 Wt. W4973 M687 750,000 8/16 D. D. & L. Ltd. Forms/C.2118/13.

Instructions regarding War Diaries and Intelligence Summaries are contained in F. S. Regs., Part II. and the Staff Manual respectively. Title pages will be prepared in manuscript.

WAR DIARY
or
INTELLIGENCE SUMMARY.
(*Erase heading not required.*)

Army Form C. 2118.

Place	Date	Hour	Summary of Events and Information	Remarks and references to Appendices
Boiry Becquerelle	23		Nos 1 + 3 Secs + 2 A+S.H as before No 2 Sec Commenced work in wiring the reserve line and putting shelters in post C.6 No 4 Sec commenced billets for the Company closer to the line 4th Kings helping them. 1st Mx + 4th Suffolks as before no work night work not possible owing to an attack on our right.	
	24.		Nos 1+2, 3 + 4 Secs as before also 2 A+S.H. and 4th Kings 1st Mx + 4th Suffolks continued in their work ~~completed the digging~~ No other night work owing to operations However in this sector night was quiet.	
	25		As before. 1st Mx + 4th Suffolks ~~[illegible]~~ completed digging the ~~[illegible]~~ dump.	
	26.		do — do Karl Trench continued. 6 Platoons 1st Mx + 4th Suffolks Continued carrying stores to the dump	
	27.		As before no work in Karl trench possible owing to shell fire	
	28		as before KARL TR abandoned I.C. 97th F^d Co R.E. came up and shewn round so as to take over.	

A5834 Wt. W4973 M687 750,000 8/16 D. D. & L. Ltd. Forms/C.2118/13.

Instructions regarding War Diaries and Intelligence Summaries are contained in F. S. Regs., Part II. and the Staff Manual respectively. Title pages will be prepared in manuscript.

WAR DIARY
or
INTELLIGENCE SUMMARY.
(Erase heading not required.)

Army Form C. 2118.

Place	Date	Hour	Summary of Events and Information	Remarks and references to Appendices
	29		No 1 Section as before. 17 bomb shelters completed & 8 shelters for men completed in the 10 days work. C. 11 post 19 completed.	
			No 2 Sec. another 120x of wire of the reserve line were wired with help of 12 men of 4th Suffolks.	
			No 3 Sec. Continued with tunnel, also 25 men 2nd A & S.H. Job 15 completed.	
			No 4 Sec. Went on with advanced Co Billets accomodation provided for 100 men. 4th Suffolks 12 men & 24 men of 1st Middlesex carried on with stocking advanced battle dump.	[initials]
	30.		Co with attached Infantry moved to MONCHY-AUX-BOIS	[initials]

A5834 Wt. W4973 M687 750,000 8/16 D. D. & L. Ltd. Forms/C.2118/13.

Instructions regarding War Diaries and Intelligence Summaries are contained in F. S. Regs., Part II. and the Staff Manual respectively. Title pages will be prepared in manuscript.

WAR DIARY
or
INTELLIGENCE SUMMARY.

(Erase heading not required.)

Army Form C. 2118.

Vol 31

Place	Date	Hour	Summary of Events and Information	Remarks and references to Appendices

– CONFIDENTIAL –

WAR DIARY

OF

11th Field Co. R.E.

from 1-7-17 (VOLUME) to 31-7-17

A L Balcombe Captain R.E.
for O.C. 11th Field Co. R.E.

A5834 Wt. W4973/M687 750,000 8/16 D. D. & L. Ltd. Forms/C.2118/13.

Instructions regarding War Diaries and Intelligence Summaries are contained in F. S. Regs., Part II. and the Staff Manual respectively. Title pages will be prepared in manuscript.

WAR DIARY
or
INTELLIGENCE SUMMARY.
(Erase heading not required.)

Army Form C. 2118.

Place	Date	Hour	Summary of Events and Information	Remarks and references to Appendices
MONCHY	1/7/17		Company rested	
ACHEUX	2/7/17		marched to ACHEUX no Casualties	
NAOURS	3/7/17		marched to NAOURS very hot dusty 15 miles - Casualties 5 men fell out	
LACHAUSSÉE	4/7/17		marched to LA CHAUSSÉE no Casualties	
CONDÉ-FOLIE	5/7/17		marched to CONDÉ-FOLIE no Casualties	
do	5 & 7th		inspection of equipment etc. Company rested.	
	8 & 9th		Company drill etc.	
	9th 31st		Company trained in line of attached training programme	appendix I

[illegible]

A5834 Wt. W4973/M687 750,000 8/16 D. D. & L. Ltd. Forms/C.2118/13.

Training Programme of 11th (Field) Co. R.E.
from July 16th 1917 to July 21st 1917

Date	Unit	Discription of Training	Area.	Remarks.
July 16th	11th Field Co R.E.	Company Training Pontooning	Folie	
July 17th.	— ditto —	Section Training	do.	Horse Show.
July 18th	— ditto. —	— ditto — ditto —	do	
July 19th	— ditto —	Company Training Pontooning	do	
July 20th	— ditto. —	— ditto —	do	Drill Exercises.
July 21st.	— ditto —	— ditto. —	do.	

for Capt

Training Programme of 11th (Field) Co R.E.
from July 9th to July 14th 1917.

Appendix I

Date	Unit	Description of Training	Area	Remarks
July 9th 1917	11th Field Co R.E.	Section Training, Infantry Drill	Folie.	Lack of any accommodation for Company Drill or Rigging work.
July 10th 1917	— ditto —	— do — do —	Folie	
July 11th 1917	— ditto —	Route March, Section Training	Folie	
July 12th 1917	— ditto —	Mapreading, Engineer Reconnaissance.	— do —	
July 13th 1917	— ditto —	Section Training		[illegible]
July 14th 1917	— ditto —	Section Training		

Major R.E.
O.C. 11th (Field) Co R.E.

HINDENBURG LINE AND SENSEE VALLEY.
SCALE: 1/10,000.
Enemy Front Line
Divisional Boundary
Cat Trench
Fontaine les Croisilles
33 Div

11th (Field) Co. R.E.

MARCHING - IN - STATE.

PERSONNEL.

OFFICERS. 7

OTHER RANKS. 210

HORSES & MULES 76

VEHICLES. —

FOUR-WHEELED (including Limbers) 14

TWO-WHEELED 2

Capt, R.E.
for. Commdg. 11th Coy. R.E

11
~~212~~ } Field Coy RE.
~~222~~

Reference 33rd Division No S.G 578 of 19th inst forwarded under this Office No 4315.

Herewith copy of the special print referred to in para 2.

The following amendments will be made in third line of para. 4 of the above:–

Delete U.2.d and U.2.d.5.8 and substitute U.2.c and U.2.c.5.8.

J E Anderson
Lieut. RE.
Adjt. RE. 33rd Div.

Instructions regarding War Diaries and Intelligence Summaries are contained in F. S. Regs., Part II. and the Staff Manual respectively. Title pages will be prepared in manuscript.

WAR DIARY
or
INTELLIGENCE SUMMARY.
(Erase heading not required.)

Army Form C. 2118.

Vol 32

Place	Date	Hour	Summary of Events and Information	Remarks and references to Appendices
			CONFIDENTIAL.	
			WAR DIARY	
			OF	
			11th (Field) Company R.E.	
			(VOLUME.)	
			From 1st ~~Apr~~ Aug. 1917. To 31st. August. 1917.	

A5834 Wt. W4973/M687 750,000 8/16 D. D. & L. Ltd. Forms/C.2118/13.

Army Form C. 2118.

Instructions regarding War Diaries and Intelligence Summaries are contained in F. S. Regs., Part II. and the Staff Manual respectively. Title pages will be prepared in manuscript.

WAR DIARY
or
INTELLIGENCE SUMMARY.

(Erase heading not required.)

Place	Date	Hour	Summary of Events and Information	Remarks and references to Appendices
CONDÉ-FOLIE	1/8/17		Company entrained for DUNKERQUE	
BRAY-DUNES	2/8/17		Company arrived at BRAY-DUNES.	
	3/8/17 to 15/8/17		Company at BRAY DUNES 2 rifle ranges built and remainder of time spent in training mostly musketry as special facilities for firing existed. Whole put through a short course in Lewis gun.	
	16/8/17		Marched to AUSTRALIA-CAMP near COXYDE. joined by 100 inf & 4 officers 169th Bde. attached inf.	
	17/8/17		Nos 1 & 3 section worked on "Gas works track" & "artillery track" with 100 inf all leading into NIEUPORT. Nos 2 & 4 section worked in narrow ("yellow") line just west of NIEUPORT.	
	18/8/17		do do ~~[illegible]~~	
	19/8/17		do do Nos 2 & 4 sections had help of 400 inf	

A5834 Wt. W4973/M687 750,000 8/16 D. D. & L. Ltd. Forms/C.2118/13.

Instructions regarding War Diaries and Intelligence Summaries are contained in F. S. Regs., Part II. and the Staff Manual respectively. Title pages will be prepared in manuscript.

WAR DIARY
or
INTELLIGENCE SUMMARY.
(Erase heading not required.)

Army Form C. 2118.

Place	Date	Hour	Summary of Events and Information	Remarks and references to Appendices
NIEUPORT	20/8/17		No 4 Section worked with 4th inf in "yellow line"	
			Whole company moved into NIEUPORT relieving work of 57th Co RE taking	
			over billets from 456 field CoRE	[illegible]
	21/8/17		Company worked in LOMBARTZYDE area	
			No 1 Sect with attached infantry (cleaning + revetting) NASAL WALK	
			No 2 ——————— NOSE ALLEY	
			No 3 ——————— NOSE AVENUE	[illegible]
			No 3 ——————— NASAL LANE	
			No 4	
			1 O.R. wounded.	[illegible]
	22/8/17		do ——— do	
	23/8/17		do do 3 O.R. RE wounded & 2 O.R. att inf (gas) [illegible]	

A5834 Wt. W4973/M687 750,000 8/16 D. D. & L. Ltd. Forms/C.2118/13.

Army Form C. 2118.

Instructions regarding War Diaries and Intelligence Summaries are contained in F. S. Regs., Part II. and the Staff Manual respectively. Title pages will be prepared in manuscript.

WAR DIARY
or
INTELLIGENCE SUMMARY.
(Erase heading not required.)

Place	Date	Hour	Summary of Events and Information	Remarks and references to Appendices
NIEUPORT.	24/8/17		[illegible] No work done owing to impending attack on German GELEIDE POST	8
	25/8/17		Nos 1, 3 & 4 sections as before and attached inf of no 2 section & other sections. No 2 Section with 104 attached infantry started work on a dam across Evacuation Canal into YSER just below bridge 66 to keep water out of this canal. All work was very much interrupted by shell fire. The enemy making a counter attack to recapture post which they had lost the night before.	
	26/8/17		No work owing to our offensive Gas operations.	
	27/8/17		Nos 1, 2, 3 & 4 sections as before. Dams made by No 2 Section now above low water level.	
	28/8/17		Company relieved by 206 Fd Co RE. Marched to COXYDE.	

A5834 Wt. W4973/M687 750,000 8/16 D. D. & L. Ltd. Forms/C.2118/13.

Instructions regarding War Diaries and Intelligence Summaries are contained in F. S. Regs., Part II. and the Staff Manual respectively. Title pages will be prepared in manuscript.

WAR DIARY
or
INTELLIGENCE SUMMARY.
(Erase heading not required.)

Army Form C. 2118.

Place	Date	Hour	Summary of Events and Information	Remarks and references to Appendices
COXYDE	29/8/17		Company moved by barge to Pt SYTHE. Transport by road.	
Pt SYNTHE	30/8/17		Company rested.	
	31/8/17		Company marched to TETEGHEM	
			[illegible] Maj RE. O.C. [illegible]	

A5834 Wt. W4973/M687 750,000 8/16 D. D. & L. Ltd. Forms/C.2118/13.

Instructions regarding War Diaries and Intelligence Summaries are contained in F. S. Regs., Part II. and the Staff Manual respectively. Title pages will be prepared in manuscript.

WAR DIARY
or
INTELLIGENCE SUMMARY.
(Erase heading not required.)

Army Form C. 2118.

Vol 33

Place	Date	Hour	Summary of Events and Information	Remarks and references to Appendices
			CONFIDENTIAL WAR DIARY OF 11TH (FIELD) COMPANY R.E. (VOL.) SEPTEMBER 1917.	

C. L. Balcombe, R.E.
Commdg. 11th Coy. R.E

A5834 Wt. W4973/M687 750,000 8/16 D. D. & L. Forms

Instructions regarding War Diaries and Intelligence Summaries are contained in F. S. Regs., Part II. and the Staff Manual respectively. Title pages will be prepared in manuscript.

WAR DIARY
or
~~INTELLIGENCE SUMMARY.~~

(Erase heading not required.)

Army Form C. 2118.

Place	Date	Hour	Summary of Events and Information	Remarks and references to Appendices
~~TETEGHEM~~	1.9.17		The Coy. remained at TETEGHEM	C.M.B.
	2.9.17		Dismounted portion of Coy. remained at TETEGHEM. Mounted portion moved off under 2 Lt. GARROD to PROVEN Area.	C.M.B.
	3.9.17		Dismounted portion of Coy moved by bus to a camp at RIDGEWOOD, by X roads 1 km. N of Groote VIERSTRAAT. Mounted portion marched via POPERINGHE & LA CLYTTE joining up with the Coy in the evening. The Mounted portion moved back to horse lines 1/4 mile S of Swan & Edgar's Corner.	C.M.B.
	4.9.17		The Coy rested & dug shelters & generally improved the camp accomodation	C.M.B.
	5.9.17		Nos 1 & 2 Sects erecting Nissen Huts in RIDGEWOOD. Nos 3 & 4 Sect dug shelters for the Coy. this being found necessary on a/c of bombing by aeroplanes at night.	C.M.B.
	6.9.17		Nos 1 & 2 Sects erecting Nissen Huts in RIDGEWOOD Nos 3 & 4 " completed work on camp	C.M.B.
	7.9.17		The Coy commenced work with our Div. Arty. No 1 Sect: was employed at MANOR FARM (Group H.Q) strengthening etc. No 2 " " " by 156 Bde. R.F.A. & was apportioned out to Batteries – digging gun positions & making command posts	C.M.B.

A5834 Wt. W4973/M687 750,000 8/16 D. D. & L. Ltd. Forms/C.2118/13.

Army Form C. 2118.

Instructions regarding War Diaries and Intelligence Summaries are contained in F. S. Regs., Part II. and the Staff Manual respectively. Title pages will be prepared in manuscript.

WAR DIARY
or
INTELLIGENCE SUMMARY.
(Erase heading not required.)

Place	Date	Hour	Summary of Events and Information	Remarks and references to Appendices
			continued.	
	7.9.17		No 3 Sect. Making a mule track to Batteries for carriage of ammunition & on making ammunition racks.	
			No 4 Sect. being attached to 162 Bde R.F.A. for work on gun positions, command posts etc.	CRB
	8.9.17		Work continued as on previous Day	CRB
	9.9.17		do do	
	10.9.17		do do Mule track completed.	
	11.9.17		do do. Casualties 1 O.R. wounded. "At Duty"	
	12.9.17		do do. No 3 Sect: making light bridges for Guns. Casualties 1 O.R. wounded "At Duty"	
	13.9.17		do do 2/Lt. ROBERTS wounded "at Duty" 1 O.R. wounded	
	14.9.17		do do 2/Lt RICHARDS wounded.	
	15.9.17		do do	
	16.9.17		do do	
	17.9.17		do do	CRB
	18.9.17		The Coy marched to BOESCHEPE Area. 1 N.C.O. & 8 sappers being left behind to assist 156 Bde: R.F.A. 1 O.R. accidentally killed.	
	19.9.17		The whole Coy was employed in erecting Nissen Huts on the Mont des CATS	
	20.9.17		" " " do do	
	21.9.17		do do.	

A5834 Wt. W4973/M687 750,000 8/16 D. D. & L. Ltd. Forms/C.2118/13.

Instructions regarding War Diaries and Intelligence Summaries are contained in F. S. Regs., Part II. and the Staff Manual respectively. Title pages will be prepared in manuscript.

WAR DIARY

or

INTELLIGENCE SUMMARY.

(Erase heading not required.)

Army Form C. 2118.

Place	Date	Hour	Summary of Events and Information	Remarks and references to Appendices
	22.9.17.		The Coy was still at BOESCHEPE	CPLB
	23.9.17		Major H.A.S. PRESSEY & Capt BALCOMBE went to billets of 101st Field Coy R.E. (23rd Div) at LAKESIDE CAMP DICKEBUSCH to take over work etc. Nos 1 & 3 Sects. marched off from BOESCHEPE and took over forward Billets of 101 Coy. in dug outs in Rly. Embankments at SHRAPNEL CORNER	CPLB
	24.9.17		Nos 2 & 4 Sects & transport marched off from BOESCHEPE & took over Camp at DICKEBUSCH four off. & 100 O.R. of 98th Bdy. joined the Coy. 2 off. & 50 men with 1 & 3 Sect in forward Billets & 2 off. & 50 men at H.Q. with 2 & 4 Sects.	CPLB
	25.9.17		The Coy standing by for orders. The attached inf. started a forward dump near FITZCLARENCE FARM. Casualties 2 O.R. wounded. 1 attached inf.	CPLB
	26.9.17		At 3. am. Nos 1 & 3 Sects & 100 attached inf. moved forward to a position in SANCTUARY WOOD near 98th (Inf.) Bdy. H.Q. & Nos. 2 & 4. Sects moved up from Coy H.Q. to Rly. dugouts. The Division attacked at 5.40 am. The two forward Sects (Nos 1 & 3) tried to go out & make a strong point in the neighbourhood of CAMERON HOUSE at about 4 & pm This was found to be impossible. The 2 Sects then returned to SANCTUARY WOOD & spent the night there. Nos 2 & 4 Sects. remained in Rly. dug outs. Casualties Lt. HUME M.C. 4th SUFFOLK Regt (attached inf.) was wounded & 2 O.R killed & 3 O.R. wounded. Sapper Casualties 3 O.R. wounded.	See Appendix A CPLB

A5834 Wt. W4973 M687 750,000 8/16 D. D. & L. Ltd. Forms/C.2118/13.

Instructions regarding War Diaries and Intelligence Summaries are contained in F. S. Regs., Part II. and the Staff Manual respectively. Title pages will be prepared in manuscript.

WAR DIARY
or
INTELLIGENCE SUMMARY.

(*Erase heading not required.*)

Army Form C. 2118.

Place	Date	Hour	Summary of Events and Information	Remarks and references to Appendices
	27.9.17		Nos 1 & 3 Sects still in SANCTUARY WOOD & Nos 2 & 4 in Rly. Dugouts. No work was done until the afternoon when 2/Lt ROBERTS & 2/Lt FORBES taped out a trench to run from CLAPHAM JUNCTION – & then to BLACK WATCH CORNER nr. VERBEEKE FARM. No work was found possible owing to shell fire, & whilst Major H.A.S. PRESSEY M.C. & 2/Lt ROBERTS & FORBES were talking over the situation outside Bde. H.Q. a shell burst just above wounding Major H.A.S. PRESSEY M.C. & 2/Lt ROBERTS & 2/Lt FORBE was killed. The shelling continued to increase & Nos 1 & 3 Sects were sent back to Coy. H.Q. The Div. Inf. were relieved by 23rd Div.	CHLB
	28.9.17		Nos 2 & 4 Sect & 1 Coy Pioneers & 200 infantry commenced work on the C.T. taped out on the previous day. The trench was carried through up to just N of FITZCLARENCE FARM. Casualties 3 O.R. (including Sgt WARWICK) wounded 2 at duty & 3 attached inf. Nos 1 & 3 Sects rested. (attached inf. from 68th Bde)	CHLB
	29.9.17		Nos 2 & 4 Sects continued work on trench getting same up to LONE HOUSE. 2/Lt FORBES was buried at HOT CEMETRY DICKEBUSCH. Ref. map. BELGIUM 28 NW 1/20000 H.27.c.2.6	CHLB
	30.9.17		Forward Sections (Nos 2 & 4) rejoined Coy at Coy H.Q. Attached inf. rejoined their Bgde. & the Coy. handed over work to 491st Fd Coy R.E. (5th Div). the Coy coming under C.R.E. X Corps Troops for work & remaining in their Billets at LAKESIDE CAMP DICKEBUSCH	CHLB

A5834 Wt. W4973 M687 750,000 8/16 D. D. & L. Ltd. Forms/C.2118/13.

Appendix

A

SECRET

Ref. GHELUVELT
Sheet 1/10,000.
Edition 6 B (local).
Map A.

Copy No ...95...

33 Div. Order No. 230.

September 24, 1917.

1. (a) At Zero hour on "K" Day (to be notified later) the 33rd Division will attack the enemy in conjunction with the 39th Division on its right, and the 5th Australian Division on its left.

(b) Map A showing starting line (BROWN), first objective (RED), and final objective (BLUE), will be issued to all concerned.

(c) The objective of the 39th Division (116th Inf. Bde. on the left), is the RED line, the possession of which will improve the observation over the valley south of GHELUVELT.

(d) The objectives of the 5th Australian Div. (15th Australian Inf. Bde. on the right), are the RED and BLUE lines.

2. The 33rd Division will attack in order to cover the right flank of the I Anzac Corps, of which the 5th Australian Div. forms part, and to occupy a line giving observation to the south and east over the REUTELBEEK Valley.

3. (a) The 100 Inf. Bde., (with 4 King's (Liverpool) R. attached), will attack with its right on the YPRES - MENIN Road (inclusive), and its left on the REUTELBEEK.

(b) The 98 Inf. Bde. (less 4 King's (Liverpool) R.) will attack with its right on the REUTELBEEK and its left on the road (inclusive) which runs along the southern edge of POLYGON WOOD.

(c) The 19 Inf. Bde. will be in divisional reserve in the BEDFORD HOUSE Area, with Report Centre at that house. G.O.C., 19 Inf. Bde., will have reconnoitred, by 6 p.m. on the 25th inst., assembly positions for two Bns. of his Bde. in the area J.13.c. and d, J.19.a. and b. These Bns. will be prepared to dig themselves in if sufficient cover is not available.

Sketches showing proposed assembly areas for these two Bns. and positions of Bn. H.Q., will be sent by 8 p.m. on the 25th inst. to Advanced Div. H. Q. and to 98th and 100 Inf.Bdes.

(d) Map A (issued separately) shews the positions of Bns. of the 98th and 100 Inf. Bdes. at Zero hour on "K" Day. Troops will be in their positions 30' before Zero hour.

4. Forward of the BROWN (Starting) line the infantry will be preceded by an artillery and machine gun barrage, details of which (with Barrage maps) are being issued to all concerned, by the C.R.A. and General Staff, respectively.

(a) The Artillery barrage will be about 1,000 yards in depth, and will consist of five separate barrages of guns and howitzers of varying calibre.

(b) The machine gun barrage, owing to the forward slope of the ground, will be kept at a minimum distance of 600 yards in front of the infantry.

P. T. O.

5. The movements of the 18 pdr. barrage nearest the Infantry (known as Barrage "A") will be as follows :-

(a) At Zero the barrage will come down 150 yards in front of the Infantry starting line.

(b) At Zero plus 3 minutes, the barrage will advance and will move for the first 200 yards at 100 yards in 4'.

(c) The barrage will then slow down to 100 yards in 6' until the barrage line protecting the RED line is reached at Zero plus 29'. At this stage smoke shells will be fired to indicate that the RED line has been reached.

(d) There will be a pause of 71' on the RED line.

(e) At Zero plus 97' smoke shells will be fired and the rate of fire quickened to warn the Infantry that the barrage is about to lift again.

(f) At Zero plus 100' the barrage will continue at the rate of 100 yards in 8' until the protective barrage in front of the final objective (BLUE line) is reached.
The actual moment for reaching this line will vary according to the distance from the RED line, but each battery as it reaches the line will fire 3 smoke shells.

(g) After reaching the final protective barrage line, a slow rate of fire will be maintained for one hour, after which fire will cease unless especially asked for by S.O.S. call or Artillery Liaison Officers.

(h) If the wind is favourable, there will be smake barrages across the ridge in J.22.a. and along the trench from J.11.c.0.4. to J.17.a.4.7.

TANKS. 6. (a) One section to assemble just west of LONE HOUSE - BLACK WATCH CORNER ROAD during night preceding "K" day, and move on at Zero hour, keeping to north of JERK HOUSE - CAMERON HOUSE, then turning south east towards J.16.a.6.6. to deal with dugouts and ruins on west edge of CAMERON COVERT.
This section is placed at the disposal of G.O.C., 98 Inf. Bde.

(b) Tanks supporting the 39th Division attack may be expected to move through the Divisional Area along the YPRES - MENIN Road, thence south to TOWER HAMLETS RIDGE.

MACHINE GUN BARRAGE 7. The 19th, 207th, 248th (less 2 sections) and 70th (less 2 sections) Machine Gun Companies will provide covering barrage fire under the instructions of D.M.G.O.
One Company will be located in 98 Inf. Bde. Area., and the remainder in 100 Inf. Bde. Area.
D.M.G.O. will have his headquarters near 100 Inf. Bde. H.Q.
Details are being issued separately to those concerned under Appendix "C" to this order.

P. T. O.

STRONG POINTS. 8. Strong Points will be made approximately at the following points :-

(a) In Right Infantry Brigade Sector

		To be constructed by.
(i)	J.16.c.85.00	100 Inf. Bde.
(ii)	J.16.c.95.55.	100 Inf. Bde.
(iii)	J.21.b.95.10.	100 Inf. Bde.
(iv)	J.21.b.95.55.	100 Inf. Bde.
(v)	J.15.d.85.05.	Pioneers.
(vi)	J.15.d.90.45.	Pioneers.

(b) In Left Infantry Brigade Sector.

		To be constructed by.
(vii)	J.16.a.70.15.	98 Inf. Bde.
(viii)	J.16.a.70.80.	98 Inf. Bde.
(ix)	J.16.a.65.95.	98 Inf. Bde.
(x)	J.15.d.40.95.	Pioneers.
(xi)	J.15.b.65.45.	Pioneers.
(xii)	J.15.b.70.85.	Pioneers.

R. E. & PIONEERS 9. Detail of R.E. and Pioneers works will be issued later (but vide para 8) under Appendix "D" to this order.

LIAISON PATROLS. 10. (a) In addition to the usual liaison parties to be detailed between adjoining Inf. Bdes. and battalions, special parties will be detailed by the 98 Inf. Bde. to establish connection with the 15th Aust. Inf. Bde. on the RED line about J.10.c.2.0. and, on the BLUE line about J.16.b.30.95.

(b) Liaison will be established with the 116 Inf. Bde at a post which they will push forward to about point J.21.d.60.98

S. O. S. 11. The S. O. S. Signal will be a parachute rifle grenade with tree coloured lights - RED over GREEN over YELLOW.

SYNCHRONIZATION OF WATCHES. 12. Instructions for the synchronization of watches are contained in Appendix "E" to be issued separately.

REPORTS. 13. (a) Situation Reports will be sent in by Inf. Bdes. after reaching their objectives, and every hour after Zero hour. The fact that touch has been kept or lost with adjoining troops of other Divisions, on reaching the objectives, will be immediately reported.

4

REPORTS (contd.) (b) Locations of various Headquarters at Zero Hour are given in Appendix "B".

Acknowledge

J Maxwell Scott.

Lieut. Colonel, G.S.,

Issued at 11 am. 33rd Division.

Distribution :-

1 - 10	Div. H.Q.	Map A
		Copy No. 1
11 - 13	Inf. Bdes.	Copies 2 - 4. *
14 - 22	Div. Art.	Copy No. 5
23	"B" Echelon, D.A.C.	
24 - 27	33 Div. Eng.	
28	Pioneers.	
29	Div. Train.	
30	248 M. G. Co.	
31	207 M. G. Co.	
32	70 M. G. Co.	
33 - 34	X Corps.	Copy No. 6.
35	X Corps R.A.	
36	X Corps H.A.	
37	Left Double Bombt.Group, X Corps H.A.	
38	21 Div.	
39	23 Div.	
40	39 Div.	Copy No. 7.
41	5 Aust. Div.	" " 8.

(*) No. 2 - 19 Bde.
3 - 98 Bde.
4 - 100 Bde.

==*

S E C R E T

Appendix "B" to 33 Div. Order No. 230.

Ref. Sheet 28.
N.W. ZILLEBEKE.

SIGNALLING COMMUNICATIONS.

1. POSITIONS OF HEADQUARTERS.

Advanced 33 Div. H.Q. -	DICKEBUSCH, H.34.a.5.8.
33 Div. Artillery Group H.Q.	" "
Left Double Bombardment Group H.Q.	" "
100 Inf. Bde. H.Q.	TORR TOP Subway, I.24.d.
98 Inf. Bde. H.Q.	J.~~15~~ 13.c.~~6~~ 5.0.
19 Inf. Bde. H.Q.	BEDFORD HOUSE, I.26.a.9.4.
116 Inf. Bde. H.Q. (39 Div.)	HEDGE STREET Tunnels, I.34.b.4.8.
5 Aust. Inf. Bde.H.Q. (5 Aust. Div.)	HOOGE.

R. F. A. Centre Group.	MANOR FARM.	I.22.c.7.5.
Right Group.	BEDFORD HOUSE,	I.26.a.9.4.
Left Group.	DORMY HOUSE.	I.23.a.6.4.

2. COMMUNICATIONS FROM DIVISIONS TO BRIGADES.

(a) Telegraph and Telephone.

Alternative buried routes exist to Headquarters of 98th and 100th Inf. Bdes. on the Corps Buried System.

This will be supplemented by some overland cable north of ZILLEBEKE.

(b) Visual.

Divisional Signals will man a central Visual Station at I.17.d.1.2, working forward to both 98th and 100th Inf. Bde. H.Q., and also to a Visual Station at CLAPHAM JUNCTION (J.13.d.6.8.) which will be manned by 98th Inf. Bde.Signals.

It will also work back to a station at BEDFORD HOUSE to be manned by 19th Inf. Bde. Signals.

Two Runners will be available at the Divisional Station to take messages to a D.R. Post at MANOR FARM.

(c) Wireless.

Wireless Sets will be erected at each of 98th and 100th Inf. Bde. H.Q. working to the Corps Directing Station at RIDGE WOOD, which has telephone communication to X Corps Exchange. It is not thought advisable to take Wireless Sets on to the forward slope owing to the visibility of the Aerial.

(d) Despatch Riders.

Despatch Riders will run to a D.R. Post at MANOR FARM, whence messages will be sent by Runner relays to 100th and 98th Inf. Bdes.

P.T.O.

Relay Posts are at :-

(i) MANOR FARM - - I.22.c.7.5.
(ii) VALLEY COTTAGES - I.23.c.95.60.
(iii) RUDKIN HOUSE - I.24.c.05.15.
(iv) TORR TOP - - 100 Inf. Bde.H.Q.
(v) J.13.c.5.0 - - 98 Inf. Bde. H.Q.

Each Bde. is providing eight Runners for this purpose. D.R's will run direct to BEDFORD HOUSE

3. COMMUNICATIONS FROM BRIGADES TO BATTALIONS.

98th and 100th Inf. Bdes.

(a) There is an existing buried route from TORR TOP to CLAPHAM JUNCTION via 98th Inf. Bde. H.Q., which is beingextended by a buried route of 20 pairs to dugout at J.14.d.9.1, via dugouts at J.14.b.3.3 and J.14.b.20.05.

98th Inf. Bde. will use dugout at J.14.b.3.3 as cable head, and the 100th Inf. Bde. will use dugout at J.14.d.9.1 as Cable head.

No telephones will be used forward of Bde. H.Q. before Zero hour.

Fullerphones may be used at all times.

After Zero hour,

Communications will be arranged on the principle of S.S.148.

Bdes. will select likely points in the area to be captured for establishing Bde. Forward Station.

The Bde. Forward Station will be established as soon as the situation permits, and all means of communication established there.

Bdes. will inform all units and Artillery the position selected.

(b) Visual.

98 Inf. Bde. will establish a Visual Station at CLAPHAM JUNCTION, working back to Divisional Visual Station (I.17.d.1.2.) and 98th Inf. Bde. H.Q., and receiving from Bns. in front.

100th Inf. Bde. will establish a Visual Station in J.19.c. for receiving from Bns.in front.

(c) Amplifier and Power Buzzer.

Combined Amplifier and Power Buzzer Sets will be established at 100th Inf. Bde. H.Q., CLAPHAM JUNCTION (J.13.d.6.7.) and in a dugout at J.14.b.3.3.

A Power Buzzer will be established at J.14.d.9.1. to work to J.13.d.6.7 and J.14.b.3.3.

One more Power Buzzer is allotted to each Bde. to send forward.

The amplified set at J.14.b.3.3. should be taken forward to the Left Bde. Forward Station as the situation permits.

(d) Pigeons.

16 Pigeons per Bde. will be available. Bdes. will arrange to collect these from Railway Dugout (I.20.d.7.8). The greater number of these should be issued to Bns. assaulting the final objective.

(e) Runners.

Will be arranged under Bde. Signal Office.

4. ARTILLERY COMMUNICATIONS.

The R.A. Signal Officerwill make his own arrangements about R.A. Communication.

About twelve pigeons will be available for F.O.O's and they may also make use of the Amplifier and Power Buzzer System when required.

A Visual Receiving Station is being established at Dugout at J.14.b.20.05.

Five pairs will be allotted to the R.A. on the new bury from CLAPHAM JUNCTION to J.14.d.9.1.

5. CONTACT AEROPLANES.

Communication between Infantry and Aeroplane will be as laid down in S.S.148.

Divisional Dropping Station will be at DICKEBUSCH, H.34.a.5.8.

Aeroplane Calls are as follows :-

19 Inf. Bde. H.Q.	-	CG	98 Inf.Bde.H.Q.	CH
20 R. Fus.	-	CGW	4 King's -	CHW
2 R. W. Fus.	-	CGX	4 Suff.R. -	CHX
1 Cams.	-	CGY	1 Middx.R.-	CHY
5 Sco. Rif.	-	CGZ	2 A.& S.H.-	CHZ

100 Inf. Bde. H.Q.		CJ
1 Queens	-	CJW
2 Worc. R.	-	CJX
16 K.R.R.C.	-	CJY
9 H.L.I.	-	CJZ

39 Div.			5 Aust. Div.		
116 Inf. Bde.	-	CA	8 Inf.Bde.	-	MM
117 Inf. Bde.	-	CB	14 Inf.Bde.	-	MN
118 Inf. Bde.	-	CK	15 Inf.Bde.	-	MV

6. SIGNAL BALLOON.

Will be ready to take messages from the left attacking Bn. of each Bde.; but will also take urgent messages from any unit if possible.

Aeroplane calls will be used.

The Balloon can only answer by "T" after each Group and "RD" at the end of a message.

This balloon will only be available for signalling at night, though it can be recognized during the day by two square black flags 200 feet below the balloon on the balloon cable. At night it can be recognized by frequent flashes on the lamp. For testing, the above mentioned unit will call up the balloon every hour from 11.30 p.m. to 4.30 a.m., and the balloon will answer by "QQ".

An alignment should be taken by day

7. WIRELESS TANK.

Should a Wireless Tank be allotted to X Corps, it will be recognized by a Blue and White square on it.

P.T.O.

It will take messages from any unit and despatch them by Wireless to Corps Advanced Intelligence Report Centre, where they will be telephoned direct to Divisions.

Notice will be given later if a Wireless Tank is available, and the position it will occupy to receive messages.

8. CODE.

All messages sent by Wireless must be sent in Code, unless the urgency of the messages warrant them being sent in Clear, in which case it must be franked "IN CLEAR" by the Officer writing it.

Power Buzzer messages should be sent in code, if possible, but P.B. should only be used in emergency and then messages in clear are usually necessary.

Bdes. must provide the necessary office at Wireless Stations for encoding and decoding.

From Zero hour, only code names will be permitted in address "To" and address "From".

Positions Calls will be used for calling up; if no position is allotted, Code Calls as issued will be used.

9. RUNNERS.

All runners will be sent in pairs, a distance of fifty yards being maintained between the two men. All messages will be carried in the right breast pocket, unless a satchel is provided.

10. GENERAL.

(a) Liaison.
Units are responsible for providing communications to the unit on their right.

(b) Dump.
A cable dump is being formed near YEOMANRY POST. Inf.Bdes. and Bdes. R.F.A. may draw their requirements from there.

11. SUBSCRIBERS TO 33 DIVL. ADVANCED EXCHANGE.

33 Div. "G"
" " "A" Mess.
G.S.O. I.
G.O.C.
X Corps Exchange.
X " Intelligence Report Centre.
19 Inf. Bde.
98 Inf. Bde.
100 Inf. Bde.
39 Divl. Exchange.
5 Australian Divl. Exchange.
23 Divl. Exchange (In reserve).
C. R. E.
O.C. Signals.
Three Bde. "B" Echelons.
R.E. and Ammunition Dumps.
Divl. P. of W. Cage. (For A.P.M.)
"Q" Exchange. (N.6.d. 33 Divl. Rear.)
{ "Q" D.A.D.O.S.
A.D.M.S. Train
Signals. }

(5)

VISUAL SCHEME

Clapham Junction

From Battn.

Artillery Receiving Visual Station J14 c.20.05.

Yeomanry Post

93rd Bde J13 c.

Div. Vis. Station

Telephone or Runner

From Battn.

J19c

100th Bde

I24d.

Bedford House 19th Bde.

P.1.0

6

5.

WIRELESS · AND · POWER · BUZZER · SCHEME

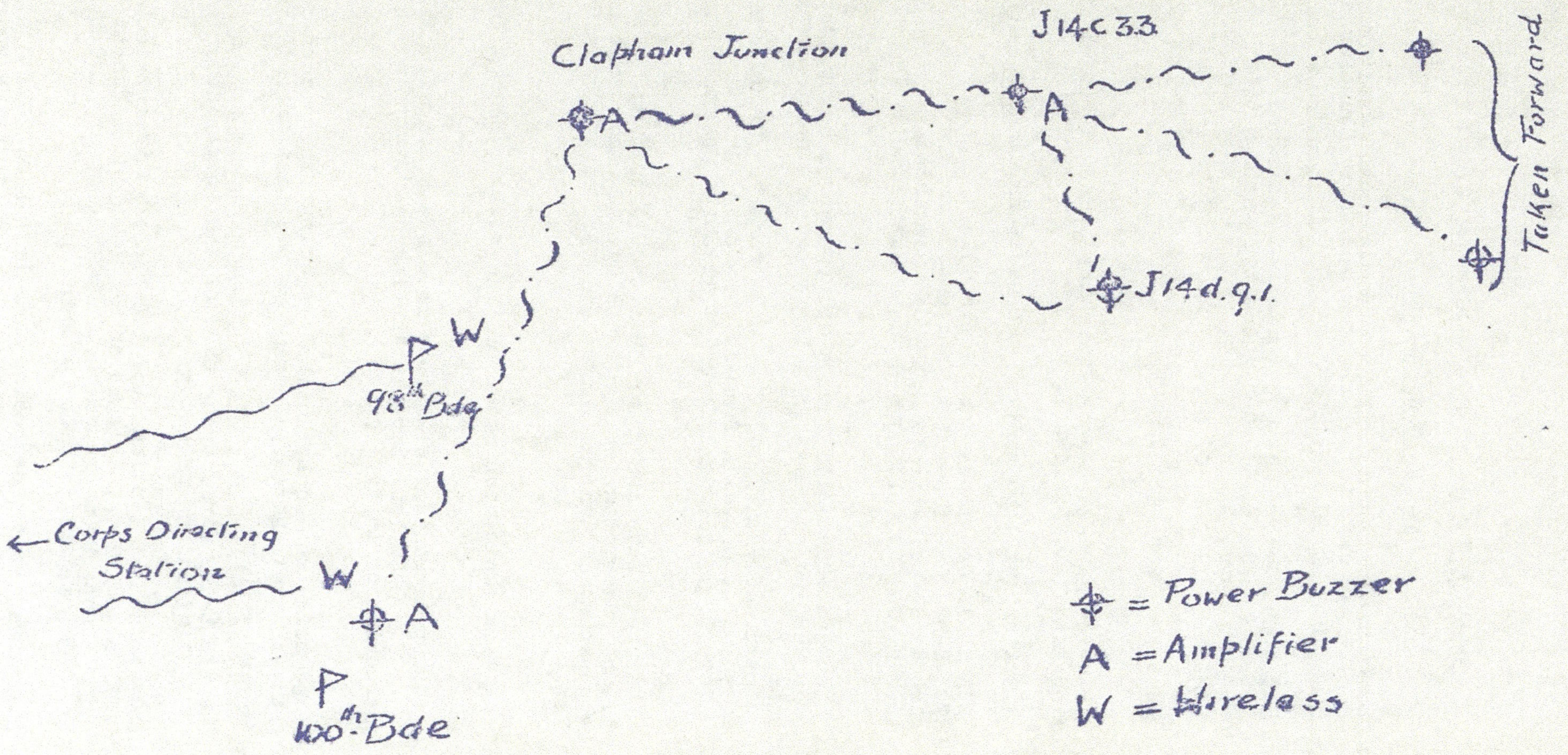

J14c33

Clapham Junction

A

A

J14d.9.1.

Taken Forward

W

98th Bde

← Corps Directing Station

W

A

100th Bde

= Power Buzzer

A = Amplifier

W = Wireless

24/9/17. Mansell Scott Lt Col. G.S. 33 Div.

S E C R E T

Appendix "C" to 33 Div. Order No. 230.

MACHINE GUN BARRAGE.

The attack will be supported by a Machine Gun Barrage. Guns are allotted as under :-

1. Right. 248 M. G. Co. (Less two Sections).
70 M. G. Co. (Less two Sections).

Centre. 19 M. G. Co.

Left. 207 M. G. Co.

2. For the Barrage, each of the above Machine Gun Cos. will be organized as follows :-

A Battery will consist of two Sections under a Battery Commander.
248 M. G. Co. (Less two Sections).
70 M. G. Co. (Less two Sections).
19 M. G. Co. will form C and D Batteries.
207 M. G. Co. will form E and F Batteries.

3. Two Batteries will form a Group under a Group Commander. Groups are numbered from Right to Left on the Divisional Front.
248th and 70th M. G. Cos. will form "A" Group BLUE.
19 M. G. Co. will form "B" Group - RED.
207 M. G. Co. will form "C" Group - BROWN.

4. Barrage lines are shewn on attached tracing. The Barrage will be independent of the Artillery Barrages, but it will be superimposed on the latter and will move forward with them.

5. A Time Table with rates of fire will be issued later.

6. Group Commanders will keep in close touch with G.O's C. 100 Inf. Bde. (attacking on right) and 98 Inf.Bde. (attacking on left).

7. By using map square method of quick fire concentration, with which all Battery Commanders are familiar, all guns will be able -

(a) to bring fire on any part of the front, subject to limitations of safety.

(b) to assist Sections to place barrage against counter-attacks; or, in case of temporary dislodgment of troops from ground won, a supplementary S.O.S. line can immediately be formed.

(c) Arrangements are being made by D.M.G.O. with D.M.G.O's 5th Aust. Div. and 39th Div. for mutually supporting fire also.

P.T.O.

8. No alteration of targets will be made during Barrage period except in an emergency. An immediate report of such change will be made to Div. H.Q. by the Bdes. making them, and to DMM.G.O., whose exact battle location will be communicated later.

9. Information will be passed by Right and Left Groups to Centre Group.

10. One Section 248 M. G. Co. not before detailed, will be maintained to engage low flying enemy aircraft. This section will be maintained on Divl. front. Guns will be maintained in action from one hour before dawn until darkness. Tracer bullets will be used in proportion of one in ten.

11. (a) The days prior to "K" Day will be utilised for reconnaissance of positions by Group, Battery and Section Commanders.

(b) A party of 48 O.R's from Infantry has been detailed, and will be used as Carrying and Working Party under orders of D.M.G.O. On "K" Day this party will be equally apportioned between Batteries.

12. Batteries will be in position by dawn on the 25th inst.

13. Battery Commanders will take every precaution that movement by daylight in vicinity of Battery positions, does not expose them to enemy observation either before the barrage commences or during lulls in the attack.

14. It is unlikely that more than one dugout will be available for each Group Commander. Odd trenches, shafts, and shelters exist and must be opened up by Group Commanders as shelter and cover for gun personnel.

15. 100th and 98th M. G. Cos. each will send to D.M.G.O. eight Clinometers on loan, for use of Cos. engaged in Barrage.

16. Present location of D.M.G.O. - H.34.a.8.8.

17. Two days Barrage and Emergency rations will be issued to Cos. and taken up to positions on "J" Day.

18. Position of Barrage Groups.

"A" Group Right - J.14.c.45.35, facing 25° E.S.E. True Bearing.

"B" Group Centre - J.14.c.97.80, facing 15° E.S.E.

"C" Group Left - J.14.b.55.37, facing due east.

(3)

Group Commanders will reconnoitre these positions forthwith and dispose Battery positions. No restrictions are placed upon Group Commanders availing themselves of the immediate local topography, and moving Batteries forward or to the flank, in order to improve position or be closer to cover for belt filling machines, spare personnel, S.A.A., etc. A report will be made if this is done.

Maxwell Scott

24/9/17.

Lieut. Colonel, G.S.,
33rd Division.

SECRET

Appendix "E" to 33 Div. Order No. 239.

SYNCHRONIZATION OF WATCHES.

1. The following procedure will be carried out in regard to the Synchronization of Watches, for the next few days, during active operations.

2. An Officer from X Corps H.Q. will visit 33 Div. H.Q. daily at 2.30 p.m., and will synchronize watches with an Officer on the 33 Div. Staff, especially detailed for this purpose.

3. An Officer from 33 Div. H.Q. will visit Bdes. as follows, and will synchronize watches with an Officer on each Bde. H.Q. Staff :-

September 24 -	19 Inf. Bde.	3.30 p.m.
	100 Inf. Bde.	4.15 p.m.
	98 Inf. Bde.	5 p.m.
September 25 -	19 Inf. Bde.	9 a.m., 3.30 p.m.
	100 Inf. Bde.	9.45 a.m., 4.15 p.m.
	98 Inf. Bde.	10.30 a.m., 5 p.m.
Following days	19 Inf. Bde.	3.30 p.m.
	100 Inf. Bde.	4.15 p.m.
	98 Inf. Bde.	5 p.m.

4. C.R.A. will be responsible for the synchronization of watches of all R.F.A. under the command of the 33 Div.

An Officer from C.R.A. Staff will be present at "G" Office, 33 Div., to meet the Corps Synchronizing Officer at 2.30 p.m. daily.

5. The D.M.G.O., 33 Div., will be responsible for the synchronization of watches of the M. G. Cos. employed on the Machine Gun barrage.

D.M.G.O. will synchronize daily with 100 Inf. Bde.

24/9/17.

W Maxwell Scott

Lieut. Colonel, G.S.,

33rd Division.

SECRET

33 Div.
GS.175.

All recipients of Appendix "C", 33 Div. Order No. 230.

Amendment to para 3 -

"207 Machine Gun Co. will form Group C"

for "BROWN"

read "GREEN".

ACKNOWLEDGE.

R.M. Bankier. Capt
for Lieut. Colonel, G.S.,
33rd Division.

24/9/17.

Issued at 10.30 p.m.

==*

APPENDIX "D" to 98th INF. BDE. ORDER NO. 170.

1. Headquarters

98th Inf. Bde.	J.13.c.5.0.
1st Midd'x Regt.	J.14.central.
4th Suff. Regt.	J.15.a.5.3.
2nd Arg. & Suth'd H.	J.14.d.3.9.

2. Communications from Bde. to Battns.

(a) There is a Corps bury past Bde. Hd. Qrs. to Clapham Junction in which the Bde. has been allotted 4 pairs.

(b) A Divisional bury has been made, and runs from CLAPHAM JUNCTION via. dug-outs at J.14.b.3.3. and J.14.b.20.05 to J.14.d.9.1. Four pairs have been allotted to Bde.
These buries are in all cases supplemented by Overland lines.

(c) Bde. Visual Station will be established at CLAPHAM JUNCTION working to BATTN. HD. QRS. at J.14.central, to BDE. HD. QRS. at J.13.c.5.0. and to Divisional Visual Station at I.27.d.1.2.

(d) Amplifier and P.B.
Combined Amplifier and P.B. sets will be established at Bde. Hd. Qrs. J.13.d.6.7 and at J.14.central.

(e) Pigeons.
24 pigeons will be available. These will be distributed equally among battalions.

(f) Runners.
Runner posts will be established at STIRLING CASTLE (J.13.d.4.1) and CLAPHAM JUNCTION (J.13.d.6.7).
Runners will be sent in pairs fifty yards between the two men.

(g) Contact Aeroplanes.
Communication between Infantry and Aeroplane will be as laid down in S.S. 148.
Calls for this Bde. will be :-

98th Inf. Bde. Hd. Qrs.	C.H.
4th King's (L'pool) Regt.	C.H.W.
4th Suff. Regt.	C.H.X.
1st Midd'x Regt.	C.H.Y.
2nd Arg. & Suth'd High'rs.	C.H.Z.

(h) Signal Balloon.
Will be ready to take messages from the left battalion, but will take urgent messages from any unit if possible.
Alignment on the balloon (recognised during the day by two square black flags 260 feet below the balloon on the cable at night by frequent flashes) will be taken by day.

(i) Wireless Tank.
If a Wireless Tank is allotted by Corps instructions re. same will be issued later.

(j) Code. All wireless messages must be in Code unless in cases of great urgency, when they may be sent in clear.
Power Buzzer messages must be sent only as a last resource, and in such a case messages in clear may be sent but only code names will be permitted in address "TO" and "FROM".
Position Calls will be used for calling up. If no position call is allotted, Code Calls as issued will be used.

General.
Units are responsible for providing communication to the Unit on their Right.
No telephones will be used forward of BDE. Hd. Qrs. before Zero hour.
Fullerphone may be used at all times.

Bde. Forward Station.
Will be established in cable head about J.15.b.2.7. From there lines will be run out to Battn. Hd. Qrs. when established after objectives have been gained.

APPENDIX "E" TO 98th INF. BDE. ORDER NO. 170.

INSTRUCTIONS REGARDING PRISONERS.

1. All prisoners will be sent under escort to Bde. Hd. Qrs.

2. The escort will not exceed 10% of the prisoners - 5% should be sufficient.

Each Battn. will establish a Police Post to ensure that this is carried out.

3. Enemy Officers and N.C.O's are to be kept separate from the men and care must be taken to prevent the destruction of documents en route.

4. Two intelligent N.C.O's per. Battn. are to be detailed to collect documents from the battlefield in their Battn. area. Brassards marked "Intelligence" will be worn by those men and will be provided, if available, by Div. Hd. Qrs.

These N.C.O's will search Dugouts and Headquarters particularly and the documents recovered will be sent to Bde. Hd. Qrs. immediately.

Identity discs will on no account be removed from German dead bodies.

Wounded prisoners will be sent to dressing station at WOODCOTE HOUSE and a receipt obtained.

APPENDIX "B" to 98th INF. BDE. ORDER NO. 170.

ARTILLERY BARRAGE.

The movements of the 18 pdr. barrage nearest the Infantry (known as Barrage "A") will be as follows :-

(a) At Zero the barrage will come down 150 yards in front on the Infantry starting line.

(b) At Zero ~~the barrage~~ plus 3 minutes, the barrage will advance and will move for the first 200 yards at 100 yards in 4'.

(c) The barrage will then slow down to 100 yards in 6' until the barrage line protecting the RED line is reached at Zero plus 29'. At this stage smoke shells will be fired to indicate that the RED line has been reached.

(d) There will be a pause of 71' on the RED line.

(e) At Zero plus 97' smoke shells will be fired and the rate of fire quickened to warn the Infantry that the barrage is about to lift again.

(f) At Zero plus 100' the barrage will continue at the rate of 100 yards in 8' until the protective barrage in front of the final objective (BLUE line) is reached.
The actual moment for reaching this line (Protective Barrage) will vary according to the distance from the RED line, but each battery as it reaches the line will fire 3 smoke shells.

(g) After reaching the final protective barrage line, a slow rate of fire will be maintained for one hour, after which fire will cease unless especially asked for by S.O.S. call or Artillery Liaison Officers.

(h) If the wind is favourable, there will be smoke barrages across the ridge in J.22.a. and along the trench from J.11.c.0.4. to J.17.a.4.7.

10. Reports
Situation Reports will be sent in by Battns on reaching their objectives, and as often afterwards as circumstances admit.
The fact that touch has been kept or lost with adjoining troops of other Bdes., on reaching the objectives, will be immediately reported.

11. Signal Communications are given in attached Appendix D.

12. Flares.
Contact aeroplanes will call for Flares by firing a white light and sounding a Klaxon horn, at approximately the following times
On 1st Objective. Zero plus 60 minutes
On 2nd Objective. Zero plus 2 hours 45 minutes.
In addition to lighting flares, maps, papers, etc, will be waved by leading Infantry on above taking place.
Leading Infantry however will wait until Aeroplane calls for flares.

13. Battle Hd. Qrs. of Units will be as follows :-

1st Midd'x Regt.	J.14. .central.
4th Suff. Regt.	J.15.a.5.3.
2nd Arg. & Suth'd High'rs.	J.14.d.1.9.
No. 98 M. G. Coy.	Trenches just N. of Bde. H. Q.
98th T. M. Battery.	J.13.d.6.7.

If Units, for any reason, desire to occupy Hd. Qrs. other than above application will be made to Bde. Hd. Qrs.

Cancelled 9.30 pm 8 mar RI
14. ~~The 11th Field Coy., R.E. will arrange to mark out the assembly areas with tape.~~ HW.

15. Bde. Hd. Qrs. will be at J.13.C.5.0.

16. ACKNOWLEDGE.

H Wailes Capt.,
B.M.,
98th Inf. Bde.

Issued at 8 a.m.
through Signals :-

1. G.O.C.
2. 1st Midd'x Regt.
3. 2nd Arg. & Suth'd High'rs.
4. 4th Suff. Regt.
5. No. 98 M. G. Coy.
6. 98th T. M. Battery.
7. 11th Field Coy., R.E.
8. 33rd Divn. "G".
9. C.R.A., 33rd Divn.
10. 100th Inf. Bde.
11. 15th Australian Bde.
12. No. 2. Sect., No. 1 Coy., "A" Battn. Tanks.
13. B. Barrage Group, M. G.
14. 1st Midd'x Regt. (Pioneers).
15. 98th Bde. Signals.
16. Staff Capt.
19. O. O. File.
20) 21) War Diary.

S E C R E T.

Copy No. 7

98th INF. BDE. ORDER NO. 170.

Ref. Maps: Sheet 28, 1/40,000,
SHREWSBURY FOREST, OOSTHOEK, WESTHOEK
and KRUISEECKE Sheets. 1/10,000.
GHELUVELT, Edition 6 B local, 1/10,000.

25th September, 1917.

1. Attack will be carried out at Zero hour on "K" day to be notified later.

2. Assembly positions are given on attached map C.
Units will be in their positions as follows :-
1st Midd'x Regt. by Zero - 6 hours.
2nd Arg. & Suth'd High'rs.) by Zero - 2 hours, not to commence
4th Suff. Regt.) before Zero - 5 hours.

3. Artillery.
Artillery Barrage vide. Appendix "B" issued with 98th Inf. Bde. Preliminary Order No. 170 is cancelled and the attached Appendix "B" substituted

(a) The Artillery barrage will be about 1,000 yards in depth, and will consist of five separate barrages of guns and howitzers of varying calibre.
An officer of the Artillery Group supporting the attack of this Bde. will be attached as Liaison Officer to one of the Battns. carrying out attack on 2nd Objective. He will accompany the Battn. Hd. Qrs. throughout the attack and be withdrawn at dusk.

4. Machine Guns.
C Group forming a barrage across the front of this Bde. will have its Hd. Qrs. at about J.14.B.55.37.
The Barrage owing to the forward slope of the Ground will be kept at a minimum distance of 600 yards in front of the Infantry.

5. Tanks.
One section is placed at the disposal of this Bde. and will assemble just west of LONE HOUSE - BLACK WATCH CORNER ROAD during night preceding "K" day, and move on at Zero hour, keeping to North of JERK HOUSE - CAMERON HOUSE, then turning south east towards J.16.a.6.6. to deal with dugouts and ruins on west edge of CAMERON COVERT.

6. Strong points will be made approximately at the following points:

	To be constructed by
(a) J.16.a.70.15.	4th Suff. Regt.
(b) J.16.a.70.80.	2nd Arg. & Suth'd High'rs.
(c) J.16.a.65.95.	2nd Arg. & Suth'd High'rs.
(d) J.15.d.40.95.	Pioneers.
(e) J.15.b.65.45.	Pioneers.
(f) J.15.b.70.85.	Pioneers.

7. Liaison Patrols.
In addition to the usual liaison parties to be detailed between adjoining Inf. Bdes. and Battns, special parties will be detailed by the 1st Midd'x Regt. and 2nd Arg. & Suth'd High'rs. to establish connection with the 15th Australian Inf. Bde. on the RED Line about J.10.c.2.0. and on the BLUE Line about J.16.b.30.9½ respectively.

8. S.O.S.
The S.O.S. Signal will be a parachute Rifle Grenade with three coloured lights - RED over GREEN over YELLOW.

9. Synchronisation of Watches.
An officer will be sent by each unit to Bde. Hd. Qrs.,
SEPT. 25th.
at 10. 40 a.m. and 5. 10 p.m.
on following days
at 5. 30 p.m.

SECRET

Appendix "D" to 33 Div. Order No. 230.
of September 24, 1917.

WORK OF R.E. AND PIONEERS.

1. Two Sections, 11 F. Co. R.E. and the 100 attached infantry will be at the disposal of the Bde. Comdr., 98 Inf. Bde.

2. Two Sections, 222 F. Co. R. E., and the 100 attached infantry will be at the disposal of the Bde. Comdr., 100 Inf. Bde.

3. The remainder of the 11 F. Co. R.E. and 222 F. Co. R.E., will be at the disposal of the C.R.E. to supplement or relieve the Sections working with Bdes.

4. The 212 F. Co. R.E., less one Section, will be in reserve. One Section will assist the Artillery.

5. One Co. of the Pioneers will complete C.T. through NORTHAMPTON FARM to present front line and continue the trench eastwards.

6. One Co. Pioneers will continue track "W" through KANTINTJE CABARET to front line.

7. Five platoons Pioneers will construct the Strong Points mentioned in para 8 of 33 Div. Order No. 230.
These platoons will assemble at Railway dugouts - I.20.b. and d. and two liaison officers from these platoons will be sent, one to 98 Inf. Bde. H.Q. and one to 100 Inf. Bde. H.Q., before Zero hour.
The parties for the Strong Points will be ready to proceed to work at dusk on "K" Day.

8. One Co. Pioneers (less one platoon) will be in reserve.

H. Denison Pender
Major for
Lieut. Colonel, G.S.,
33rd Division.

24/9/17.

==*

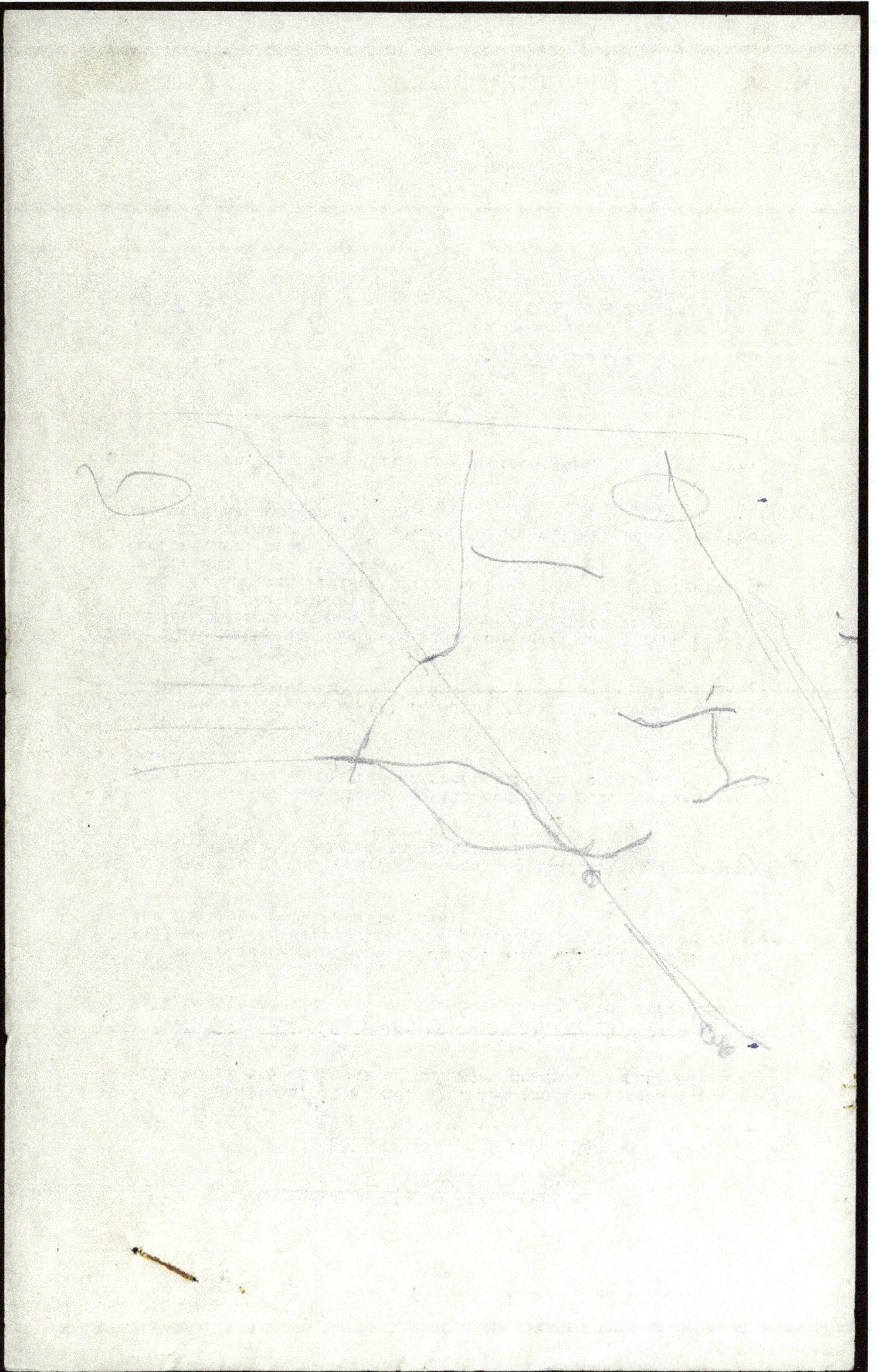

No. 9. **MESSAGE MAP.** Trenches &c. corrected to 10-9-17.

Polygoneveld

POLYGONE de ZONNEBEKE

Jetty Wood

Polygonebeek

J

5th Aust Div

Joist Fm

Black Watch Corner

Jark Ho.

Cameron Ho.

Cameron Covert

Verbeek Fm

98 Inf Bde

Lone Ho

Carlisle Fm

Jut Farm

Reutelbeek

Northampton Fm

4th Kings

Veldhoek

Polderhoek

Present Right Flank of 4 Kings L'pool Regt

100 Inf Bde

Kantintje Cabt

Scherriebeek

TRENCH

JOHNSON

116 Inf Bde

Gheluvelt Wood

Tower Hamlets

Lewis Ho.

Ambrose Fm

Gheluvelt

9 10 15 16 21 22

R.E. C.S. 1136 22.9.17

Scale. 1:10,000.

Yds. 500 400 300 200 100 0 500 1000 Yds.

Printed by No. 2 Advanced Section, A.P. & S.S.

MESSAGE FORM.

To:— No.

1. I am at.......................... (Note:—Either give Map Reference or mark your position by a X on the Map on back.

2. I have reached limits of my Objective.

3. My Platoon / Company is at........................ and is consolidating.

4. My Platoon / Company is at..and has consolidated.

5. Am held up by (a) M.G. / (b) Wire at........................(Place where you are).

6. Enemy holding strong point ....

7 I am in touch with..............................on Right / Left. at.............

8. I am not in touch with..on Right. / Left.

9. Am shelled from.........................

10. Am in need of —

11. Counter Attack forming at ....

12. Hostile (a) Battery / (b) Machine Gun / (c) Trench Mortar active at ....

13. Reinforcements wanted at ....

14. I estimate my present strength at .... rifles.

15. Add any other useful information here:—

Name.................................

Platoon..............................

Time .... m. Company....................

Date .... 1917. Battalion....................

(A). Carry no maps or papers which may be of value to the Enemy.

(B). Give no information if captured, except the following, which you are bound to give:—

Name and Rank.

(C). Collect all captured maps and papers and send them in at once.

SECRET.

Copy No. ____

98th Inf. Bde. Order No. 171.

Ref Maps: Sheet 28, 1/40,000,
SHREWSBURY FOREST, OOSTHOEK, WESTHOEK
and KRUISEECKE Sheets, 1/10,000.

September 25th, 1917

---

1. The enemy have gained possession of our front line and driven us back to Line approximately J.15.C.9.8. to J.15.A.9.8.

2. It is reported that ~~1st Midd'x Regt. are in touch with Right flank, but~~ touch with ~~left~~ both flank uncertain.

3. The original front line from J.15.D.4.8. to J.9.D.4.0 will be re-established by a Counter-attack which will take place at Zero, 25th instz

   The attack will be carried out by the 1st Midd'x Regt.

   2nd Arg. & Suth'd High'rs. will, in addition to the Coy. already sent, place a second Coy. at disposal of 1st Midd,x Regt.

4. Zero will be 2. 0 p.m.

5. Artillery Barrage.

   n Artillery Barrage will come down at Zero, 150 yards in front of present line.

   Lift 100 yards at Zero plus 3 minutes and continue at the rate of 100 yards per 6 minutes until it reaches a line 200 yards beyond objective.

   The Artillery has been asked to ensure safety from barrage of flanks of Bdes on North and South.

6. 98th T. M. Battery will send up at once 4 guns to report to 1st Midd'x Regt. at J.14.central for co-operation in attack.

7. ACKNOWLEDGE.

[signature]

Capt.,
B.M.,
98th Inf. Bde.

Issued at 11. 15 a.m.
through Signals to :-

No. 1 G.O.C.
" 2 1st Midd'x Regt.
3 2nd Arg. & Suth'd High'rs.
4 4th Suff. Regt.
5. No. 98 M. G. Coy.
6. 98th T. M. Battery.
7. "G" 33rd Div.
8. 100th Inf. Bde.
9. 15th Australian Bde.
10. Left Group, R.F.A.
11. 11th Field Coy., R.E.
12. Bde. Signals.
13. Staff Captain.
14. O. O. File.
15
16 War Diary.

Duplicate

S E C R E T

Copy No..25....

33 Div. Order No. 231.

25th Sept., 1917.

1. Owing to the attacks made by the enemy on the 33 Div. front to-day, the role of the 33 Div. in to-morrow's operations, has to be altered, and the Division will attack at Zero hour from its present front line as follows :-

(a) 1 Cams. are placed under the orders of G.O.C.,100 Inf.Bde.

5 Sco. Rif.are placed under the orders of G.O.C.,98 Inf.Bde.

(b) The RED Line (first objective) will, instead of starting on the right from the YPRES - MENIN Road, will start at a point on the present front of the 100 Inf. Bde. about J.15.d.55.30 and will run in a north-easterly direction to a point on the REUTELBEEK, where it will join the original RED Line about J.16.c.3.8, immediately south of JUT FARM. From this point the new RED Line will follow the original RED Line due north to the Divisional Boundary at point J.10.c.3.0.

(c) The BLUE Line will be considerably altered, as follows :-

It will only start where the new RED Line crosses the REUTELBEEK, and will continue in a north-north-easterly direction to the Divisional Boundary at point J.16.a.7.9, whence it will continue in a north-easterly direction to join the original BLUE Line about point J.10.d.1.4.

(d) The only portion of the RED Line, i.e., first objective, to be taken by 100 Inf. Bde., is the RED Line from where it starts in our present front line to as far as the point where it crosses the REUTELBEEK. The troops detailed for this attack will consolidate on this line, and will cover the right flank of the 98 Inf. Bde. when the latter moves forward to the ~~BLUE~~ RED Line.

(e) 98 Inf. Bde. from its present front (whether it is on the BROWN Line or further west) will carry out the original instructions and take the RED Line between the REUTELBEEK and POLYGON WOOD. In moving forward to the attack on the new BLUE Line, it will pivot on its right in close touch with the 100 Inf. Bde., and will gain the BLUE Line in order to cover the right flank of the 5 Australian Division.

(f) South of the point where the new RED Line starts on the front of the 100 Inf. Bde., our present front line will remain as it is, with the exception that if the troops immediately to the right of the 100 Inf. Bde. have lost ground since this morning's operations started, they will retake the portion lost at Zero hour and gain touch on the original BROWN Line with the 116 Inf. Bde.

P. T. O.

(g) It is to be impressed on all concerned that the role of the 33 Div. in tomorrow's operations, is to cover the right flank of the 5 Australian Division.
The success of the Second Army's operations depends on the holding, at any cost, of the ground gained.

2. No alterations will be made in the Artillery Creeping Barrage programme, except that protective barrage lines will halt in conformity with the new objectives - RED and BLUE Lines described in para 1.

3. The D.M.G.O. will issue such amendments to his instructions as will ensure efficient machine gun barrage, particular attention being paid to the ground just north of the YPRES - MENIN Road, and to CAMERON COVER.

4. The 19 Inf. Bde. (less two Bns. and the 19 M. G. Co.) will be in Divisional Reserve near BEDFORD HOUSE, with its two Bns. ready to move at half an hour's notice.

5. A message map shewing the new RED and BLUE Lines, is attached.

6. ACKNOWLEDGE.

W Maxwell Scott

Issued at 8.45 p.m.

Lieut. Colonel, G.S.,
33rd Division.

Distribution :-

1 - 8	Div. H.Q.
11 - 13	Inf. Bdes.
14 - 22	Div. Art.
24 - 27	Div. Eng.
28	Pioneers.
30	248 M. G. Co.)
31	207 M. G. Co.) per D.M.G.O.
32	70 M. G. Co.)
33 - 34	X Corps.
35	X Corps R.A.
36	X Corps H.A.
37	Left Dbl.Bombt.Group, X Corps H.A.
38	21 Div.
39	23 Div.
40	39 Div.
41	5 Aust. Div.
42	No. 6 Squadron, R.F.C.
43	"A" Bn. Tank Corps.

==*

SPECIAL ORDER OF THE DAY

by

MAJOR-GENERAL P. WOOD, C.B., C.M.G.

Commanding 33rd Division.

1. I have received the following messages in connection with the operations in which the 33rd Division took part on September 25th, 26th and 27th, 1917.

I.

From

The Field-Marshal Commanding-in-Chief,
British Armies in FRANCE.

To

General Sir H.C.O. PLUMER,
Commanding 2nd Army.

G. H. Q., 27th September, 1917.

"The ground gained by the 2nd Army yesterday under your command, and the heavy losses inflicted on the enemy in the course of the day, constitute a complete defeat of the German forces opposed to you. Please convey to all Corps and Divisions engaged, my heartiest congratulations, and especially to the 33rd Division whose successful attack following a day of hard fighting, is deserving of all praise."

II.

From X Corps.

To 33rd Division.

G. G. 131. 26th September, 1917.

"Following received from General PLUMER begins AAA Please accept my congratulations on success of to-day's operations, and convey them to the troops engaged AAA The 33rd Division have done fine work under extraordinarily difficult circumstances, and the 39th Division have carried out their task most successfully AAA message ends AAA The Corps Commander adds his own congratulations."

2. In circulating the above messages, I wish to congratulate all Officers, Non-commissioned Officers and men of the Division, on having gained, by their fine fighting qualities, such marks of appreciation from the Commander-in-Chief, and from the Army and Corps Commanders.

P. T.O.

Captured enemy documents, from which extracts and translations are attached, show what efforts the enemy made, on the 25th September 1917, against the front held by the Division between the YPRES - MENIN Road and the southern edge of the POLYGON WOOD.

3. I wish this order to be read on parade to all ranks of the Division, as a mark of my appreciation of their gallant conduct in the past, and as a proof of my confidence in their being able to maintain their high reputation in the future.

P. Wood

September 29th, 1917.

Major-General,

Commanding 33rd Division.

Distribution made on scale of 1 per Officer throughout the Division.

Instructions regarding War Diaries and Intelligence Summaries are contained in F. S. Regs., Part II. and the Staff Manual respectively. Title pages will be prepared in manuscript.

WAR DIARY
or
INTELLIGENCE SUMMARY.
(Erase heading not required.)

Army Form C. 2118.

Place	Date	Hour	Summary of Events and Information	Remarks and references to Appendices
TROISVILLES REF MAP 57 B.	1		Infantry training and general cleaning up. Memorial Service held in Barn in afternoon.	
	2		do do do do	
	3		do and packing up wagons	
WAGGONVILLE	4		Coy moved from TROISVILLE to WAGGONVILLE	
SARTBARA REF MAP 51. $\frac{1}{40,000}$	5		Coy working on roads through Forest and moved into SARTBARA in evening	
	6		No 2 & 3 Section working on approaches to bridge over Canal Bank, Eleven casualties one killed Sapper Tofield.	
BERLAIMONT SHEET 51.	7th		moved to BERLIAMONT. - No 2 & 3 Section ahead of Coy with 19th I.B. advancing on MAUBERGE - AVESNES ROAD.	
	8th		Section withdrawn from line remainder of Coy working on approaches to Bridge	
	9th		Built footbridge over Canal	
	10th		Salving pontoons from side of Canal. 1 Section on footbridge afterwards repairing road by CROISIL INN	
	11th		ARMISTICE SIGNED. Making double road for horse transport by CROISIL INN.	
	12th		Cleaning up vehicles, checking pontoon equipment	
	13th		General cleaning up & Drill	
	14th		do do do do	

D. D. & L., London, E.C.
(A5004) Wt W1771/M2031 750,000 5/17 Sch. 32 Forms/C2118/14

Instructions regarding War Diaries and Intelligence Summaries are contained in F. S. Regs., Part II. and the Staff Manual respectively. Title pages will be prepared in manuscript.

WAR DIARY
or
INTELLIGENCE SUMMARY.
(Erase heading not required.)

Army Form C. 2118.

Place	Date	Hour	Summary of Events and Information	Remarks and references to Appendices
LOCQUIGNOL REF MAP 51.	15th		Coy marched to LOCQUINAL	
	16th		do do FOREST	
	17th		do do CLARY	
CLARY SHEET 57 B.	18th		Cleaning Vehicles	
	19th		do do	
	20th		Infantry Training	
	21		do do	
	22		do do.	
	23		Coy employed on Salvage work	
	24.		Brigade Manoeuvre & Blanks firing Church Parade	
	25th		Infantry Training	
	26th		Salvage work	
	27th		Infantry Training	
	28th		Salvage work	
	29th.		Infantry Training & Lecture on Demobilisation, & Educational Scheme.	
	30th		Packing Wagon Transport moved under Lieut Russel to PIPERS OUTBREAK.	

D. D. & L., London, E.C. (A8604) Wt W1771/M2031 750,000 5/17 Sch. 52 Forms/C2118/14

Army Form C. 2118.

Instructions regarding War Diaries and Intelligence Summaries are contained in F. S. Regs., Part II. and the Staff Manual respectively. Title pages will be prepared in manuscript

WAR DIARY
or
INTELLIGENCE SUMMARY.
(Erase heading not required.)

Vol 34

Place	Date	Hour	Summary of Events and Information	Remarks and references to Appendices
			CONFIDENTIAL	
			— WAR DIARY —	
			OF	
			— 11TH FD COY R.E. —	
			FROM 1ST OCTOBER TO 31ST OCTOBER 1917. VOLUME	
			C.P.L. Balcombe Major, R.E. Commdg. 11th Coy. R.E	

A5834 Wt. W4973/M687 750,000 8/16 D. D. & L. Ltd. Forms/C.2118/13.

Army Form C. 2118.

WAR DIARY
or
INTELLIGENCE SUMMARY.
(*Erase heading not required.*)

Instructions regarding War Diaries and Intelligence Summaries are contained in F. S. Regs., Part II. and the Staff Manual respectively. Title pages will be prepared in manuscript.

Place	Date	Hour	Summary of Events and Information	Remarks and references to Appendices
DICKEBUSCH	1.10.17		They Coy was put under orders of C.E. X^th^ Corps for construction of a road for 6" guns – running from BEDFORD HOUSE grounds on to SANDBAG TRACK the idea being that the road was eventually to join up with MIDDLESEX ROAD at LA CHAPELLE FARM. A reconnaissance of the road was made, & work laid out.	[initials] Sketch attached Marked A
do	2.10.17		Work commenced on road. Making formation, & filling shell holes etc; & felling & removing old trees.	[initials]
do	3.10.17		Work as for the 2nd inst. In the evening orders received to work on road in SANCTUARY WOOD – switch road off PLUMER DRIVE to CLAPHAM JUNCTION	[initials]
do	4.10.17		Work commenced on road in SANCTUARY WOOD. Owing to heavy shelling no actual work on road possible – but all men were put on to carrying material to the job.	[initials]
do	5.10.17		Work continued in SANCTUARY WOOD on PLUMER DRIVE. General road work done. Casualties 3 O.R. wounded. Cpl LOXLEY, Pion. STEVENS, Spr COGLAN } No 2 Sec	[initials]

A5834 Wt. W4973 M687 750,000 8/16 D. D. & L. Ltd. Forms/C.2118/13.

Instructions regarding War Diaries and Intelligence Summaries are contained in F. S. Regs., Part II. and the Staff Manual respectively. Title pages will be prepared in manuscript.

WAR DIARY
or
INTELLIGENCE SUMMARY.
(Erase heading not required.)

Army Form C. 2118.

Place	Date	Hour	Summary of Events and Information	Remarks and references to Appendices
DICKEBUSCH	6.10.17		Work carried on in SANCTUARY WOOD, on PLUMER DRIVE SOUTH	[illegible] map [illegible] B
do / WESTOUTRE	7.10.17		Work carried on as yesterday. Orders received to move back to WESTOUTRE. The Mounted portion of Coy moved off at 2.0 p.m. independently. Sappers moved off in lorries from SHRAPNEL CORNER at 5.0 p.m. on completion of days work, arriving WESTOUTRE 7.0 p.m. Coy was relieved by 61st Field Coy. 14th (Lt) Div.	[illegible]
Sheet 28 Trench [illegible] on [illegible] NEUVE EGLISE ROAD.	8.10.17		Coy marched off & clear of WESTOUTRE by 9.15 am. arriving in new billets at 12.0 noon. Work reconnaissances for tomorrow were carried out.	[illegible]
do	9.10.17		Work commenced in the Sector. No 1 Sect. O.P.s 47th Bty. R.F.A. No 2 " MULE TRACK No 3 R. Batt. H.Q. No 4 Corps Line.	[illegible]
do.	10.10.17		Work carried on with as in yesterdays report.	[illegible]

A5834 Wt. W4973 M687 750,000 8/16 D. D. & L. Ltd. Forms/C.2118/13.

Army Form C. 2118.

Instructions regarding War Diaries and Intelligence Summaries are contained in F. S. Regs., Part II. and the Staff Manual respectively. Title pages will be prepared in manuscript.

WAR DIARY
or
INTELLIGENCE SUMMARY.
(Erase heading not required.)

Place	Date	Hour	Summary of Events and Information	Remarks and references to Appendices
Sheet 28 T.10 a 5.9 on NEUVE EGLISE – WOLVERGHEM Road.	11		Work carried on with as yesterday. 4 men in addition being sent to help 46 Bde. RFA with O.P's. Lt RUSSELL took over the duties of Div. Drainage Officer. Three reinforcements (drivers) arrived.	
	12		Work carried on as usual. Bad weather.	
do	13		Work carried on as usual. Bad weather.	
do	14		Work as usual.	
do	15		Work as usual	
do	16		Work as usual Bad weather	
do	17		Work carried on as usual. Bad weather	
do	18		Work carried on as usual. Major Balcombe left on leave for England.	
do	19		Work as usual. Eight reinforcements joined (Sappers). Lower Cathcart accidentally wounded	

A5834 Wt.W4973 M687 750,000 8/16 D. D. & L. Ltd. Forms/C.2118/13.

24047

Instructions regarding War Diaries and Intelligence Summaries are contained in F. S. Regs., Part II. and the Staff Manual respectively. Title pages will be prepared in manuscript.

WAR DIARY
or
INTELLIGENCE SUMMARY.
(Erase heading not required.)

Army Form C. 2118.

Place	Date	Hour	Summary of Events and Information	Remarks and references to Appendices
Sheet 28	20		Work carried on as usual weather fine	
T.10 a 5.9 on	21		Work carried on as usual weather fine	
Neuve Eglise WULVERGHEM ROAD	22		Work carried on as usual Court Martial of Driver McGuck held at SHANKHILL CAMP. II LIEUT W.H.E GARROD prosecuted. (Cpl Rugby wounded)	
	23		Work carried on as usual. of C.R.E called with reference to Rt Battn HQ and Mule TRACK. Weather very bad	
	24		Work carried on as usual on Rt BATTN HQ, MULE TRACK & O.P's weather bad	
	25		Work on Mule track suspended for one night under CRE's instructions. Nos 2.3 & 4 Sections worked on Rt BATTN HQ Sergt Fox wounded (at duty).	
	26		Work continued on Mule track, Rt BATTN HQ and O.P's Working party for Mule Track lent to No 3 Section for carrying party.	
	27		Work on all these jobs as usual. Weather good	
	28		Work carried on as usual, fine weather,	
	29		Work as usual. Major C.P.A. BALCOMBE returned from leave	

A5834 Wt. W4973 M687 750,000 8/16 D. D. & L. Ltd. Forms/C.2118/13.

Army Form C. 2118.

Instructions regarding War Diaries and Intelligence Summaries are contained in F. S. Regs., Part II. and the Staff Manual respectively. Title pages will be prepared in manuscript.

WAR DIARY
or
INTELLIGENCE SUMMARY.
(*Erase heading not required.*)

Place	Date	Hour	Summary of Events and Information	Remarks and references to Appendices
Sheet 28 T.10.a.5.9. on NEUVE EGLISE	30		Work as usual. Bad weather. Increased activity in enemy artillery fire.	
WULVERGHEM ROAD	31.		Work as usual. Fine day.	

A5834 Wt. W4973 M687 750,000 8/16 D. D. & L. Ltd. Forms/C.2118/13.

Army Form C. 2118.

WAR DIARY
or
INTELLIGENCE SUMMARY.

(*Erase heading not required.*)

Instructions regarding War Diaries and Intelligence Summaries are contained in F. S. Regs., Part II. and the Staff Manual respectively. Title pages will be prepared in manuscript.

Place	Date	Hour	Summary of Events and Information	Remarks and references to Appendices
LA SOTIERE	23/10/18		Coy standing by.	
	24/10/18		Coy at work in line 2 sections digging new line and Coy at night moved to FOREST.	
FOREST	25/10/18		Coy moved to CROIX No 3 Section going to live in billets at Poix du Nord.	
CROIX	26/10/18		Coy digging assembly trenches. Major C.R.L. Balcombe. M.C. RE severely wounded.	
TROISVILLES	27/10/18		Coy moved out of line to TROISVILLES.	
	28/10/18		Bath for Coy at BERTRY. 2 sections cleaning up 2 working on town Concert party's hall.	
	29/10/18		do do do. Notification received that MAJOR C.R.L. Balcombe. M.C. RE had died of wounds at CAMBRAI.	
	30/10/18		Cleaning up vehicles for G.O.C.'s Inspection.	
	31/10/18		Inspection by G.O.C. 33rd Divn. 1/Cpl. [illegible] & Sapper Sandy [illegible] awarded M.M's for operations on night of 3rd and 11/12th.	

D. D. & L., London, E.C. (A8004) Wt W1771/M2031 750,000 5/17 Sch. 52 Forms/C2118/14

B

SHEET 28. J. (BELGIUM).

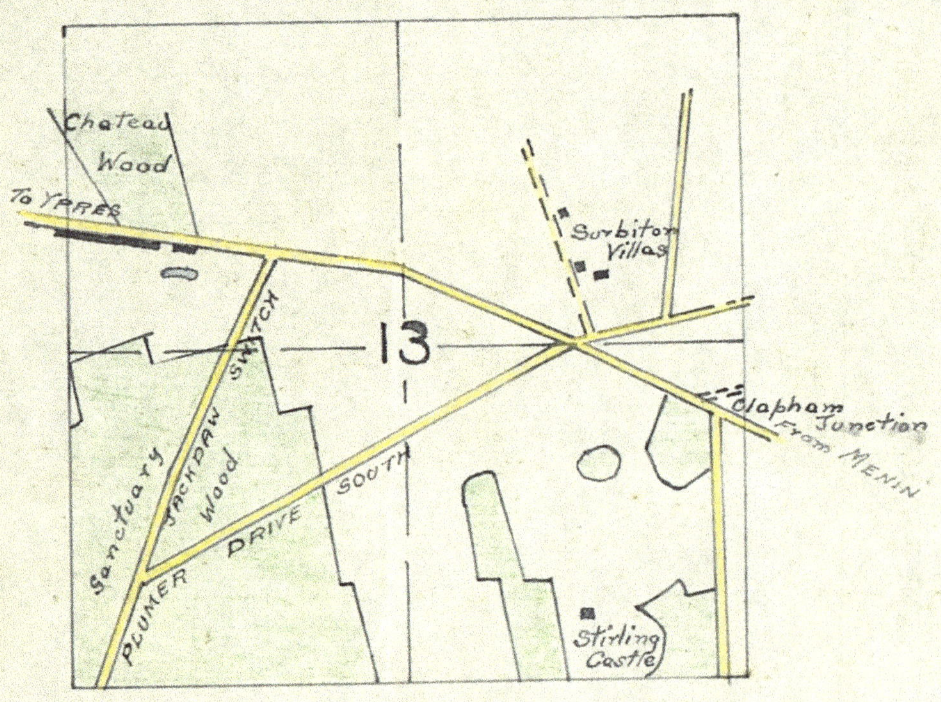

SCALE 1:10,000.

5.10..17.

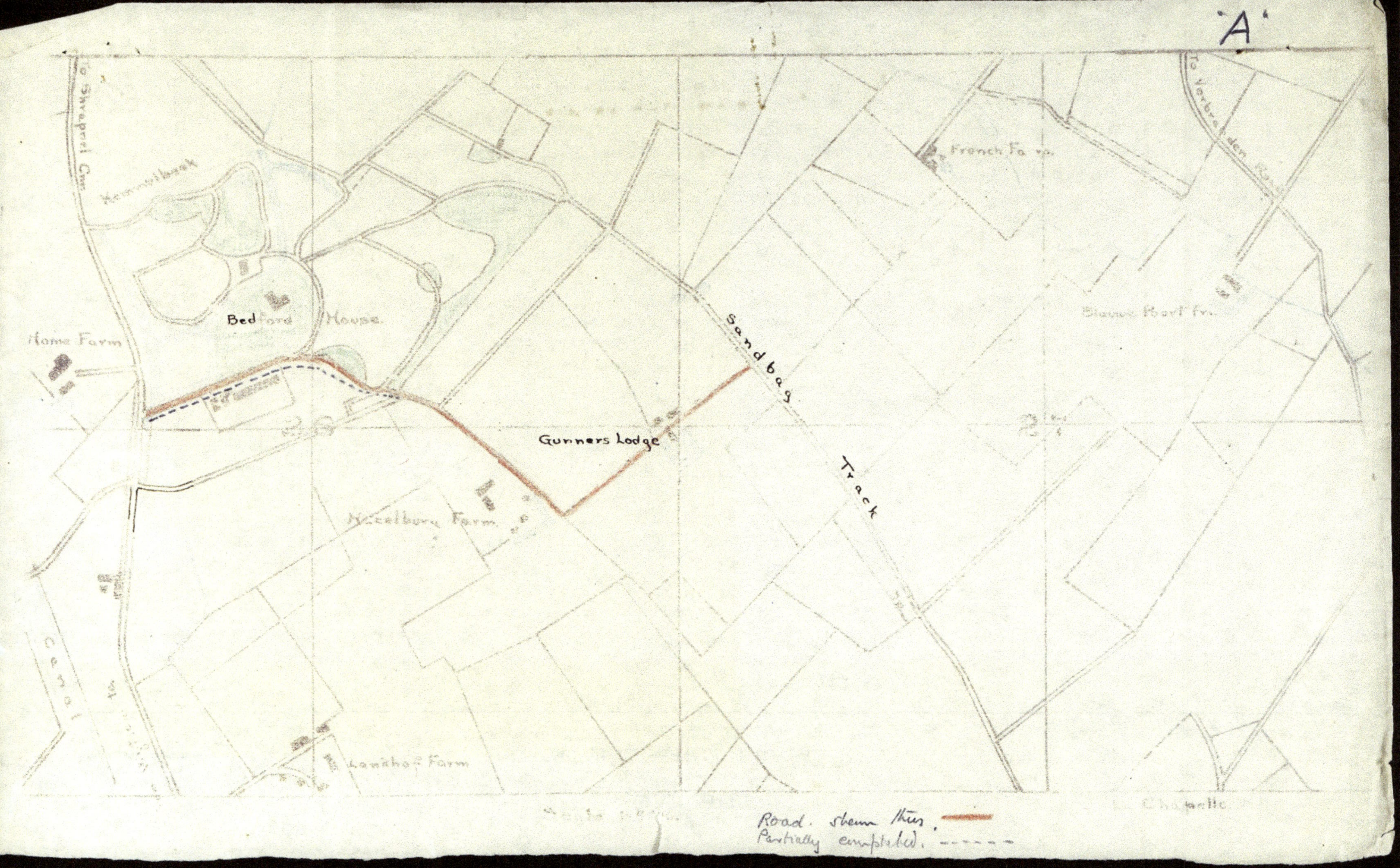

'A'
To Shrapnel Cnr.
To Verbranden Rd.
French Farm
Blauwe Poort Fr.
Bedford House.
Home Farm
Sandbag Track
Gunners Lodge
Canal
Lankhof Farm
Chapelle
Road. shewn thus.
Partially completed.

Instructions regarding War Diaries and Intelligence Summaries are contained in F. S. Regs., Part II. and the Staff Manual respectively. Title pages will be prepared in manuscript.

WAR DIARY
or
INTELLIGENCE SUMMARY.
(*Erase heading not required.*)

Army Form C. 2118.

Vol 35

Place	Date	Hour	Summary of Events and Information	Remarks and references to Appendices

CONFIDENTIAL

WAR DIARY

OF

11th Field Company R.E.

(VOLUME)

From November 1st 1917 To 30th November 1917.

C R L Balcombe
Major RE
O.C. 11th Field Coy RE

A5834 Wt. W4973 M687 750,000 8/16 D. D. & L. Ltd. Forms/C.2118/13.

Instructions regarding War Diaries and Intelligence Summaries are contained in F. S. Regs., Part II. and the Staff Manual respectively. Title pages will be prepared in manuscript.

WAR DIARY
or
INTELLIGENCE SUMMARY.
(Erase heading not required.)

Army Form C. 2118.

Place	Date	Hour	Summary of Events and Information	Remarks and references to Appendices
On NEUVE-EGLISE – WULVERGHEM Road T.10.a.5.9. (Sheet 28)	Nov 1	1917	Coy employed as follows No 1 Sect. Concrete O.P.s for 47th Bde. R.F.A. N.E of MESSINES. No 2 Sect. Commenced work on New Reserve Line with inf. party consisting of 4th Kings Regt. No 3 Sect. R. Batt H.Q., "C" type shelters covered with concrete. No 4 Sect. Mule track from PETIT DOUVE DUMP – WHITE SPOT CUTTING	CHR
	Nov 2		As yesterday. No 4 Sect. stopped MULE TRACK & went to work on New CROSS St.	CHR
	Nov 3		As yesterday. The enemy artillery seem to be gradually lengthening & shows more activity than formerly	CHR
	Nov 4		Work as usual, fair amount of gas shelling on early morn.	CHR
	Nov 5		As before. Bad weather	CHR
	Nov 6		Work as usual	CHR

A5834 Wt. W4973 M687 750,000 8/16 D. D. & L. Ltd. Forms/C.2118/13.

Army Form C. 2118.

WAR DIARY
or
INTELLIGENCE SUMMARY.
(*Erase heading not required.*)

Instructions regarding War Diaries and Intelligence Summaries are contained in F. S. Regs., Part II. and the Staff Manual respectively. Title pages will be prepared in manuscript.

Place	Date	Hour	Summary of Events and Information	Remarks and references to Appendices
On WOLVERGHEM – NEUVE EGLISE Rd	Nov 7.		Work as before. Lt. W.H.E. GARROD proceeded on leave to U.K.	CPKB
	Nov 8.		Work as usual. No night work on Res. Line owing to relief of 19 I.B. by [illegible] I.B.	CPKB
T.10.a.5.9 (sheet 28)	Nov 9		Work as usual. Increased activity of shelling	CPKB
	Nov 10		Work as usual. Wet all day.	CPKB
	Nov 11		Work as usual	CPKB
	Nov 12		Work as usual	CPKB
	Nov 13.		Officer from 5th Aus. Div. 8th Aus. Fld Coy. came to look over trench. work as usual.	
	[illegible]		Major FARQUARSON 8th Aust. Fld Coy came & went over work & all maps etc handed over to him.	CPKB
HAZEBROUCK Sheet 5A. [illegible] of 1st R in MERRIS	Nov 14		Coy. moved off from Billets at 9.15 am. joining 19th I.B. on march at Rd. Junction T 20.a.8.0 (sheet 28). Marched to MERRIS via BAILLEUL. Arrived MERRIS 2-0 p.m. Good weather for marching.	CPKB
	Nov 15		Coy at MERRIS. General clean up. Played football v. 212 Fld Coy R.E. & lost 3-1.	[illegible]

A5834 Wt. W4973 M687 750,000 8/16 D. D. & L. Ltd. Forms/C.2118/13.

Army Form C. 2118.

WAR DIARY
or
INTELLIGENCE SUMMARY.
(Erase heading not required.)

•Instructions regarding War Diaries and Intelligence Summaries are contained in F. S. Regs., Part II. and the Staff Manual respectively. Title pages will be prepared in manuscript.

Place	Date	Hour	Summary of Events and Information	Remarks and references to Appendices
HAZEBROUCK Sheet 5A. 100 yds N of 1st R in MERRIS	16		Rested in MERRIS. Mounted v. Dismounted at Football. Mounted won 7-4.	CRLH
	17		Coy moved off at 5.45 am. & embussed on the STRAZEELE - PRADELLES road at 9.0 am. Debussed at the Asylum - Ypres, & marched to camp at I.2.c.5.5 (sheet 28). ~~Dis~~ Mounted marched under Bde arrangements to camp at GOLDFISH CH. H 11. central.	CRLH
Camp in Ypres I 2 c.5.5. (sheet 28)	18		Coy cleaning camp etc. General reconnaissance	CRLH
	19		Nos 2 & 3 Sects. on 'K' & 'H' tracks respectively. Tracks lead off ZONNEBEKE - YPRES Road to PASCHENDAELE. Nos 1 & 4 Sect work in camp.	CRLH
	20.		Nos 2, & 3 on Secs. work on tracks as above. No 1 Sect work in camp	CRLB
	21		As above no change.	CRLB
	22.		As above. Lt. W.H.E. GARROD returned from leave	CRLB.

A5834 Wt. W4973 M687 750,000 8/16 D. D. & L. Ltd. Forms/C.2118/13.

Instructions regarding War Diaries and Intelligence Summaries are contained in F. S. Regs., Part II. and the Staff Manual respectively. Title pages will be prepared in manuscript.

WAR DIARY
or
INTELLIGENCE SUMMARY.
(Erase heading not required.)

Army Form C. 2118.

Place	Date	Hour	Summary of Events and Information	Remarks and references to Appendices
Camp in YPRES. I.2.c.5.5. Horse lines H.11 Central (Sheet 28)	23		Nos 1, 2 & 3 Sect on tracks – with addition of improvements on Arsenal R.A.M.C. Posts. No 4 Sec. placed under orders of C.R.A. 33rd Div. for purposes of assisting artillery. 1 shell (5.9 H.V.) dropped in Coy Billet. Spr WALTERS was killed. This man was proceeding on leave this night.	[initials]
	24		Work as usual.	[initials]
	25.		Work as usual	[initials]
	26		Work as usual	[initials]
	27		Work as usual	[initials]
	28		Work as usual	[initials]
	29		Work as usual	[initials]
	30		Work as usual tracks all damaged by heavy shelling. Enemy Barrage at 6.45 am. & there was considerable shelling all day. L/Cpl MORLEY & of 3 sappers wounded whilst working at TRANSIT DUMP YPRES Stn.	[initials]

A5834 Wt. W4973 M687 750,000 8/16 D. D. & L. Ltd. Forms/C.2118/13.

Instructions regarding War Diaries and Intelligence Summaries are contained in F. S. Regs., Part II. and the Staff Manual respectively. Title pages will be prepared in manuscript.

WAR DIARY
or
INTELLIGENCE SUMMARY.
(Erase heading not required.)

Army Form C. 2118.

Vol 36

Place	Date	Hour	Summary of Events and Information	Remarks and references to Appendices

CONFIDENTIAL

WAR DIARY

OF

11th (Field) Co. R.E

VOLUME ( ).

From 1st December 1917 To 31st December 1917.

C.P.L. Balcomb Major R.E.
Commdg. 11th Coy. R.E

A5834 Wt. W4973/M687 750,000 8/16 D. D. & L. L. L.

Instructions regarding War Diaries and Intelligence Summaries are contained in F. S. Regs., Part II. and the Staff Manual respectively. Title pages will be prepared in manuscript.

WAR DIARY
or
INTELLIGENCE SUMMARY.
(Erase heading not required.)

Army Form C. 2118.

Place	Date	Hour	Summary of Events and Information	Remarks and references to Appendices
I.2.c.5.5. (Ref map Sheet 28) on YPRES – St. JEAN Rd.	1/12/17		Coy Employed as usual. No 1 Sec on Improvements to forward R.A.M.C. aidposts. No 2 Sec on K track. No 3 Sec on H track. No 4 Sec under C.R.A. 33rd Div. generally assisting the R.F.A. in forward areas	CWLB
	2nd		Work as usual. Track consistently shelled – especially in vicinity of ABRAHAM HEIGHTS.	CWLB
	3rd		Work as usual. Usual area shoot round KANSAS CROSS – where No 4 Sect are making road to guns.	CWLB
	4th		Work as usual. Enemy aircraft very active – & several low flying machines were in evidence	CWLB
	5th		Work as usual.	CWLB
	6th		Work as usual. No 3 Sec commenced building new Coy Billets at I.8.b.5.5. just E of MENIN GATE on ZONNEBEKE Rd.	CWLB
	7th		Work as usual	CWLB
	8th		Work as usual. Tracks moderately shelled all day	CWLB
	9th		Work as usual.	CWLB
	10th		Work as usual	CWLB
	11th		Work as usual	CWLB
	12th		Work as usual. Major CHIVERS O.C. 447 Fld Coy R.E. 50th Div. arrived to take over work etc – on relief of the Div.	CWLB

Instructions regarding War Diaries and Intelligence Summaries are contained in F. S. Regs., Part II. and the Staff Manual respectively. Title pages will be prepared in manuscript.

WAR DIARY
or
INTELLIGENCE SUMMARY.
(Erase heading not required.)

Army Form C. 2118.

Place	Date	Hour	Summary of Events and Information	Remarks and references to Appendices
I.2.C.5.5. on St Jean YPRES Road	13.12.17.		The Coy rested today - & work was carried on by relieving Coy. (244) Fld Coy R.E.)	[initials]
	14.12.17.		New work under VIII Corps commenced ① Upkeep of main ZONNEBEKE E of FREEZENBERG - as far as DEVILS CROSSING 2 sections sappers (Nos 2 & 4), 'B' Corps Works Coy, & 18) Labour Coy. ② Construction of New Plank road - from just W. of DEVILS CROSSING - SEINE Rd via WINDMILL CABARET Nos 1 & 4 Sects & 2 Coys of 16th K.R.R	[initials]
	15.12.17		Work as yesterday. Enemy aircraft active.	[initials]
	16.12.17		Work as yesterday.	[initials]
	17.12.17.		Work on plank road was handed over to the 18th Mdxx (Pioneers). Nos 1 & 2 Sect continued on Maintenance of Southern Road. Nos 3 & 4 Sect commenced on New CORPS LINE; consisting of an observation line - running from VAMPIRE (on ZONNEBEKE RD) - BRIDGEHOUSE (St JEAN RD) - VANHEULE (St Julian Rd) The main line runs from FREEZENBERG X RDS - GREY RUIN - & crosses St JEAN RD (200yds W of RAT Fm - St Julian RD - S of CHECKERS Fm.	[initials]

A5834 Wt. W4973 M687 750,000 8/16 D. D. & L. Ltd. Forms/C.2118/13.

Army Form C. 2118.

Instructions regarding War Diaries and Intelligence Summaries are contained in F. S. Regs., Part II. and the Staff Manual respectively. Title pages will be prepared in manuscript.

WAR DIARY
or
INTELLIGENCE SUMMARY.
(Erase heading not required.)

Place	Date	Hour	Summary of Events and Information	Remarks and references to Appendices
YPRES - St JEAN Rd. I.2.c.5.5. (sheet 28)	18.12.17		Work as usual. Nos 1 & 2 on Road, & 3 & 4 on Corps Line	[illegible]
	19.12.17		Work as usual. Very heavy frost.	[illegible]
	20.12.17		Work as usual. Still freezing hard	[illegible]
MENIN GATE I8.b.3.4. (sheet 28)	21.12.17		No 2 Sec. moved to STEENVOORDE. Dismounted by lorry, mounted & cyclists by road. They relieved one sec 212 Fd Coy. Work to be generally assisting the Divn. (on rest) Coy H.Q. changed to MENIN GATE I 8.b.3.4. (sheet 28), took over & handed over work to 212 Fd Coy RE. Work on new horse lines.	[illegible]
	22.12.17		Work as yesterday, on new horse lines & improving new camp.	[illegible]
	23.12.17		Work as above. The frost still holds, & the ice is about 2" thick on Canal.	[illegible]
	24.12.17		Work as above.	
	25.12.17		Xmas Day. No work. Church service in morning. No 2 Sec. remained at STEENVOORDE. Nos 1, 3 & 4 Secs. had a good feed here, provided out of Canteen Funds. Breakfast 8.0am Sausages & bacon. Dinner 1.0pm Roast beef, cabbage & potatoes. Plum Pudding & 1 pint of beer per man. Tea 4.30pm Tinned salmon, bread, butter & jam etc. Supper. 8.0pm Ham sandwiches ½ pint beer.	[illegible]
	26.12.17		Work on horse lines as usual.	

A5834 Wt. W4973 M687 750,000 8/16 D. D. & L. Ltd. Forms/C.2118/13.

Instructions regarding War Diaries and Intelligence Summaries are contained in F. S. Regs., Part II. and the Staff Manual respectively. Title pages will be prepared in manuscript.

WAR DIARY
or
INTELLIGENCE SUMMARY.
(Erase heading not required.)

Army Form C. 2118.

Place	Date	Hour	Summary of Events and Information	Remarks and references to Appendices
MENIN GATE. I8. b. 3. 4. (Sheet 28)	27.12.17		Work on Horse Lines no change.	CRLB
	28.12.17		do as above.	
	29.12.17		Handed over work on Horse Lines to 222nd Coy, & took over work from them. Work Nos 1. 2 Sects under No 5 Army Tramway Coy – maintenance of the KANSAS CROSS – SEINE line.	CRLB
			Nos 3 & 4 Sec. Maintenance & doubling of KANSAS X – ZONNEBEKE Plank Rd.	CRLB
	30.12.17		Work as above.	CRLB
	31.12.17		Work as above. Maj. C.R.L. BALCOMBE moved to H.Q.R.E. for purpose of taking over control of all forward roads in Corps Area (with Corps)	CRLB

A5834 Wt. W4973 M687 750,000 8/16 D. D. & L. Ltd. Forms/C.2118/13.

Instructions regarding War Diaries and Intelligence Summaries are contained in F. S. Regs., Part II. and the Staff Manual respectively. Title pages will be prepared in manuscript.

WAR DIARY
or
INTELLIGENCE SUMMARY.
(Erase heading not required.)

Army Form C. 2118.

Vol 37

Place	Date	Hour	Summary of Events and Information	Remarks and references to Appendices
			CONFIDENTIAL	
			WAR DIARY OF	
			11th Field Coy R.E.	
			(Volume)	
			From 1st ~~February~~ January 1918. To 31st January 1918.	
			P L Brabant Major RE. O.C. 11th Field Coy RE.	

A5834 Wt. W4973 M687 750,000 8/16 D. D. & L. Ltd. Forms/C.2118/13.

Instructions regarding War Diaries and Intelligence Summaries are contained in F. S. Regs., Part II. and the Staff Manual respectively. Title pages will be prepared in manuscript.

WAR DIARY
or
INTELLIGENCE SUMMARY.
(Erase heading not required.)

Army Form C. 2118.

Place	Date	Hour	Summary of Events and Information	Remarks and references to Appendices
MENIN GATE I 8.b 3.4 (Sheet 28)	1.1.18		Coy working on Corps Work Forward Rd. Plank Rd. KANSAS X - ZONNEBEKE RD and Light RAILWAY MAJOR BALCOMBE a/ CRE FORWARD ROADS	H.D.J.
	2.1.18		Work as on 1st.	H.D.J.
	3.1.18		do do do	H.D.J.
	4.1.18		do do do JUDAH TRACK and DIV. HQ (1 SECTION).	H.D.J.
	5.1.18		do do do and working on	H.D.J.
	6.1.18		MAJOR BALCOMBE RE a/ CRE 33RD DIVISION. Nos 1 & 4 SECTIONS plus Carpenters & Painters from No 2 Section working on DIVISIONAL HQ THE RAMPARTS YPRES. DIVINE SERVICE 3-30 PM (CAPT LEWIS C.F.) No 2 & 3 SECTIONS JUDAH TRACK.	H.D.J.
	7.1.18		Work as on 6th Lieut Harper a/2nd Cpl KARK. J. to VIII CORPS GAS SCHOOL	H.D.J.
	8.1.18		do do	H.D.J.
	9.1.18		do do	H.D.J.
	10.1.18		do do	H.D.J.
	11.1.18		do do	H.D.J.
	12.1.18		do do and 2 Sappers working for D 156 BATTY 2 FROST House DRESSING STN and 2 BRIGADE H.Q.	H.D.J.
	13.1.18		Same as 12th plus 2 Sappers repairing SQUARE Fm PILL BOX. DIVINE SERVICE AT 3.PM SERMON BY MAJOR MAYNE SENIOR CHAPLAIN FORCES CE 33RD DIVn	
	14.1.18		Work as on 13th	H.D.J.

Instructions regarding War Diaries and Intelligence Summaries are contained in F. S. Regs., Part II. and the Staff Manual respectively. Title pages will be prepared in manuscript.

WAR DIARY
or
INTELLIGENCE SUMMARY.
(Erase heading not required.)

Army Form C. 2118.

Place	Date	Hour	Summary of Events and Information	Remarks and references to Appendices
Menin Gate I 8.b.3.4	27-1-18		Work of Coy taken over by 447th Field Coy. Dismounted portion of Coy entrained at St Jean Station at 3.40 for St. Omer and marched to Salperwick arriving about 9.30 pm.	N.D.J
Salperwick. Hazebrouck 5A Edition 2 Belgium	28-1-18		No 1 & 4 Sections marched off 10 AM under Lieut Feary for Mortbecourt 4th Army Musketry School. No 2 & 3 Sections drill parade 9 AM – dismissed for cleaning up. Lieut Harper proceeded on leave to UK.	N.D.J
Sheet 27A SE R 21 d.1.2	29-1-18		The Bridging Wagons left 8 AM under Lieut Garrod to dump Bridging Equipment at Pontoon Park. No 2 & 3 Sections paraded full marching order for inspection 9 AM. Kit Inspection 10.30 AM. dinner 12.30 pm afternoon off.	N.D.J
	30-1-18		Major Balcombe rejoined Coy. No 2–3 Sections drilling in morning till 10.30. Rifle Exercises 11.0 – 12 noon. dinner 12.30 pm. Afternoon Run.	N.D.J
	31-1-18		No's 2 & 3 Sections rifle drill & movement of arms. Football in the afternoon.	

Army Form C. 2118.

Instructions regarding War Diaries and Intelligence Summaries are contained in F. S. Regs., Part II. and the Staff Manual respectively. Title pages will be prepared in manuscript.

WAR DIARY
or
INTELLIGENCE SUMMARY.
(Erase heading not required.)

VR 38

Place	Date	Hour	Summary of Events and Information	Remarks and references to Appendices

CONFIDENTIAL

WAR DIARY OF

11TH FD COY R.E.

(Volume)

From 1st February 1918
To 28th February 1918

P.L. Balcombe [signature]
Major, R.E.
Commdg. 11th Coy. R.E.

A5834 Wt. W4973 M687 750,000 8/16 D. D. & L. Ltd. Forms/C.2118/13.

Army Form C. 2118.

Instructions regarding War Diaries and Intelligence Summaries are contained in F. S. Regs., Part II. and the Staff Manual respectively. Title pages will be prepared in manuscript.

WAR DIARY
or
INTELLIGENCE SUMMARY.
(Erase heading not required.)

Place	Date	Hour	Summary of Events and Information	Remarks and references to Appendices
SALPERWICK Sheet 27a SE R21.d.1.2	1.2.18		No 2 & 3 Section Squad Drill movement of Ammn. football in afternoon. Nos 1 & 4 Sections at 4th Army Musketry School HORTBECOURT.	H.J.
	2.2.18		do do do do do	H.J.
	3.2.18		Voluntary Church Parade at 2.30 pm	H.J.
	4.2.18		Squad Drill, Lecture on Gas by Coy Gas N.C.O. movement of Ammn. football in afternoon. 30 Sappers & Drivers inoculated	H.J.
	5.2.18		Mounted Parade as usual all Sappers not inoculated employed in cleaning and painting wagons.	H.J.
	6.2.18		Squad Drill. Lecture on R.E. Reconnaissance. Football match in afternoon v. 102nd Field Ambulance. 1st Coy winning 4-2. Smoking Concert in School from 6-9 pm.	H.J.
	7.2.18		Gas Drill in Battle order, football in afternoon. Squad drill. 1 N.C.O. & 10 Sappers working for 19th A.B.	H.J.
	8.2.18		No 2 & 3 Sections proceeded to HORTBECOURT to relieve Nos 1 & 4 Sections	H.J.

Army Form C. 2118.

Instructions regarding War Diaries and Intelligence Summaries are contained in F. S. Regs., Part II. and the Staff Manual respectively. Title pages will be prepared in manuscript.

WAR DIARY
or
INTELLIGENCE SUMMARY.

(*Erase heading not required.*)

Place	Date	Hour	Summary of Events and Information	Remarks and references to Appendices
SALPERWICK SHEET 27 SE R21 d 1.2	9.2.18		Capt N J Johnson RE went to Course for OC's + 2nd in Command at ~~[illegible]~~ BLENDECQUES SHEET 5A RE School of Instruction. Aiming Drill. Squad drill football in afternoon Lt S Geary RE took over Command of Coy	SA
	10.2.18		Musketry Squad Drill Handling of Arms. Football in afternoon	SA
	11.2.18		Squad Drill. RE Reconnaissance Football match against 212 Lost 1-3	SA
	12.2.18		Nos 2 + 3 Sections returned from NORBECOURT for scheme against low flying Aeroplanes	SA
	13.2.18		Scheme against Low flying Aeroplanes postponed owing to bad visibility. Musketry Drill Handling of Arms Gas lecture	SA
	14.2.18		Scheme again postponed. Squad Drill. Washed and painted remaining wagons	SA
	15.2.18		Squad Drill, RE Reconnaissance. Trial match Possibles v Probables for Divisional RE team against Winners of Div Football Competition.	SA
	16.2.18		Inspection of Coy by GOC 33rd Division at 12 noon Football in afternoon	SA
	17.2.18		Presentation of medal ribbons by GOC 33rd Division. Transport of Nos 2 + 3 Sections returned from NORBECOURT.	SA
	18.2.18		Transport left for YPRES. All NCOs + men put through Gas.	SA

A5834 Wt. W4973 M687 750,000 8/16 D. D. & L. Ltd. Forms/C.2118/13.

Instructions regarding War Diaries and Intelligence Summaries are contained in F. S. Regs., Part II. and the Staff Manual respectively. Title pages will be prepared in manuscript.

WAR DIARY
or
INTELLIGENCE SUMMARY.
(Erase heading not required.)

Army Form C. 2118.

Place	Date	Hour	Summary of Events and Information	Remarks and references to Appendices
SALPERWICK SHEET 27 SE R21d, 2	19.2.18		Scheme against Low flying Aeroplanes. Nos 2 & 3 Sections returned from NORBÈCOURT football in afternoon	SJ
YPRES SHEET 28 I8b34	20.2.18		Coy moved to YPRES. relieved the 446th Field Coy. RE	SJ
	21.2.18		MAJOR C.P.L BALCOMBE RE resumed command of the Coy Work taken over as follows	
			No1 Sec opening up cellars in PASSCHENDALE	
			No2 & 3 " HILLSIDE DEFENCES. HAALEN SWITCH Defences	SJ
			No 4 " CREST FARM Defences. BELLEVUE SWITCH LINE Defences HILLSIDE Defences	
			No1 Sec proceeded to CREST FARM Dugouts	
	22.2.18 27.2.18		Work continued on above	SJ
	28.2.18		No3 Sec relieved No1 Sec at CREST FARM Dugouts after days work	SJ

A5834 Wt. W4973 M687 750,000 8/16 D. D. & L. Ltd. Forms/C.2118/13.

Instructions regarding War Diaries and Intelligence Summaries are contained in F. S. Regs., Part II. and the Staff Manual respectively. Title pages will be prepared in manuscript.

WAR DIARY
or
INTELLIGENCE SUMMARY.
(Erase heading not required.)

Army Form C. 2118.

WO 39

Place	Date	Hour	Summary of Events and Information	Remarks and references to Appendices

CONFIDENTIAL.

WAR DIARY

OF

11th Field Company. R.E.

(Volume)

From 1st March 1918.

To 31st March 1918

P. L. Balm[illegible] Major R.E.
O.C. 11th Field Coy R.E.

A5834 Wt. W4973 M687 750,000 8/16 D. D. & L. Ltd. Forms/C.2118/13.

Instructions regarding War Diaries and Intelligence Summaries are contained in F. S. Regs., Part II. and the Staff Manual respectively. Title pages will be prepared in manuscript.

WAR DIARY
or
INTELLIGENCE SUMMARY.
(Erase heading not required.)

Army Form C. 2118.

Place	Date	Hour	Summary of Events and Information	Remarks and references to Appendices
YPRES	1.3.18		Sections employed on works in forward area. No 3 Section PASSCHENDAELE No 1. HILLSIDE DEFENCES No 2. HAALEN SWITCH No 4 CREST FARM Defences.	
	2.3.18		ditto	
	3.3.18		ditto Sappers UNSWORTH. P. + KNEALE J. killed night of 3/4 March	
	4.3.18		ditto work on 24 Sa + Sb HAALEN SWITCH Defences commenced	
	5.3.18		ditto Sapper OFFEN W. wounded. HAALEN SWITCH No 2 finished	
	6.3.18		ditto	
	7.3.18		Working on 12 R. 14 R. 18 S. 20 S. The Hut. DOCTORS HOUSE and CREST FARM DEFENCES.	
	8.3.18		do do and HAALEN SWITCH No 3	
	9.3.18		do do and WINDMILL and BELLVUE SWITCH	
	10.3.18		do do and Posts 24 Sa + 24 Sb.	
	11.3.18		do do do	
	12.3.18		do do do.	
	13.3.18		do do and draining + building sand bag walls at Pill Box No 11 INFIRM.	

A5834 Wt. W4973 M687 750,000 8/16 D. D. & L. Ltd. Forms/C.2118/13.

Instructions regarding War Diaries and Intelligence Summaries are contained in F. S. Regs., Part II. and the Staff Manual respectively. Title pages will be prepared in manuscript.

WAR DIARY
or
INTELLIGENCE SUMMARY.
(Erase heading not required.)

Army Form C. 2118.

Place	Date	Hour	Summary of Events and Information	Remarks and references to Appendices
YPRES I.8.b.3.4	14.3.18		Sections working on Posts 12.R. 14 R. 24 S.b. CREST F^M Defences Pill Box No 11 INFIRM. PRIMUS POST	
			do do do and PRIMUS O.P. and R^T COY. H.Q.	
	15.3.18		do do do do do	
	16.3.18		do do do do do	
	17.3.18		do do do do do.	
	18.3.18		Posts 12 R. 14 R. 24 Sb HALLEN N^o3 CREST F^M DEFENCES Pill Box No 6 INCLINE PRIMUS. O.P. R^T COY H.Q	
	19.3.18		do do do do and 26. S.D. and 17.18.20 S	
	20.3.18		do do do do do do	
	21.3.18		do do do do do	
	22.3.18		Posts 12 R. 17.18.19. S. PRIMUS. O.P. 24 S.d. HALLEN SWITCH N^o3. CREST F^M DEFENCES PILL BOX No8 TYNE COTT	
	23.3.18		do. do do do do	
	24.3.18		do do do do.	
	25.3.18		do do do do.	

A5834 Wt. W4973 M687 750,000 8/16 D. D. & L. Ltd. Forms/C.2118/13.

Instructions regarding War Diaries and Intelligence Summaries are contained in F. S. Regs., Part II. and the Staff Manual respectively. Title pages will be prepared in manuscript.

WAR DIARY
or
INTELLIGENCE SUMMARY.

(Erase heading not required.)

Army Form C. 2118.

Place	Date	Hour	Summary of Events and Information	Remarks and references to Appendices
			SECTIONS WORKING ON.	
YPRES	26.3.18		PRIMUS O.P. 18 S 23 S Post 24 S.b HAALEN SWITCH No3, CREST	
I8 b.3.4			FARM DEFENCES RT COY POST 26 S d.	
	27.3.18		do do do do do do	
	28.3.18		do do do do do do.	
	29.3.18		Post 23 b PRIMUS O.P. HAALEN SWITCH No3 POST 18 R	
			CRES FM DEFENCES, 26 S d. 18 S. 20 S.	
	30.3.18		do do do do	
	31.3.18		do do do do	

A5834 Wt. W4073 M687 750,000 8/16 D. D. & L. Ltd. Forms/C.2118/13.

33rd Divisional Engineers

11th FIELD COMPANY R.E. ::::: APRIL 1918.

Army Form C. 2118.

*Instructions regarding War Diaries and Intelligence Summaries are contained in F. S. Regs., Part II. and the Staff Manual respectively. Title pages will be prepared in manuscript.

WAR DIARY
or
INTELLIGENCE SUMMARY.
(Erase heading not required.)

VR 40

Place	Date	Hour	Summary of Events and Information	Remarks and references to Appendices
			CONFIDENTIAL WAR DIARY OF 11TH FD COY R.E. Volume ______ P.L. Balcombe Major, R.E. Commdg. 11th Coy. R.E. From 1st April 1918 To 30th April 1918.	

A5834 Wt. W4973/M687 750,000 8/16 D. D. & L. Ltd. Forms/C.2118/1

Instructions regarding War Diaries and Intelligence Summaries are contained in F. S. Regs., Part II. and the Staff Manual respectively. Title pages will be prepared in manuscript.

WAR DIARY
or
INTELLIGENCE SUMMARY.
(Erase heading not required.)

Army Form C. 2118.

Place	Date	Hour	Summary of Events and Information	Remarks and references to Appendices
MENIN Gate YPRES I.8.b.3.4 (Sheet 28)	1		No 1 Sect working on S.Ps. on PASSCHENDAELE – BROODSEINDE Rd. + O.P in same place. No 2 Sect. " " on HAALEN SWITCH Line No 3 Sect " CREST FARM Defences No 4 Sect " HILLSIDE Defences.	
	2.		O.C 510 Field Coy RE came to take over work in line (29th Div). Secs working as usual.	
	3.		Secs working as usual. Officers + NCOs of 510 Field Coy RE went round works. Relief was complete by 6.0 p.m.	
RIDGE CAMP BRANDHOEK	4.		Coy moved off 8.0 am. to RIDGE CAMP BRANDHOEK Arrived in camp 10.30 am. Billets at MENIN GATE handed over to 467 Field Coy RE (59th Div) 2/Lt SUMMERS joined.	
	5.		Coy Remained at RIDGE CAMP. General cleaning up.	
	6.		Coy Remained at RIDGE CAMP. Played football v. 222 Field Coy RE lost 1–0.	
GRANDE RULLECOURT BILLET 71	7.		Coy moved off (Transport 2.0 am) 4.0 am. + entrained at HOPOUTRE Siding (W. of Pop) + moved off by train 6.15 am. Detrained AUBIGNY + marched to GRAND RULLECOURT arriving 6.0 p.m. Wet day.	

A5834 Wt. W4973 M687 750,000 8/16 D. D. & L. Ltd. Forms/C.2118/13.

Instructions regarding War Diaries and Intelligence Summaries are contained in F. S. Regs., Part II. and the Staff Manual respectively. Title pages will be prepared in manuscript.

WAR DIARY
or
INTELLIGENCE SUMMARY.
(Erase heading not required.)

Army Form C. 2118.

Place	Date	Hour	Summary of Events and Information	Remarks and references to Appendices
Billet 71 GRAND ROLLECOURT	8		Coy paraded for musketry instruction. Range allotted to us on GRAND ROLLECOURT — SOMBRIN Rd. Officers & N.C.O's attended lecture by Maj. Gen. R. PINNEY CB. in afternoon. Wet day.	
	9.		Coy carried out musketry all day. Firing on range.	
	10.		Coy fired on range in morning. Lt FLATTERS & C.M. went to reconnoitre "purple line" near FICHEUX - BLAIREVILLE - MONCHY. Coy ordered to stand by for a move at once. Moved off at moment's notice 8.45 pm. Marched to AUBIGNY & entrained. Transport went by road.	
Farm at X9d27. (Ref sheet 27)	11.		Detrained at CAESTRE at 12.0 noon. Marched to METEREN. Everything was fairly quiet. Roads full of refugees etc. Coy arrived in billets about 7.0 pm. very done up. ~~Tool~~ forage carts arrived about midnight.	
	12.		Enemy commenced shelling Meteren. Place was on fire by nightfall. No 4 Sect. put in M.G. emplacements on roads S & SE of Meteren. Heavy shell fire on village. Remainder of Coy standing to. I went to Bde H.Q. (19th I.B.) wildest rumours were afloat but the situation calmed down considerably.	
	13.		Rode with B.G. MAYNE (G.O.C 19th I.B.) round line etc & saw Battn. commanders. The situation was very obscure. Billet ~~got~~ heavily shelled. In afternoon went to reconnoitre a line to join us up with 1 Australian Bde on Right, & to join switch line on main BAILLEUL Rd on left. Went to STRAZEELE & saw C.O. 4th Aus. Battn. got full details. Got back & found Bde had shifted, everyone standing to, manning ditches etc. The situation was cleared up shortly & all was well.	
	14.		Nos 3 & 4 Sects. went dug themselves in in posts connecting up support line to 1st Queens on left & Australians on right. Heavy Hun attack in progress. Spr. GIBSON killed. Nos 1 & 2 relieve 3 & 4 at 10.0 pm. holding the posts.	

A5834 Wt. W4973/M687 750,000 8/16 D. D. & L. Ltd. Forms/C.2118/13.

Instructions regarding War Diaries and Intelligence Summaries are contained in F. S. Regs., Part II. and the Staff Manual respectively. Title pages will be prepared in manuscript.

WAR DIARY
or
INTELLIGENCE SUMMARY.
(Erase heading not required.)

Army Form C. 2118.

Place	Date	Hour	Summary of Events and Information	Remarks and references to Appendices
X 2 c 2 2 (Sheet 27)	15		Coy moved to H.Q. Bde having taken over H.Q. Heavily shelled before leaving. 1/Cpl GENTLE R.A.M.C. killed. I was recalled to Bde H.Q. as it was reported that enemy was advancing along main BAILLEUL – METEREN road, some 1 kilo W. of BAILLEUL. Nos 1, 2 still occupying posts. Nos 3 & 4 working. I remained at Bde H.Q.	
	16		Heavy enemy attack all along our front. Bde H.Q. heavily machine gunned & shelled & moved to X 1 d 2 1. Coy was shelled out of Billets & lined in the road. The French came up in support (133 Div). Nos 1 & 2 Sects who were holding the posts under Lt FEARY & Lt SUMMERS were about to be relieved by 5th S.R. when attack commenced. The 2 Sects were shortly after sent to support 1st Kings on left. They then counter attacked a farm at X 14 d 9 1. This they captured with 3 machine guns, & 18 prisoners were sent back to Bde. At least 30 of the enemy were bayonetted in the farm, & severe casualties in addition inflicted by rifle fire. This was in all a most brilliant piece of work, & encouraged the inf. & also restored what might have been a very serious situation. The position ~~held~~ taken was held by Nos 1 & 2 Sects until I went up & brought them back at about midnight on the French having passed through us. The French attacked through us at 7.0 p.m. & the result was a quiet night. Lt FEARY wounded. 10 OR killed & 6 wounded.	
R. 34. a. 50. 85 (Sheet 27)	17.		Coy moved 8.0 am to R. 34 a 50 85. A minor move. Billets heavily shelled. Orders to work on "Green line" were given – but this was cancelled later.	
	18.		Coy under orders of 19th I.B. to support 34th Div. Took over work from 57th Field Coy R.E. Nos 1 & 2 fortifying houses in ST JAN CAPEL. No 3 digging C.T. along road to BAILLEUL – No 4 working. On going up to Bde	

Army Form C. 2118.

Instructions regarding War Diaries and Intelligence Summaries are contained in F. S. Regs., Part II. and the Staff Manual respectively. Title pages will be prepared in manuscript.

WAR DIARY
or
INTELLIGENCE SUMMARY.

(Erase heading not required.)

Place	Date	Hour	Summary of Events and Information	Remarks and references to Appendices
R 34 a 50.85 (Sheet 27)	18		HQ at Mont NOIR. Lt HARPER, 2Lt FLATTERS + 3 attached inf officers Lt Spence (1st Cams) Lt RAYNOR (1st Queens) Lt FORD (5th J.R.) were all wounded. All slightly except Lt HARPER who was serious. Billet heavily shelled. 1 ox. killed & 3 wounded.	
	19		Same work, billet.	
	20.		Moved off at 8.0 p.m. on being relieved by French. Bivouacked for the night with the Bde in fields near KRUYSTAATE.	
Aerodrome P 25 central (Sheet 27)	21.		Moved off from Bivouac at 9.30 am & marched off via Eecke & St Sylvestre Capel to Aerodrome. Arrived in Billets 6.0 p.m.	
	22.		All day at Aerodrome generally cleaning up etc.	
Q. 8 C. (Sheet 27)	23.		Inspected by Maj Gen PINNEY C.B. who was very complimentary to the Coy. The Coy moved off to fields at Q.8.C. Gen Mayne marched out with the Coy who were headed by the bands of the 1st Queens & pipes of 5th S.R's. Coy arrived & pitched tents.	
	24.		Working on WATOU - CAESTRE line.	
	25.		Working on WATOU - CAESTRE line.	

A5834 Wt. W4973/M687 750,000 8/16 D. D. & L. Ltd. Forms/C.2118/13.

Army Form C. 2118.

Instructions regarding War Diaries and Intelligence Summaries are contained in F. S. Regs., Part II. and the Staff Manual respectively. Title pages will be prepared in manuscript.

WAR DIARY
or
INTELLIGENCE SUMMARY.
(Erase heading not required.)

Place	Date	Hour	Summary of Events and Information	Remarks and references to Appendices
Q. 8 C (sheet 27)	26		Working on WATOU-CAESTRE line	
	27		do do	
	28		do do	
	29		do do. Line handed over to the French	
	30.		Working on switch line between WATOU line – POPERINGE line.	

A5834 Wt. W4973/M687 750,000 8/16 D. D. & L. Ltd. Forms/C.2118/13

Army Form C. 2118.

Instructions regarding War Diaries and Intelligence Summaries are contained in F. S. Regs., Part II. and the Staff Manual respectively. Title pages will be prepared in manuscript.

WAR DIARY
or
INTELLIGENCE SUMMARY.

(Erase heading not required.)

Vol 41

Place	Date	Hour	Summary of Events and Information	Remarks and references to Appendices
			Confidential.	
			War Diary	
			of	
			11th (Field) Coy. R.E.	
			Volume ____	
			From 1st May 1918. To 31st May 1918.	
			C.P.L. Balmain Major, R.E Commdg. 11th Coy. R.E	

D. D. & L., London, E.C.
(A8004) Wt W1771/M2031 750,000 5/17 Sch. 52 Forms/C2118/14

Instructions regarding War Diaries and Intelligence Summaries are contained in F. S. Regs., Part II. and the Staff Manual respectively. Title pages will be prepared in manuscript.

WAR DIARY
or
INTELLIGENCE SUMMARY.
(Erase heading not required.)

Army Form C. 2118.

Place	Date	Hour	Summary of Events and Information	Remarks and references to Appendices
STEENVOORDE Q. 8. C. (sheet 27)	1/5/18		Whole Coy working on the WATOU Line.	
	2/5/18		do do do	
	3/5/18		do do do	
Sheet 27 L9d01	4/5/18		Coy moved to new camp just outside POPERINGHE.	
	5/5/18		Coy started work on VLAMERTINGHE Line, in OTTAWA Camp. Proceeding to work by L.R.	
	6/5/18		do do	
	7/5/18		do do	
	8/5/18		do do	
	9/5/18		Supervising work on the HUBERTSHOEK Line. This line ran S.W. DICKEBUSCH – N.W. HALLEBAST CORNER – to join with French on LA CLYTTE – RENINGHELST road. No 3 Sect. supervised their work done by 600 inf. at night. Remainder of Coy as before.	
	10/5/18		Work on VLAMERTINGHE Line as usual. No 3 Sect. standing by.	
	11/5/18		Handed over work to the 7th Co. de Genie 44th French Inf. Div.	
	12/5/18		Coy went on the E POPERINGHE Support Line. Construction of new line, & shelters etc	
	13/5/18		do do	
	14/5/18		do do	
	15/5/18		do do	

Instructions regarding War Diaries and Intelligence Summaries are contained in F. S. Regs., Part II. and the Staff Manual respectively. Title pages will be prepared in manuscript.

WAR DIARY
or
INTELLIGENCE SUMMARY.
(*Erase heading not required.*)

Army Form C. 2118.

Place	Date	Hour	Summary of Events and Information	Remarks and references to Appendices
Sheet 27 (L9d01)	16/5/18		Coy training. Drill. Signalling. Extended order drill etc.	
	17/5/18		do do.	
	18/5/18		Coy took over work on VLAMERTINGHE Line. Construction of trenches & 2 concrete shelters.	
	19/5/18		do do	
	20/5/18		do do	
			On 20th 20 men from Coy under Capt. JOHNSTON were inspected on a general Div. Parade by Gen PLUMER G.O.C. 2nd Army.	
	21/5/18		Coy on VLAMERTINGHE Line as before.	
	22/5/18		Coy Training. Trestle bridging & use of Weldon Trestles, & bridging generally.	
	23/5/18		do do do	
	24/5/18		Coy on E POPERINGHE SUPPORT Line.	
	25/5/18		do	
	26/5/18		do	
	27/5/18		do	
	28/5/18		Coy Training. Trestle Bridging & demolitions.	
	29/5/18		do do.	

A5834 Wt. W4973/M687 750,000 8/16 D. D. & L. Ltd. Forms

Instructions regarding War Diaries and Intelligence Summaries are contained in F. S. Regs., Part II. and the Staff Manual respectively. Title pages will be prepared in manuscript.

WAR DIARY
or
INTELLIGENCE SUMMARY.
(Erase heading not required.)

Army Form C. 2118.

Place	Date	Hour	Summary of Events and Information	Remarks and references to Appendices
Sheet 27	30/5/18		Coy. working on VLAMERTINGHE Line.	
L9 d 0 1	31/5/18		do do.	
			During the month the honours for the Coy. gained in the recent operations in fighting around METEREN were awarded as below.	
			D. S. O. Lt. STEPHEN FEARY R.E.	
			Bar to M. C. Maj. C. P. L. BALCOMBE M.C. R.E.	
			D. C. M. No 20100 Sgt. DORRINGTON. A. G.	
			No 22630 Sgt LAWES. F. M.M.	
			Bar to M.M. No 167455 L/Cpl JAGO, C. K.	
			M. M. No 13232 L/Cpl AUSTIN, W.	
			No 20571 do LONG W.	
			No 21768 2/Cpl PIRIE R.	
			No 26133 Spr. WARD W.	

D. D. & L., London, E.C.
(A8004) Wt W1771/M2031 750,000 5/17 Sch. 52 Forms/C2118/14

Instructions regarding War Diaries and Intelligence Summaries are contained in F. S. Regs., Part II. and the Staff Manual respectively. Title pages will be prepared in manuscript.

WAR DIARY
or
INTELLIGENCE SUMMARY.
(Erase heading not required.)

Army Form C. 2118.

Vol 32

Place	Date	Hour	Summary of Events and Information	Remarks and references to Appendices

SECRET

WAR DIARY

of

11th Fd. Coy. R.E.

Volume ______

From
1st June 1918.

To.
30th June 1918.

[signature]
Major, R.E.
Commdg. 11th Coy. R.E.

D. D. & L., London, E.C.
(A8004) Wt W1771/M2031 750,000 5/17 Sch. 52 Forms/C2118/14

Army Form C. 2118.

Instructions regarding War Diaries and Intelligence Summaries are contained in F. S. Regs., Part II. and the Staff Manual respectively. Title pages will be prepared in manuscript.

WAR DIARY
or
INTELLIGENCE SUMMARY.
(Erase heading not required.)

Place	Date	Hour	Summary of Events and Information	Remarks and references to Appendices
Sheet 27 L9d01 SW of POPERINGHE	June 1st 1918		All Coy working on E. POPERINGHE Line.	
	2.6.18		do do do	
	3.6.18		Training. Trestle Bridging. Weldon trestles - lashings etc.	
	4.6.18		Training. Bayonet fighting, & extended order drill	
	5.6.18		Day off - preparatory to taking over work in Line - from 6th Div. (12th Field Coy.)	
	6.6.18		Party went up & took over bridges over YPRES - COMINES Canal, & sects sent parties to take over works in line.	
Sheet 28 G.10.b.20	7.6.18		Coy moved to billets of 12th Field Coy., & took over work from them. Horse Lines remained at old billets. Work taken over as below.	
			No 1 Sect. Concrete Command Posts for R.F.A.	
			No 2 Sect. Belgian Chateau. Road screening. Concrete Shelters for I.B.	
			No 3 Sect. G.H.Q. 1 Line.	
			No 4 Sect. do & demolitions.	
	8.6.18		Coy worked as usual. Sector appears to be a quiet one. Shelling on middle areas principally. Forward of G.H.Q. 1 Line practically no shelling. Certain amount of gas shelling between G.H.Q. 1 Line & Main Pop. YPRES Road.	
	9.6.18		As usual	

D. D. & L., London, E.C.
(A8004) Wt W1771/M2031 750,000 5/17 Sch. 52 Forms/C2118/14

Instructions regarding War Diaries and Intelligence Summaries are contained in F. S. Regs., Part II. and the Staff Manual respectively. Title pages will be prepared in manuscript.

WAR DIARY
or
INTELLIGENCE SUMMARY.
(Erase heading not required.)

Army Form C. 2118.

Place	Date	Hour	Summary of Events and Information	Remarks and references to Appendices
G.10.b.2.0 Sheet 28	10/6/18		Work as before. Artillery work being done in for 156 Bde & 162 Bde (Div Arty) & for 11th Bde RFA (Army). Fine weather. A fair amount of aeroplane activity — in which our planes are easily the superior.	
	11		Work as usual. The Enemy are expected to make a show up here — but so far no signs of this. The French on our right are constantly taking & retaking Ridge Wood.	
	12		Work as usual. Nothing of import happening	
	13.		Work as usual. Party at Belgian Battery Corner at night — got in for a heavy gas shelling, but no casualties	
	14		No change in work. We are now working on G.H.Q. Line by day, a successful change	
	15.		Sector still very quiet in spite of repeated rumours of attacks by the Enemy.	
	16		Work as usual. No 2 Sect got heavily shelled at Belgian Chateau.	
	17.		All work the same. Master Engineer SADLER U.S. Army (Engineers) was attached to us for instruction. Spr. Miller wounded	
	18.		Work as before. Concrete work is slow on account of lack of material.	
	19.		Work as before. 3 Enemy planes brought down. This was seen from G.H.Q. Line	

D. D. & L., London, E.C. (A8004) Wt W1771/M2031 750,000 5/17 Sch. 52 Forms/C2118/14

Instructions regarding War Diaries and Intelligence Summaries are contained in F. S. Regs., Part II. and the Staff Manual respectively. Title pages will be prepared in manuscript.

WAR DIARY
or
INTELLIGENCE SUMMARY.

(*Erase heading not required.*)

Army Form C. 2118.

Place	Date	Hour	Summary of Events and Information	Remarks and references to Appendices
G. 10. b. 2. 0. Sheet 28	20/6/18		Work as usual. The front except for a few shell storms has been very quiet lately	
	21		Work as usual – no change.	
	22.		Work as usual. Great air activity in early morning. Our planes were nearly always	
	23.		Night party on G H Q 1 Line got badly shelled. Spr HAWKIE wounded.	
	24.		Work the same. One of our planes must have been hit (direct) by a shell this morning. It was flying quite quietly at about 8000 ft – when all of a sudden it crumpled up & fell in pieces. No "Archies" were firing neither were any E.A. in sight. Plane was seen to fall on rear side of Observation Ridge.	
	25.		No change. All quiet.	
	26.		All work as usual	
	27.		No work on G.H.Q. 1 Line owing to Operation further S. & demonstration on our front.	
	28.		Bridges at I 19 d 5.7. I 19 d 75 05, I 25 b 7 9 across YPRES – COMINES canal were blown at 11.30 pm. This synchronized with raid of Div on left. The demolitions were quite successfull.	
	29.		No change.	
	30.		Work as usual.	

D. D & L., London, E.C.
(A8004) Wt W1771/M2031 750,000 5/17 Sch. 52 Forms/C2118/14

Army Form C. 2118.

Vol 43

Instructions regarding War Diaries and Intelligence Summaries are contained in F. S. Regs., Part II. and the Staff Manual respectively. Title pages will be prepared in manuscript.

WAR DIARY
or
INTELLIGENCE SUMMARY.
(Erase heading not required.)

Place	Date	Hour	Summary of Events and Information	Remarks and references to Appendices
			Confidential	
			War Diary	
			of	
			11th (Field) Company, R. E.	
			(Volume)	
			From 1st July 1918 To 31st July 1918.	
			C. P. L. Balcombe Maj RE O.C. 11th Field Coy RE	

D. D & L., London, E.C. (A8094) Wt W1771/M2051 750,000 5/17 Sch. 52 Forms/C2118/14

Army Form C. 2118.

WAR DIARY
or
INTELLIGENCE SUMMARY.
(Erase heading not required.)

Instructions regarding War Diaries and Intelligence Summaries are contained in F. S. Regs., Part II. and the Staff Manual respectively. Title pages will be prepared in manuscript.

Place	Date	Hour	Summary of Events and Information	Remarks and references to Appendices
Sheet 28. G.10.b.0.0.	1.7.18		The Coy working in L. Brigade Sector as under.	
			No1 Sect. Concrete Command Posts for R.F.A.	
			No 2 Sect. Strengthening of BELGIAN CHATEAU O.P. in Ramparts at Lille Gate	
			No 3 Sect. } No 4 Sect. } Re-claiming G.H.Q. 1 Line.	
	2.7.18		Work as usual	
	3.7.18		Nos 3 & 4 Sects took over work from Nos 1 & 2 Sects. & vice versa.	
	4.7.18		Work as usual. The sector has been much quieter lately, & an almost complete absence of gas shelling.	
	5.7.18		Work as usual.	
	6.7.18		Work as usual. Lt. RUSSELL left Coy. for course at ROUEN	
	7.7.18		Work as usual	
	8.8.18		Work as usual. Weather seems inclined to break, & more wind about.	
	9.8.18		Work as usual.	
	10.8.18		Work as usual.	
	11.8.18		Work as usual	
	12.8.18		Work as usual	
	13.8.18		Work as usual.	

D. D & L., London, E.C.
(A8064) Wt W1771/M2031 750,000 5/17 Sch. 52 Forms/C2118/14

Army Form C. 2118.

Instructions regarding War Diaries and Intelligence Summaries are contained in F. S. Regs., Part II. and the Staff Manual respectively. Title pages will be prepared in manuscript.

WAR DIARY
or
INTELLIGENCE SUMMARY.

(*Erase heading not required.*)

Place	Date	Hour	Summary of Events and Information	Remarks and references to Appendices
Sheet 28. G10.b.0.0.	14/7/18		Taking over & handing over work with 222nd Field Coy RE. Work as usual.	
	15.7.18		Commenced new work as taken over from 222nd Field Coy RE, as Coy in Div. Reserve. No1 Sect. Road screening New Water Point at L.16.b.2.7 (Sheet 27) New Div Baths at L.3. Central (Sheet 27) No 2 Sect. Brown Line. No 3 Sect. Road screening No 4 Sect. Green Line.	
	16.7.18		Work as usual. 1 Platoon from C Coy. 105th Regt. American Engineers joined Coy for training. Lt. PESCHAU in command of platoon.	
	17.7.18		Work as usual. Americans put to work with No 2 Sect.	
	18.7.18		Work as usual.	
	19.7.18		Work as usual	
	20.7.18		Work as usual. A MOIR M.G. Emp. at G.18.b.3.7 in Yellow Line was completed. This was the first we had seen. They appear to be a very excellent idea, & very good. Given materials on site. 8 men erect same in 4 days.	

D. D. & L., London, E.C. (A8004) Wt W1771/M2031 750,000 5/17 Sch. 52 Forms/C2118/14

Army Form C. 2118.

Instructions regarding War Diaries and Intelligence Summaries are contained in F. S. Regs., Part II. and the Staff Manual respectively. Title pages will be prepared in manuscript.

WAR DIARY
or
INTELLIGENCE SUMMARY.

(Erase heading not required.)

Place	Date	Hour	Summary of Events and Information	Remarks and references to Appendices
Sheet 28. G.10 b. 0.0.	21/7/18		Work as usual. Night work commenced on Brown Line.	
	22/7/18		Work as usual.	
	23/7/18		Work as usual.	
	24/7/18		The Platoon of American Engineers was relieved by 1 Platoon from F Coy 105th Regt. American Engineers. Lt. MORPHY in command of Platoon.	
	25/7/18		Work as usual. Americans put with No 2 Sect.	
	26/7/18		Work as usual. Night 26th 27th. camp heavily shelled from 10.30 p.m. – 4.0 am. by 5.9 H.V. Gun. Average rate of fire 3 rounds every 15 minutes. 1st shell took the heating apparatus for Off. Bath. 2nd Shell " " shower bath 3rd Shell outside the door of the mess. 4th Shell just by office One shell dropped short & fell in Field Farm where some men were sleeping. 11 Cpl KARK was killed. Rest of men were fortunately out on night work.	
	27/7/18		Work as usual. Wet weather.	
	28/7/18		Work as usual.	

D. D. & L., London, E.C.
(A8004) Wt W1771/M2031 750,000 5/17 Sch. 52 Forms/C2118/14

Army Form C. 2118.

Instructions regarding War Diaries and Intelligence Summaries are contained in F. S. Regs., Part II. and the Staff Manual respectively. Title pages will be prepared in manuscript.

WAR DIARY
or
INTELLIGENCE SUMMARY.
(Erase heading not required.)

Place	Date	Hour	Summary of Events and Information	Remarks and references to Appendices
Sheet-28. G.10.b.0.0.	29/7/18		Work as usual. Fine weather.	
	30/7/18		Work as usual.	
	31/7/18		Work as usual.	

D. D. & L., London, E.C.
(A8004) Wt W1771/M2031 750,000 5/17 Sch. 52 Forms/C2118/14

Instructions regarding War Diaries and Intelligence Summaries are contained in F. S. Regs., Part II. and the Staff Manual respectively. Title pages will be prepared in manuscript.

WAR DIARY
or
INTELLIGENCE SUMMARY.
(Erase heading not required.)

Army Form C. 2118.

Vol 44

Place	Date	Hour	Summary of Events and Information	Remarks and references to Appendices
			Secret War Diary of 11th Field Coy. R.E. Volume — From 1st August 1918. To. 31st August, 1918.	

C. R. L. Balcombe
Major, R.E.
Commdg. 11th Co. R.E.

D. D. & L., London, E.C.
(A8004) Wt W1771/M2031 750,000 5/17 Sch. 52 Forms/C2118/14

Army Form C. 2118.

Instructions regarding War Diaries and Intelligence Summaries are contained in F. S. Regs., Part II. and the Staff Manual respectively. Title pages will be prepared in manuscript.

WAR DIARY
or
INTELLIGENCE SUMMARY.
(Erase heading not required.)

Place	Date	Hour	Summary of Events and Information	Remarks and references to Appendices
Sheet 28 G 10 b. 0. 0.	1.8.18.		Coy working as under. 1st Sect. On 'Q' work for DIV. 2nd " Mois Pill Box & Concrete shelters at Ambulance Farm 3rd " Mois Pill Box & Brown Line 4th " Green Line & maintenance of road screening.	
			Platoon of 'F' Coy 105th Regt. U.S. Engineers left & was relieved by '4' Platoon 'A' Coy of same Regt. under Lt. TAYLOR.	
	2.8.18.		Work as usual. Fine morning cloudy later, turning to rain in the Evening.	
	3.8.18.		Work as usual.	
	4.8.18.		Work as usual.	
	5.8.18		Lt. RUSSELL rejoined Coy from R.E. training school Rouen.	
	6.8.18		Lt. Jenkins proceeded to R.E. training school Rouen	
	7.8.18.		Work as usual	
	8.8.18		Work as usual.	
	9.8.18		Camp slightly shelled at night, no damage.	
	10.8.18		Work as usual	
	11.8.18.		Work as usual	

D. D & L., London, E.C.
(A8004) Wt W1771/M2031 750,000 5/17 Sch. 52 Forms/C2118/14

Army Form C. 2118.

WAR DIARY
or
INTELLIGENCE SUMMARY.
(Erase heading not required.)

Instructions regarding War Diaries and Intelligence Summaries are contained in F. S. Regs., Part II. and the Staff Manual respectively. Title pages will be prepared in manuscript.

Place	Date	Hour	Summary of Events and Information	Remarks and references to Appendices
Sheet 28. G.10.b.o.o.	12.8.18.		Platoon of Americans left + were relieved by 2 Platoon 'B' Coy of same regt. (Capt. Stafford)	
	13.8.18.		Work as usual.	
	14.8.18.		Camp shelled but no damage.	
	15.8.18.		Excellent shooting of hostile H.V. guns on balloons. Two brought down. Parachutists landed safely.	
	16.8.18.		Handing over work, billets etc to 'B' Coy 1st Batt. 105 Regt. U.S. Engineers. Capt. Winthrop in command.	
Gaunt Farm A 25 a 2 7 Sheet 28	17.8.18.		Relief by U.S. Engineers complete at 12 noon. Coy moved to GAUNT FARM.	
	18.8.18.		Coy church parade at Gaunt Farm.	
WESTROVE (Hazebrouck sheet. N.W. of Houlle).	19.8.18.		Coy left Gaunt Farm 11.0 am + marched to PROVEN. Entrained there at 4.0 p.m. Detrained St. Omer 8.0 p.m. Marched to WESTROVE arriving in Billets at midnight.	
CAHEN (Calais sheet 13.)	20.8.18.		Coy moved off from Westrove 9.30 am. Arrived in Billets at CAHEN 2.0 p.m. Marched with 19th Brigade Group.	

D. D & L., London, E.C.
(A5004) Wt W1771/M2031 750,000 5/17 Sch. 52 Forms/C2118/14

Instructions regarding War Diaries and Intelligence Summaries are contained in F. S. Regs., Part II. and the Staff Manual respectively. Title pages will be prepared in manuscript.

WAR DIARY
or
INTELLIGENCE SUMMARY.
(Erase heading not required.)

Army Form C. 2118.

Place	Date	Hour	Summary of Events and Information	Remarks and references to Appendices
CAHEN (Calais Sheet 13)	21		Coy employed in general clean up of Equipment etc. Good Billets in pretty village.	
	22		Coy Employed cleaning etc. All wagons scrubbed & preparations made for painting etc.	
	23		Coy training. Inf. Drill, Physical training etc. Excellent training area. Bayonet fighting etc.	
	24		Coy training. Coy Drill. Possibles v. Probables football match in afternoon.	
	25		All officers & N.C.Os training in Map reading etc. Coy engaged on Coy Drill. Football Match Sappers v. A.A. Inf. Sappers won 5-1. Orders arrived midnight to stand to for a move at any moment.	
AFFRINGUES (8 miles SW WIZERNES Hazebrouck Sheet)	26.		Coy moved off by march route 5.30 pm. Arriving at Affringues at 10.30 p.m.	
	27.		At Affringues all day. Coy resting.	

D. D. & L., London, E.C.
(A6004) Wt W1771/M2031 750,000 5/17 Sch. 52 Forms/C2118/14

Instructions regarding War Diaries and Intelligence Summaries are contained in F. S. Regs., Part II. and the Staff Manual respectively. Title pages will be prepared in manuscript.

WAR DIARY
or
INTELLIGENCE SUMMARY.
(Erase heading not required.)

Army Form C. 2118.

Place	Date	Hour	Summary of Events and Information	Remarks and references to Appendices
IVERGNAY (Billet No 51 LENS 11 Sheet)	28		Coy. Left AFFRINGUES 10.30 p.m. by march route to WIZERNES. Entrained at WIZERNES 7.40 p.m. Spent Night in train.	
	29.		Detrained FREVENT 4.0 am. Marched to IVERGNAY arriving 10.am	
	30.		Coy paraded with 19th I.B. for medal riband presentation by GEN. Pinney K.C.B. The Coy marched past at the head of the Brigade. The Band of 1st Queens (RWS Regt) playing the March Past. The following were recipients of medal Ribands. Major C.P.L. Balcombe — Bar to M.C. Sgt. Lawes, Sgt. Derrington — D.C.M. 2nd/Cpl JAGO — Bar to M.M. 2nd Cpl PIKE, L/Cpl Austin, Cpl PESTER, L/Cpl LONG, Spr Ward — M. M.	
	31.		Coy still at IVERGNAY. Inf. training in morning. Football Drivers v. Sappers in afternoon. Draw 2 all.	

D. D & L., London, E.C. (A8004) Wt. W1771/M2031 750,000 5/17 Sch. 52 Forms/C2118/14

Army Form C. 2118.

WAR DIARY
or
INTELLIGENCE SUMMARY.
(Erase heading not required.)

Instructions regarding War Diaries and Intelligence Summaries are contained in F. S. Regs., Part II. and the Staff Manual respectively. Title pages will be prepared in manuscript.

9845

Place	Date	Hour	Summary of Events and Information	Remarks and references to Appendices
			Confidential War Diary of 11th (Field) Coy R.E. Volume ___ From 1st September 1918. To 30th September 1918. N. P. Johnson Capt. R.E. A/O.C. 11th Fd Coy R.E.	

D. D. & L., London, E.C.
(A8004) Wt W1771/M2031 750,000 5/17 Sch. 52 Forms/C2118/14

Instructions regarding War Diaries and Intelligence Summaries are contained in F. S. Regs., Part II. and the Staff Manual respectively. Title pages will be prepared in manuscript.

WAR DIARY
or
INTELLIGENCE SUMMARY.
(Erase heading not required.)

Army Form C. 2118.

Place	Date	Hour	Summary of Events and Information	Remarks and references to Appendices
IVERGNY Billet 51 (LENS 11 Sheet)	Sept 1st		Coy out at rest. Church Parade in morning	
	2		Coy Infantry Training in morning. Football afternoon v. 19th Field Ambulance won 9-1.	
			v. Cameronians won 2-1.	
	3		do do do do " " v. 9th H.L.I. lost 5-0	
	4		do do do do " "	
	5		do do do do " " 2nd Team played 19th I.B. lost 2-1	
	6.		Coy Trench Bridging, Knots & lashings, demolitions	
	7.		Nos 1 & 2 Sections Trench Bridging 3 & 4 Knots & lashings.	
	8.		Divine Service at 5.30 pm. Lieut P. Russell RE proceeded on leave to U.K. Football v. 5th Sco Rifles won 3-2.	
	9		Coy lecture & practice in use of Field Level & Geometry.	
	10th		do do do do do	
	11th		Route March 9 am – 1 pm.	
	12th		Coy paraded for Baths at LUCHEUX. 99th Field Ambulance gave the Coy a concert.	
	13th		All Lewis gunners firing on range at LUCHEUX. Remainder of Coy drill.	
	14th		Musketry Exercise. Lewis gunners firing on Range. Played 19th I.B. football lost 2-1	

D. D. & L., London, E.C.
(A8004) Wt W1771/M2031 750,000 5/17 Sch. 52 Forms/C2118/14

Instructions regarding War Diaries and Intelligence Summaries are contained in F. S. Regs., Part II. and the Staff Manual respectively. Title pages will be prepared in manuscript.

WAR DIARY
or
INTELLIGENCE SUMMARY.
(*Erase heading not required.*)

Army Form C. 2118.

Place	Date	Hour	Summary of Events and Information	Remarks and references to Appendices
MENIN GATE I.8.b.3.4 Sheet 28	15-1-18		Coy working on Div H.Q. Judah Track repairing [illegible] of Pill Box at Frost House. No 3 Section working for RFA. Putting in [illegible] sliding doors to Battalion H.Q.	H.J.
	16-1-18		do do do do do do do.	H.J.
	17-1-18		do do do do do do do	H.J.
	18-1-18		do do do do do do do. Lieut Russell RE granted leave to UK from 18-1-18 to 1-2-18.	H.J.
	19-1-18		Work as usual repairs to [illegible] Pill Box completed.	H.J.
	20-1-18		Work on Div H.Q. Heine House Track. Concrete Shelter for "B" 156 Batty & "C" 156 Batty. New Shelter in Ry Embankment for D 156 Batty. No 2 OP at GRA commenced.	H.J.
	21-1-18		do do do	H.J.
	22-1-18		do do do	H.J.
	23-1-18		do do do	H.J.
	24-1-18		do do do	H.J.
	25-1-18		do do do	H.J.
	26-1-18		do do do Coy Transport moved at 8 AM with 19th I.B. for Rest Area. [illegible] 447 Fd Coy arrived to take over work the section.	H.J.

A5834 Wt. W4973 M687 750,000 8/16 D. D. & L. Ltd. Forms/C.2118/13.

Instructions regarding War Diaries and Intelligence Summaries are contained in F. S. Regs., Part II. and the Staff Manual respectively. Title pages will be prepared in manuscript.

WAR DIARY
or
INTELLIGENCE SUMMARY.
(Erase heading not required.)

Army Form C. 2118.

Place	Date	Hour	Summary of Events and Information	Remarks and references to Appendices
IVERGNY. Billet 51 Lens 11 Sheet	Night 14/15		Coy entrained at 8-30 pm and detrained at YTRES.	
ETRICOURT.	15th		Coy in field at 1 Rds W.A.E. of ETRICOURT.	
SHEET 57C S.E	16		do do do do.	
	17.		do do do do.	
	18th		Coy moved at 5 am to trench system in V.11.c. near EQUANCOURT.	
	19th		Coy moved to W.19.d.15.55 an open field. Capt Johnson + Lieut [illegible] made reconnaissance to forward position. Took over work from 98th Coy. 2 & 3 Sections working on Strong Points.	
	20th		2 & 3 Sections working on Strong Points. No 4 Section building Camps. No 1 Section divisional reserve. Cpl Shepherd + 6 O.R. fixed on bridges over CANAL DU NORD.	
	21		do do do do	
	22		do do do do	
	23		do do do do	
	24		do do do do	
	25		do do do do	
	26		do do do do	

D. D. & L., London, E.C. (A8004) Wt. W1771/M2031 750,000 5/17 Sch. 52 Forms/C2118/14

Instructions regarding War Diaries and Intelligence Summaries are contained in F. S. Regs., Part II. and the Staff Manual respectively. Title pages will be prepared in manuscript.

WAR DIARY
or
INTELLIGENCE SUMMARY.
(Erase heading not required.)

Army Form C. 2118.

Place	Date	Hour	Summary of Events and Information	Remarks and references to Appendices
SHEET 57.C W.25.a.77	27.		No. 2.3.4 Sections digging trench for new Battalion H.Q. and [illegible] entrances for Dug-Outs. No. 1 Section [illegible] [illegible]	
	28.		Working on 4 Entrances to Dug Out	
	29.		Coy moves to trench System in X.19 d.35	
SHEET 57 B. S.W.	30		Coy moved to trenches in X 22. c 0.2	

D. D & L., London, E.C.
(A8604) Wt W1771/M2031 750,000 5/17 Sch. 52 Forms/C2118/14

9

Army Form C. 2118.

Instructions regarding War Diaries and Intelligence Summaries are contained in F. S. Regs., Part II. and the Staff Manual respectively. Title pages will be prepared in manuscript.

WAR DIARY
or
INTELLIGENCE SUMMARY.

(Erase heading not required.)

Vol 46

Place	Date	Hour	Summary of Events and Information	Remarks and references to Appendices
			Confidential	
			War Diary of 11th (Field) Coy R.E.	
			Volume	
			From - 1st October 1918.	
			To - 31st October 1918.	
			N. J. Johnson Capt. R.E. for O. Commdg. 11th Coy. R.E.	

D. D. & L., London, E.C.
(A8004) Wt W1771/M2031 750,000 5/17 Sch. 52 Forms/C2118/14

Army Form C. 2118.

Instructions regarding War Diaries and Intelligence Summaries are contained in F. S. Regs., Part II. and the Staff Manual respectively. Title pages will be prepared in manuscript.

WAR DIARY
or
INTELLIGENCE SUMMARY.

(Erase heading not required.)

Place	Date	Hour	Summary of Events and Information	Remarks and references to Appendices
Limerick Post Sheet 57C S.W.	1.10.18		Coy living in old trench system. Sappers working on Bde H.Q.	
X22 c 0 2	2.10.18		Coy still standing by.	
	3.10.18		Coy still standing by.	
	4.10.18		Coy still standing by.	
	5.10.18		The 19th I.B. crossed over the Canal St. QUENTIN in the morning. The Coy at once went to erect bridges over the canal. Two bridges were done. (1) a bridge for inf. in file. (2) a bridge for Horse transport & 18 pdr. The enemy was retiring & no fire of any kind was encountered. By 6.0 pm No 2 bridge was open & the Div. Artillery of 33rd & 38th Divns. passed over. Transport poured over during the whole night, & by daylight the following morning, the E. side of the Canal was a mass of tents & horse lines etc.	The bridges erected were between OSSUS & HONNECOURT
	6.10.18		The Coy carried on with strengthening the bridge & doing general repairs.	
	7.10.18		Nos 2 & 3 Sects carried on with the light traffic bridge, & Nos 1 & 4 sects repaired a heavy trestle bridge at HONNECOURT - making it fit for 6 ton axle load.	
X 18 a 25 90 Sheet 57C S.W. just S. of Honnecourt	8.10.18		Coy moved camp to new location just S. of HONNECOURT. Orders were received at 9 a.m to prepare to continue the advance with 19th I.B. starting 1.0 am 9th inst.	

D. D. & L., London, E.C.
(A8004) Wt W1771/M2031 750,000 5/17 Sch. 52 Forms/C2118/14

Instructions regarding War Diaries and Intelligence Summaries are contained in F. S. Regs., Part II. and the Staff Manual respectively. Title pages will be prepared in manuscript.

WAR DIARY
or
INTELLIGENCE SUMMARY.
(Erase heading not required.)

Army Form C. 2118.

Place	Date	Hour	Summary of Events and Information	Remarks and references to Appendices
HURTEVANT FARM O21d 3 8 Sheet 57 B.	9.10.18		Coy moved off from HONNECOURT 1.0am. marched through LA TERRIERE & AUBENCHEUL & arrived VILLERS OUTREUX at 5.0am. The 19th I.B. (3 batts inf) advanced through the 38th Div at 5.20am. The Coy moved off 12 noon via MALINCOURT to DEHERIES, arriving 3.0pm. Moved off 7.0pm. to Bde H.Q. at HURTEVANT FARM arriving there 9.0pm. At 10.0pm. the Coy was put under orders of 98th I.B. who were advancing through the 19th I.B. the following morning.	
TROISVILLES	10.10.18		The O.C. & Lt Brown went forward with G.O.C. 98th I.B. leaving HURTEVANT FARM at 4.0am. via CLARY – BERTRY & thence to TROISVILLES. The coy followed and arrived TROISVILLES 10.0am. Lt. Brown went forward to do a reconnaissance of the River SELLE, but was unable to complete same owing to heavy fire, losing his orderly & horse in the effort. The Coy had to shift billets during the day owing to shell fire.	
TROISVILLES	11.10.18		Orders were received at 3.0pm for 6 bridges to be thrown across the River SELLE between MONTAY & NEUVILLY by 4.0am the 12th inst. The enemy were holding the E bank of the river, excepting where one isolated post of A.&S.H. was across. The Coy moved off 5.0am & met the covering party of 1 Coy of 2nd Worcester Regt at 5.30pm. The whole Coy was on the works & 3 bridging wagons. After a difficult journey across country Coy arrived at site 10.0pm. A reconnaissance was then done for the sites of the bridges, & the bridging wagons were then taken to the river bank & work commenced. All bridges were completed by 2.0am 12th inst. Heavy M.G. fire & sniping but all high. No casualties. Coy returned to Billets 5.0am 12th inst.	

D. D. & L., London, E.C.
(A8004) Wt W1771/M2031 750,000 5/17 Sch. 52 Forms/C2118/14

Army Form C. 2118.

Instructions regarding War Diaries and Intelligence Summaries are contained in F. S. Regs., Part II. and the Staff Manual respectively. Title pages will be prepared in manuscript.

WAR DIARY
or
INTELLIGENCE SUMMARY.
(Erase heading not required.)

Place	Date	Hour	Summary of Events and Information	Remarks and references to Appendices
TROISVILLES	12/10/18		Standing by. Two secs went out at night on maintenance of bridges erected previous night.	
ELINCOURT	13/10/18		Coy moved to ELINCOURT to rest. The Div. being relieved by 35th Div. Arrived in new billets 2.0 p.m.	
do	14/10/18		Cleaning up. Two sects. working on baths & water points at MALINCOURT. The G.O.C. Div. Gen Sir R. Pinney KCB paraded the Div. Eng. & complimented & thanked them on their bridging of the River SELLE.	
	15/10/18		General Clean up etc.	
do	16/10/18		Church Service in morning. Coy Concert in the Evening.	
do	17/10/18		Cleaning up and Infantry training	
do	18/10/18		Coy Parade Musketry Order.	
do	19/10/18		Coy Parade full Marching Order for Inspection	
do	20/10/18		Drill Order Parade.	
do	21/10/18		do do	
do	22/10/18		Coy moved to LA SOTIERE E of TROISVILLES.	

D. D. & L., London, E.C.
(A8004) Wt W1771/M2051 750,000 5/17 Sch. 52 Forms/C2118/14

11th Field Coy. R.E. ✓
212th Field Coy. R.E.
222nd Field Coy. R.E.

The C.R.E. would like to express his appreciation of the excellent work done by the Field Companies engaged in making bridges over the Canal. Owing to the keenness displayed by all ranks it was possible for us to materially assist the Division on our right and also the Corps Heavy Artillery, as the only bridges working on the night of the 5th/6th were those erected by the 33rd Divisional Engineers.

G. F. Evans

Lieut.-Colonel, R.E.,
C.R.E., 33rd Division.

11th Field Coy. R.E.
212th Field Coy. R.E.
222nd Field Coy. R.E.

I have much pleasure in forwarding the under-mentioned message sent to me by the Division -

"General PINNEY thanks you an-d all ranks under your command for your great and successful efforts during the recent operations."

C.R.E.,
33rd DIVISION.
No. 8578
Date 27/10/18.

G. F. Evans
Lt. Colonel. R.E.
C.R.E. 33rd Division.

War Diary

COPY.
FJ-L.

COMMUNE
de
CLARY.

CLARY, le 14 Octobre 1918.

A Monsieur le Général,
Commandant l'Armée Britannique.
(33rd British Division).

Monsieur le Général,

Au nom des habitants de Clary dont je suis heureux de me faire l'interprète, je viens exprimer bien respectueusement notre admiration et notre vive et profonde reconnaissance aux si vaillantes troupes Anglaises qui, dans un élan irrésistible ont refoulé et chassé l'Envahisseur barbare et maudit dont nous subissons l'oppressant joug depuis plus de quatre longues années.

Grace a leur si vigoureuse et rapide poursuite, les braves troupes Ecossaises ont réussi a empêcher l'ennemi d'achever l'oeuvre de destruction qu'il avait commencé dans notre Commune. Il n'y a eu aucun accident de personnes a deplorer. Notre Eglise a fin être préservée a la dernière minute. La population au cours des derniers jours, des dernières heures critiques qui ont précédé son heureuse delivrance a su résister résolument aus agissements et aux menaces des Autorités Allemandes désemparées. Sa confiance a été aussi inèbraulable que justifiée.

Nous addressons l'expression émue de notre gratitude à tous les braves soldats qui ont si généreusement versé leur sang pour la Cause Sacrée du Droit de la Justice et de l'Independance de tous les peuples.

Bientôt, nous l'esperons, les vaillantes Armées Alliées, animées d'une même ardeur, d'une égale volonté de vaincre auront liberé toutes les regions envahiers et forcé le Géant Audesque à demander grace.

Honneur et Gloire a elles ! Honte éternelle a l'Oppresseur, cause de tant de deuils et de misères.

Veuillez, Monsieur le General, transmettre à leurs Majestés, le Roi Georges et à la Gracieuse Reine Mary et à leurs Chers Enfants, l'hommage de notre vénération et de notre reconnaissance; Nos voeux les plus ardents pour leur bonheur et la prospérité de la Nation Anglaise si fraternellement et indissolument unie a la France.

(OVER).

Veuillez assurer, de notre sympathie la plus vive, votrebbelle et vaillante Armée qui s'est montrée si bonne et si compatissante pour nous et recevoir pour vous,

Monsieur le Général, l'expression de notre entier et respectueux dévouement.

(Signed) BONNEVILLE.

Maire do CLARY
R. F.
(N O R D).

Maire de Clary.

TO ALL RECIPIENTS OF 33rd DIV. ROUTINE ORDERS.

TELEGRAM
TO A.D.C. for G.O.C., 33rd Division.

Sender's Number	Day of month.
140	26/10/18.

MAIRE of ENGLEFONTAINE met this afternoon in a cellar of his village begs to express you in name of the 1200 inhabitants freed by the British Army his deepest feelings of hearty gratitude. I wish to add the best congratulations of the French Mission for the last night's most successful and brilliant operation

From :- O.C. French Mission, 33rd Div.

(Signed) P. GIRARD, O.C.

TELEGRAM

To:- G.O.C. 33rd Division.

Sender's No.	Date.
G.434	26

Please convey to all ranks under your command my congratulations on the gallantry and endurance they have shewn during the recent hard fighting AAA They may well be proud of the advance from MALINCOURT to the River SELLE where all resistance was overcome until the final objective was gained and the assault and capture of ENGLEFONTAINE with 500 prisoners after 36 hours of continuous heavy fighting and hard marching over most difficult country was a magnificent piece of work well organised and most gallantly carried out AAA The present nature of fighting was a little new to the Division which made their task harder and more costly yet in spite of heavy casualties their pluck determination to win and splendid soldierlike spirit carried them through to success AAA Please convey to them my personal thanks for all they have done.

FROM :- General SHUTE.

EB TIME :- 2345

17

Instructions regarding War Diaries and Intelligence Summaries are contained in F. S. Regs., Part II. and the Staff Manual respectively. Title pages will be prepared in manuscript.

WAR DIARY
or
INTELLIGENCE SUMMARY.

(Erase heading not required.)

Army Form C. 2118.

WO 95/47

Place	Date	Hour	Summary of Events and Information	Remarks and references to Appendices
			Confidential	
			War Diary	
			of	
			11th (Field) Coy. R.E.	
			(Volume)	
			From 1st November 1918.	
			To 30th November 1918.	
			N. D. Johnson Capt. R.E. A/O.C. 11th Fd Coy. R.E.	

D. D. & L., London, E.C.
(A8004) Wt W1771/M2031 750,000 5/17 Sch. 52 Forms/C2118/14

17

Instructions regarding War Diaries and Intelligence Summaries are contained in F. S. Regs., Part II. and the Staff Manual respectively. Title pages will be prepared in manuscript.

WAR DIARY
or
INTELLIGENCE SUMMARY.
(Erase heading not required.)

Army Form C. 2118.

98/48

Place	Date	Hour	Summary of Events and Information	Remarks and references to Appendices
			Confidential.	
			War Diary of 11th (Irish) Coy. R.E.	
			Volume ( )	
			From - 1st December 1918.	
			To - 31st December 1918.	
			N. J. Johnson Capt., R.E. for O. Commdg. 11th Coy. R.E.	

D. D. & L., London, E.C. (A8004) Wt W1771/M2031 750,000 5/17 Sch. 52 Forms/C2118/14

Instructions regarding War Diaries and Intelligence Summaries are contained in F. S. Regs., Part II. and the Staff Manual respectively. Title pages will be prepared in manuscript.

WAR DIARY
or
INTELLIGENCE SUMMARY.
(Erase heading not required.)

Army Form C. 2118.

Place	Date	Hour	Summary of Events and Information	Remarks and references to Appendices
CLARY	1.12.18		Dismounted portion of Coy entrained at CAUDRY arriving at VILLERS BRETONNEUX at 10 am 2nd	
FOUILLOY	2.12.18		Coy detrained at VILLERS BRETONNEUX and marched to billets FOUILLOY.	
CORBIE	3.12.18		FOUILLOY CORBIE AREA.	
	4.12.18		do do do cleaning up. Mounted Section proceeded by road to HORNOY AREA staging at SALEUX.	
VRAIGNES	5.12.18		Dismounted marched from FOUILLOY to road junction ½ mile south of S in AMIENS & proceeded thence by Lorry to VRAIGNES.	
(DIEPPE SHEET)	6.12.18		Coy cleaning and scrubbing Equipment	
	7.12.18		do do do do	
	8.12.18		CHURCH PARADE in morning.	
	9.12.18		Nos 1 & 4 Sections proceeded on detachment to CAMPS-EN-AMIENOIS for working on billets prior to arrival of 19th I.B. Nos 2 & 3 Section working on billets and polishing up vehicles.	
	10.12.18		do do do do No 1 & 4 erecting Bath points - improving billets	
	11.12.18		do do do do do do do do	
	12.12.18		do do do do do do do do.	
	13.12.18		do do do do party of No 3 Section at ST AUBIN repairing proposed Hospital for 19th Field Ambulance & erecting Bath point.	
	14.12.18		CHURCH PARADE.	
	15.12.18		SECTIONS 1 & 4 at work in 19th Bde Area 2 & 3 improvement of billets at VRAIGNES	
	16.12.18		do do do do do do do.	
	17.12.18		Nos 1 & 4 SECTIONS returned to VRAIGNES	
	18.12.18		Party working at THIEULLOY No 3 Section erecting Baths at CAMPS-EN-AMIENOIS and Nos 1 & 4 SECTIONS cleaning up. No 2 Section improvement of billets.	
	19.12.18		do do do do do	
	20.12.18		Nos 1 & 4 SECTION erecting RECREATIONAL HUT for Coy at VRAIGNES. & No 2 & 3 improving billets	
	21.12.18		do do do do do do do.	

D. D. & L., London, E.C.
(A8004) Wt W1771/M2031 750,000 5/17 Sch. 52 Forms/C2118/14

Instructions regarding War Diaries and Intelligence Summaries are contained in F. S. Regs., Part II. and the Staff Manual respectively. Title pages will be prepared in manuscript.

WAR DIARY
or
INTELLIGENCE SUMMARY.

(Erase heading not required.)

Army Form C. 2118.

Place	Date	Hour	Summary of Events and Information	Remarks and references to Appendices
VRAIGNES (DIEPPE SHEET)	22.12.18		Working on hut in morning. Church parade in afternoon.	
	23.12.18		All Section employed on improving billets, erection of hut, making tables & forms for Hut.	
	24.12.18		do do do do do do.	
	25.12.18		XMAS DAY. Sappers had dinner in the new Recreation Hut & drawn in a barn. During dinner Sappers & drawn were visited by C.R.E. Lt Col. BINGAY R.E. In the evening a concert was held in the Recreation Hut.	
	26.12.18		Church parade in morning	
	27.12.18		General clean up and billet improvement.	
	28.12.18		do do do do	
	29.12.18		Packing up ready for move.	
	30.12.18		General SIR REGINALD PINNEY K.C.B inspected the Division R.E. at THIEULLOY. LIEUT. PETER RUSSELL & H.G.M. OUDNEY presented with M.C. ribbands. Cpl WHEELER received M.M. ribband.	
	31.12.18		Entrained at Poix for ROUEN.	

H. D. Johnson
Capt. R.E
for O.C. 11th Field Coy R.E.

D. D. & L., London, E.C.
(A8004) Wt W1771/M2031 750,000 5/17 Sch. 52 Forms/C2118/14

18

Instructions regarding War Diaries and Intelligence Summaries are contained in F. S. Regs., Part II. and the Staff Manual respectively. Title pages will be prepared in manuscript.

WAR DIARY
or
INTELLIGENCE SUMMARY.

(Erase heading not required.)

33 D W

Army Form C. 2118.

98 49

Place	Date	Hour	Summary of Events and Information	Remarks and references to Appendices
			Confidential	
			War Diary of 11th (Field) Coy. R.E.	
			Volume ( )	
			From 1st January 1919 To 31st January 1919.	
			M. J. Johnson Capt, R.E. for O. Commdg. 11th Coy. R.E.	

D. D. & L., London, E.C.
(A8004) Wt W1771/M2031 750,000 5/17 Sch. 52 Forms/C2118/14

Instructions regarding War Diaries and Intelligence Summaries are contained in F. S. Regs., Part II. and the Staff Manual respectively. Title pages will be prepared in manuscript.

WAR DIARY

or

~~INTELLIGENCE SUMMARY.~~

(Erase heading not required.)

Army Form C. 2118.

Place	Date	Hour	Summary of Events and Information	Remarks and references to Appendices
ROUEN	1.1.19.		Jany 1st 1919 Coy arrived at Rouen and proceeded to Camp 944 A E Coy.	
	2nd		Jany 2nd 1919 Erecting Hospital Nissen Huts in "C" Camp.	
	3rd		do do do do do do	
	4th		do do do do do do.	
	5th		do do do do do do.	
	6th		do do do do do do	
	7th		do do do do do do	
	8th		do do do do do do.	
	9th		Coy left Rouen for LE HAVRE Transport proceeded by road under Lieut- Russell M.C. R.E. Dismounted by train Entrained at 8 am & train left about 1.30.	
LE HAVRE	10th		Coy in Camp at GOUCRIAVILLE HARFLEUR CAMP 8A.	
	11th		do do do do	
	12th		Coy at work on delousers in Australian Camp.	
	13th		Coy at work at delousers in Australian Camp & party of 1 NCO & 10 men Erecting Nissen for Kitchen	
	14th			
	15th		do do do	
	16th		do do do	
	17th		do do do	
	18th		do do do	
	19th		do do do	
			CHURCH SERVICE. ST. PETERS CHURCH 9.00 hrs	

D. D. & L., London, E.C.
(A8004) Wt W1771/M2031 750,000 5/17 Sch. 52 Forms/C2118/14

Army Form C. 2118.

WAR DIARY
or
INTELLIGENCE SUMMARY.
(Erase heading not required.)

Instructions regarding War Diaries and Intelligence Summaries are contained in F. S. Regs., Part II. and the Staff Manual respectively. Title pages will be prepared in manuscript.

Place	Date	Hour	Summary of Events and Information	Remarks and references to Appendices
LE HAVRE	20th		Coy working on delouser in Australian Camp. 1 NCO & 10 men building Nissen Huts for Kings in Camp 15.	
	21st		do do do do do do	
	22nd		do do do do do do	
	23rd		do do do Party working for Kings [illegible] –	
	24th		Coy on delouser do do do do	
	25th		do do do do	
	26th		1 Lieut. T.H. Brown left for VERCHOQ CHURCH SERVICE at 9 am in St PETERS	
	27th		Coy working on delouser in Australian Camp.	
	28th		do do do do do	
	29th		do do do do do	
	30th		do do do do do	
	31st		do do do do do	

N. J. Johnson
Capt, R.E.
Commdg. 11th Coy. R.E

D. D. & L., London, E.C.
(A8004) Wt W1771/M2031 750,000 5/17 Sch. 52 Forms/C2118/14

17

Instructions regarding War Diaries and Intelligence Summaries are contained in F. S. Regs., Part II. and the Staff Manual respectively. Title pages will be prepared in manuscript.

WAR DIARY
or
INTELLIGENCE SUMMARY.
(Erase heading not required.)

11 Fd Coy

98 50

Army Form C. 2118.

Place	Date	Hour	Summary of Events and Information	Remarks and references to Appendices
			CONFIDENTIAL WAR DIARY of 11th (Field) Company R.E. Volume ( ) From 1st. February 1919 To. 28th February 1919. J Butler Major, R.E. Commdg. 11th Coy. R.E.	

D. D. & L., London, E.C.
(A8004) Wt W1771/M2031 750,000 5/17 Sch. 52 Forms/C2118/14

Instructions regarding War Diaries and Intelligence Summaries are contained in F. S. Regs., Part II. and the Staff Manual respectively. Title pages will be prepared in manuscript.

WAR DIARY
or
~~INTELLIGENCE SUMMARY.~~
(Erase heading not required.)

11th Field Coy. R.E.

Army Form C. 2118.

Place	Date	Hour	Summary of Events and Information	Remarks and references to Appendices
HARFLEUR near LE HAVRE	1st		Coy working on No 3 Delouser Australian Camp.	
	2nd		Church Parade at 10.00 hrs at ST PETERS Church	
	3–8		Coy working on No 3 Delouser Australian Camp	
	9th		Church Parade at ST. PETERS Church 10.00 hours	
	10–15		Coy working on No 3 Delouser Australian Camp work completed.	
	16		Church Parade at ST PETER'S church 10.00 hours	
	17–22		Coy working on erection of NISSEN BOW huts and improvement of General Base Depot camp 8 CAUCRIAVILLE under D.O.RE CAUCRIAVILLE	
	23		Church Parade at ST. PETERS Church 10.00 hrs	
	24–28		Coy working on general repairs to GENERAL BASE DEPOT.	
	7th		Capt. JOHNSON transferred to 202nd Field Coy RE as OC. (Authority:- GHQ. No. AG. 55/6352 (c) d/- 28-1-19.	
	27th		Lieut OUDNEY. M.C transferred to RE Bridging School MONCHY CAYEAUX. }	
	26th		2/Lt. BROWN. " Field Survey Bn } Authority V Corps No. V.A./286/153. d/- 29-1-19.	

D. D. & L., London, E.C.
(A8064) Wt W1771/M2031 750,000 5/17 Sch. 53 Forms/C2118/14

Instructions regarding War Diaries and Intelligence Summaries are contained in F. S. Regs., Part II. and the Staff Manual respectively. Title pages will be prepared in manuscript.

WAR DIARY
or
INTELLIGENCE SUMMARY.

(*Erase heading not required.*)

Army Form C. 2118.

Place	Date	Hour	Summary of Events and Information	Remarks and references to Appendices
			No of OR sent for dispersal during the month:- 37.	
			[signature] Major RE OC 11th [illegible] Coy. RE.	

D. D & L., London, E.C.
(A8004) Wt W1771/M2031 750,000 5/17 Sch. 52 Forms/C2118/14

Instructions regarding War Diaries and Intelligence Summaries are contained in F. S. Regs., Part II. and the Staff Manual respectively. Title pages will be prepared in manuscript.

WAR DIARY
or
INTELLIGENCE SUMMARY.
(*Erase heading not required.*)

Army Form C. 2118.

Vol 51

Place	Date	Hour	Summary of Events and Information	Remarks and references to Appendices
			CONFIDENTIAL	
			WAR DIARY	
			of	
			11th. (Field Company, R.E.	
			Volume ( )	
			From. 1st. March 1919.	
			To. 31st. March 1919.	

11TH FIELD COMPANY, R.E.
No.
Date.

[signature]
Major RE
O.C. 11th. Fd. Coy RE.

D. D. & L., London, E.C. (A8204) Wt. W1771/M2031 750,000 5/17 Sch. 52 Forms/C2118/14

Army Form C. 2118.

WAR DIARY
or
INTELLIGENCE SUMMARY.
(Erase heading not required.)

Instructions regarding War Diaries and Intelligence Summaries are contained in F. S. Regs., Part II. and the Staff Manual respectively. Title pages will be prepared in manuscript.

11th Field Coy RE

Place	Date	Hour	Summary of Events and Information	Remarks and references to Appendices
HARFLEUR near LE HAVRE	1st.		Coy working on erection of Nissen Hospital Huts and improvement of General Base Depot Camp 8 CAUCRIAVILLE under DORE CAUCRIAVILLE.	
	2nd.		Church Parade at St PETERS Church 10.00 hours.	
	3-8		Coy working on general repairs to GENERAL BASE DEPOT Camp 8.	
	9		Church Parade at St PETERS Church 10.00 hrs. Lieut F. Desborough proceeded on Leave to UK. (9.3.19 - 24.3.19)	
	10-15		Coy working on general repairs to GENERAL BASE DEPOT Camp 8.	
	13.		2/Lieut. T.H. Brown rejoined Coy. Authority GHQ No. AG. 8139/1(O) d/- 9.3.19.	
	15		2/Lieut. D. Jenkins proceeded on Leave to UK. (15.3.19 - 30.3.19)	
	16		Church Parade at St PETERS Church 10.00 hrs.	
	17-22		Coy working on general repairs to GENERAL BASE DEPOT Camp 8.	
	21.		2/Lieut J.A. Bebb joined from 210th Fd Coy RE and 2/Lt A.W. Rogers joined from 223rd Field Coy RE	
	23		Church Parade at St PETERS Church 10.00 hrs.	
	24-29.		Coy working on general repairs to GENERAL BASE DEPOT, Camp 8.	
	30		Church Parade at St PETERS Church 10.00 hrs.	
	31.		Coy working on general repairs to GENERAL BASE DEPOT, Camp 8.	

D. D. & L., London, E.C. (A8004) Wt W1771/M2931 750,000 5/17 Sch. 52 Forms/C2118/14

Army Form C. 2118.

Instructions regarding War Diaries and Intelligence Summaries are contained in F. S. Regs., Part II. and the Staff Manual respectively. Title pages will be prepared in manuscript.

WAR DIARY
or
INTELLIGENCE SUMMARY.

(Erase heading not required.)

Place	Date	Hour	Summary of Events and Information	Remarks and references to Appendices
			No of OR. sent for dispersal during the month, 58,	
			Company being reduced to Cadre 'A' Establishment:-	
			Strength of Coy on 31.3.19, 8 Officers 68 OR. 6 Light Draught Horses	
			and complete in strengths of vehicles, including one ASC Wagon and	
			one two-wheeled cart surplus to establishment, allowed by special authority	
			[illegible signature] Major. RE	
			OC 11th Fd Coy RE.	

D. D. & L., London, E.C.
(A8004) Wt W1771/M2031 750,000 5/17 Sch. 52 Forms/C2118/14

12

Instructions regarding War Diaries and Intelligence Summaries are contained in F. S. Regs., Part II. and the Staff Manual respectively. Title pages will be prepared in manuscript.

WAR DIARY
or
INTELLIGENCE SUMMARY.
(Erase heading not required.)

Army Form C. 2118.

Vol. 52

Place	Date	Hour	Summary of Events and Information	Remarks and references to Appendices
			CONFIDENTIAL —	
			WAR DIARY	
			of the	
			11th (Field) Company, Royal Engineers	
			Volume ( )	
			From - 1st. April 1919.	
			To:- 30th April 1919.	
			[signature] Capt. RE O.C 11th Fd Coy RE.	

D. D. & L., London, E.C.
(A8004) Wt W1771/M2031 750,000 5/17 Sch. 52 Forms/C2118/14

Army Form C. 2118.

Instructions regarding War Diaries and Intelligence Summaries are contained in F. S. Regs., Part II. and the Staff Manual respectively. Title pages will be prepared in manuscript.

WAR DIARY
or
INTELLIGENCE SUMMARY.
(Erase heading not required.)

Place	Date	Hour	Summary of Events and Information	Remarks and references to Appendices
Camp 8(a) HARFLEUR NR LE HAVRE	2/4/19		2/Lt T.H. BROWN (Reg) granted leave to UK from 2-4-19 to 17-4-19, Transferred to 460th (Highland) Field Coy RE on 3/4/19; Authority. AG 10336/11(0) d/- 22.3.19,	
	3/4/19		10. OR (retainable under AO.55 of 1919) despatched to CRE 33rd (Northern) Division COLOGNE, Authority - CRE 33rd Div. Wire No B232 d/- 31.3.19.	
	8/4/19		2/Lt. A.W. Rogers & 2/Lt J.A. Belile transferred to Chief Engineer No 5 Area - (Authority - AG 10336/5 Area (0) d/- 29.3.19.	
	8/4/19		2/Lt D Jenkins & 2/Lt. O.R. Slater transferred to 135 A.T. Coy RE, Authority - AG 10336/1 Area (0) d/- 29.3.19,	
	8/4/19		Major J O'SULLIVAN granted leave to UK from 8/4/19 - 23/4/19,	
	8/4/19		Capt. P RUSSELL M.C assumed command of Cadre,	
	8/4/19		16. OR (Retainables) transferred to Army of Rhine, Authority CRE 33rd Div Wire No B232 d/- 31.3.19,	
	10/4/19		Lt DESBOROUGH F.R rejoined from Leave,	
	23/4/19		Major J.O'SULLIVAN transferred to 32nd Base Park Coy RE, Authority - AG 10336/32 (0) d/- 28/3/19,	
			1OR sent Base for dispersal during month, Company reduced to Cadre Strength, Strength of Coy on 30/4/19, 2 Officers - 32 ORs	
			[signature] OC 11th Field Coy RE	

D. D. & L., London, E.C. (A8004) Wt W1771/M2031 750,000 5/17 Sch. 52 Forms/C2118/14

Instructions regarding War Diaries and Intelligence Summaries are contained in F. S. Regs., Part II. and the Staff Manual respectively. Title pages will be prepared in manuscript.

WAR DIARY
or
INTELLIGENCE SUMMARY.
(Erase heading not required.)

Army Form C. 2118.

WR 53

Place	Date	Hour	Summary of Events and Information	Remarks and references to Appendices
			CONFIDENTIAL—	
			WAR DIARY of 11th (Field) Company R.E. Volume ( )	
			From May 1st. 1919. To May 31st 1919.	
			Peter Russell Capt R.E. O.C. 11th (Field) Coy R.E.	

D. D. & L., London, E.C. (A8004) Wt W1771/M2031 750,000 5/17 Sch. 52 Forms/C2118/14

Army Form C. 2118.

Instructions regarding War Diaries and Intelligence Summaries are contained in F. S. Regs., Part II. and the Staff Manual respectively. Title pages will be prepared in manuscript.

WAR DIARY
or
INTELLIGENCE SUMMARY.
(Erase heading not required.)

Place	Date	Hour	Summary of Events and Information	Remarks and references to Appendices
CAMP 8(A)	2/5/19		1 OR transferred to 32nd Base Park Coy RE.	
HARFLEUR	14/5/19		1 OR transferred to CRE 30th (Northern) Division, Army of Rhine.	
NR. LE HAVRE	17/5/19		8 OR joined from Gen Base Depot Havre. (Authority DAG CR. No 1337/1115 C. dated 12/4/19.	
	29/5/19		7 OR sent for Dispersal.	
	30/5/19		1 OR joined from General Base Depot.	
			Strength of Unit on 31/5/19:- 2 Officers and 33 OR.	
			Remaining 6 Horses handed in to Remounts Rouen on 30/5/19. Party proceeded by road on 29/5/19, comprised of Lieut DESBOROUGH and 3 mounted OR. Returned by rail on 31/5/19.	
			Peter Russell Capt. RE OC 11th Field Coy RE.	

D. D. & L., London, E.C. (A8004) Wt W1771/M2031 750,000 5/17 Sch. 52 Forms/C2118/14

www.ingramcontent.com/pod-product-compliance
Lightning Source LLC
Chambersburg PA
CBHW080806010526
44113CB00013B/2332
* 9 7 8 1 4 7 4 5 1 6 5 5 6 *